Fundamentals of Electronic Resources Management

ALA FUNDAMENTALS SERIES

ALA FUNDAMENTALS SERIES

Fundamentals of Electronic Resources Management

Alana Verminski
Kelly Marie Blanchat

An imprint of the American Library Association

Chicago   2017

ALANA VERMINSKI is the collection development librarian at the Bailey/ Howe Library at the University of Vermont. Her interest in electronic resources management began while working at the St. Mary's College of Maryland Library in St. Mary's City, Maryland. She holds an MSIS from The University of Texas at Austin.

KELLY MARIE BLANCHAT is the electronic resources support librarian at Yale University Library. Before joining Yale, Kelly worked as the electronic resources librarian at Queens College Libraries at the City University of New York and as an account specialist at Springer Science + Business Media. Kelly earned an MLIS from Long Island University.

© 2017 by the American Library Association

Printed in the United States of America

21 20 19 18 17   5 4 3 2 1

Extensive effort has gone into ensuring the reliability of the information in this book; however, the publisher makes no warranty, express or implied, with respect to the material contained herein.

ISBN: 978-0-8389-1541-7 (paper)

Library of Congress Cataloging-in-Publication Data
Names: Verminski, Alana, author. | Blanchat, Kelly Marie, author.
Title: Fundamentals of electronic resources management / Alana Verminski, Kelly Marie Blanchat.
Description: Chicago : ALA Neal-Schuman, an imprint of the American Library Association, 2017. | Series: ALA fundamentals series | Includes bibliographical references and index.
Identifiers: LCCN 2016044178 | ISBN 9780838915417 (pbk. : alk. paper)
Subjects: LCSH: Libraries—Special collections—Electronic information resources. | Electronic information resources—Management. | Libraries and electronic publishing.
Classification: LCC Z692.C65 V47 2017 | DDC 025.2/84—dc23 LC record available at https://lccn.loc.gov/2016044178

Cover design by Alejandra Diaz. Image © -strizh-/Shutterstock, Inc. Text composition in the Melior and Din typefaces by Dianne M. Rooney.

♾ This paper meets the requirements of ANSI/NISO Z39.48-1992 (Permanence of Paper).

ALA Neal-Schuman purchases fund advocacy, awareness, and accreditation programs for library professionals worldwide.

Contents

Preface

This book aims to provide both new and seasoned information professionals with a practical foundation for electronic resources management: how it came to be, where it is today, essential tools needed to get the job done, and expectations for the future. You can anticipate an overview of the essential concepts, processes, and concerns associated with electronic resources management.

Electronic resources and their management are dynamic and ever-changing. We encourage you to consult the further readings included at the end of each chapter for historical information and context. For the most up-to-date practices, you can look to sources such as the *Journal of Electronic Resources Management,* the Electronic Resources in Libraries (ERIL) listserv, and the Electronic Resources and Libraries (ER&L) Conference.

In this book, you will be presented with scenarios that apply to the management of electronic resources. Keep in mind that the relevance of specific workflow processes will depend on the type of library, local mission, institutional goals, and library staffing and structure. Every library is unique, and an important aspect of starting in any new job or field is adapting to local processes and culture. This book aims to set the groundwork for the concepts behind workflows and the interconnection between workflows and systems.

In the world of electronic resources, librarians and their vendors use a plethora of acronyms and jargon. In this book acronyms and jargon are used as they are on the job, because the proper use of terminology—no matter how esoteric—is essential for successful communication. Some acronyms and jargon may be familiar to readers with a background in library science—such as

"MARC" and "OCLC"—while other terms may be entirely new due to their specificity to electronic resources. Readers are encouraged to consult the glossary at the end of the book for additional definitions, context, and related terms. Glossary terms are bold-faced when first used in the text of each chapter.

Finally, if you are reading this book and are new to the library profession—we welcome you! Whether you have decided to pursue electronic resources or simply are exploring the profession more broadly, this book will have something for you. Information and concepts build on each other, especially in the field of electronic resources. With that said, take in the whole book at once, or pick a chapter and skip around. One word of advice, though it may be cliché: the best way to eat an elephant is one bite at a time. Expertise comes with time, and masters of any field will tell you the same. We are glad you're here, and don't hesitate to reach out to other information professionals for help, advice, and questions.

Getting Your Feet Wet

A Background in Electronic Resources Management

Electronic Resources Management (ERM) refers to the processes associated with the acquisition and maintenance of library resources in electronic format. The last two decades have seen increased user expectations for immediate anytime anywhere access to information because of the enhanced availability of information on the Open Web. Libraries are acquiring more and more electronic resources, and as a result there is increasing demand for competent professionals to manage these resources.

Electronic resources involve new and, at times complex, acquisition models. For example, print resources are purchased outright, claimed, processed, and placed on a shelf for patron use, whereas electronic resources have individual

license agreements that govern how and when a resource is used, and once processed, they are visible only when discovered through the library's catalog systems. Electronic resources librarians need to understand some degree of legalese—beyond copyright law—to successfully negotiate license agreements that will allow access for users. Further, electronic resources affect nearly every library department because they are used by nearly every library patron, so it is important that electronic resources librarians translate jargon to public services staff and patrons alike. Therefore, to be successful electronic resources librarians should have excellent communication skills. They need to know not only whom to contact and what to ask, but also how to answer a complex array of questions from other librarians as well as end-users.

Today's electronic resources librarian works in an ever-evolving field, where workflows, tools, and technologies require not only technical know-how, but also creativity and flexibility. Perhaps not surprisingly, the evolving nature of the format requires that electronic resources librarians continually update, revise, and scale their workflows from acquisitions and implementation to access and discovery. As a result, electronic resources have spurred fundamental questions about the future of library collections, such as:

> What is the future of the library without, potentially, a physical collection?
>
> How do electronic resources serve our patrons' needs today?
>
> How can we ensure that today's electronic resources support the needs of our patrons in the future?
>
> Is the library constantly playing catch-up with the evolving field, or are there opportunities to advocate for local needs to influence change?

Acronyms and Jargon Defined

Throughout this book acronyms and jargon are used as they are on the job. Understanding terminology used by both internal and external peers will be essential for success. Look out for boldfaced terms and be sure to flip back to the glossary for a refresher on new or unfamiliar acronyms and jargon! For a full list of jargon and acronyms defined, see the glossary.

The concepts behind these questions are truly expansive, but should not be a deterrent to embarking into the field. Electronic resources management is a rewarding and stimulating career option for librarians and information professionals interested in collaborative problem-solving and new technology, and for anyone with an inclination toward life-long learning.

The Landscape of Electronic Resources

In the days before the World Wide Web, Dialog Information Systems offered users the ability to broadly search multiple indexed databases from file servers. Though Dialog may be a thing of the past, such functionality may sound similar to today's discovery interfaces, such as Summon, EBSCO Discovery Service (EDS), and even Google Scholar. Today's patrons would likely find Dialog unrecognizable, clunky, and unintuitive, especially now that patrons have begun to access information resources using mobile devices. Whether library users are inclined to use smartphones to access library resources, the ability to do so has an effect not only on how a library presents itself and markets its resources, but also how publishers and vendors design their platforms and databases for information retrieval. Electronic resources are here to stay, and as their technologies continue to change and improve, so will the technical specifications for access.

Library acquisition budgets increasingly allocate more funds to electronic resources than to print materials, yet many libraries still struggle to keep up with the services and infrastructure needed for consistent, effective, and scalable electronic resource management. The reason for this disconnect can be found in the history of library collection practices: library structures were initially developed to meet the demands of print materials, which involved linear workflows for items that moved physically from one workflow stage to the next. Electronic resources defy that traditional linear path, however, by moving through cyclical stages as intangible, digital objects, which is commonly referred to as the **electronic resources lifecycle**. Lifecycles vary from resource to resource and are comprised of repetitive stages that are not always obvious (see figure 1.1). Because electronic resources are not physically shipped and delivered, there is not an absolute marker to trigger workflows and thus more proactive, anticipatory management is needed.

Driven by the complicated nature of electronic resource renewals, libraries are continually adapting and revising management techniques. For instance, at the 2015 **Electronic Resources and Libraries (ER&L) Conference**, librarians from the Newman Library at Baruch College (CUNY) presented their analysis of local internal workflows for electronic resources, which uncovered a good deal of inefficiency and redundancy—mostly related to passing information to relevant parties via email—in day-to-day processes.[1] These kinds of workflow analyses are crucial to electronic resources management, because workflows need to be continually updated, reviewed, and revised in order to keep up with the evolving market. Such analyses can also be a great way to determine whether there is need for additional staff, staff training, or enhanced workflow software.

Modern libraries have always had some means of automating their internal workflows. The **Integrated Library System (ILS)** first appeared in libraries around 1970 and was designed to facilitate print acquisitions and discovery. For this reason, present-day functionality of the ILS generally falls short of meeting the nuanced demands of the electronic resources lifecycle. As a solution, **Electronic Resources Management Systems (ERMS)** entered the market in the early 2000s with the promise to improve information sharing and to help keep track of the full lifecycle of electronic resource holdings.

Early vendor-developed ERMS were built to accommodate the needs of libraries of all types and sizes, but did not allow for easy customization. As a result, homegrown systems began to appear, ranging from the ERMS built on Google Sites from the University of Alaska Fairbanks to the popular open source systems **CORAL** and **CUFTS**, developed by University of Notre Dame and Simon Fraser University, respectively.[2] The most recent evolution for electronic resources workflow solutions is the "next generation ILS," which promises to replace both the ILS *and* ERMS by integrating workflows for print and electronic materials. For any workflow solution to be truly successful, a good deal of manual setup and ongoing maintenance is required, such as associating each of the library's electronic resources with the correct vendor and annual subscription price, as well as entering contact information for vendor representatives and administration credentials for things like **usage statistics**. For libraries with thousands of electronic resources, this is no small task! No matter the system or trend, the most important thing to keep in mind when working with a system or considering a new one is its suitability—of price and in function—for any task at hand.

Education and Training

Dedicated electronic resources librarian positions began to emerge as early as the 1980s, with most positions created in the early 2000s.[3] The position was developed to fill a growing need for the coordination of emerging access methods for digital resources: database searching, CD-ROMs, and the Internet. These new positions did not have much focus on instruction and reference duties, but as the needs of the job became more complex, a wider range of skills and qualifications were required. These requirements bridged responsibilities from many library departments, including serials management, acquisitions, information technology, and business and legal services. Not surprisingly, existing positions in the library did not require the same set of combined skill requirements, and new electronic resources librarians learned their trade on the job. Today, this trend continues as libraries create new or modified professional roles to manage electronic resources. As electronic collections grow in scope, it is increasingly essential to librarians to understand the complex issues associated with electronic resources and communicate effectively about them.

Perhaps the most official and significant update to the work of electronic resources librarians occurred with the publication of NASIG's *Core Competencies for Electronic Resources Librarians* in 2013.[4] The publication assembles the essential skills and requirements for effective electronic resources librarians. The *Core Competencies* is the first attempt to distill electronic resources management into a single, vetted document. It can aid current electronic resources librarians in their daily work, and it has potential to be used by libraries when developing future job descriptions, planning organizational structure, assessing departmental goals, and evaluating Library and Information Science (LIS) coursework.

Despite the uptick in responsibilities, opportunities, and standards, graduate programs in LIS have been slow to incorporate true training for electronic resources into coursework and are often criticized for an imbalance of theoretical framework to practical applications. Far too frequently, recent graduates embark on careers in electronic resources management with little to no direct experience and face a steep learning curve on the job. In other areas of LIS coursework—such as cataloging, reference, and instruction—there are more opportunities for hands-on learning, including classroom activities, job shadowing, and internships. To be a successful electronic resources librarian, it is essential to have personal initiative to learn through alternative means (and reading this book accomplishes part of this task!).

Fortunately, a large network of librarians, publishers, and other information professionals are available for support. For the new or seasoned professional, becoming involved with national and international organizations can be an effective way to dive into continuing education. Library organizations that offer opportunities for training in electronic resources include:

American Association of Law Libraries (AALL)

American Library Association (ALA)

Association of College and Research Libraries (ACRL)

Association of Library Collections and Technical Services (ALCTS)

Library Information Technology Association (LITA)

National Information Standards Organization (NISO)

NASIG (formerly the North American Serials Interest Group)

Opportunities with these organizations range from pre-conference meetings and workshops to lunch-and-learn sessions with content and systems providers and webinars. Attending national conferences—such as Electronic Resources and Libraries (ER&L) Conference and the **Charleston Conference**—as well as regional conferences—such as local chapter meetings and interest groups—are excellent opportunities not only to learn about the field, but also to network with fellow electronic resources librarians and vendor representatives.

Regardless of a librarian's career stage or experience level, participation in the larger conversations surrounding electronic resources management is an effective way to stay up to date with new strategies, tools, and trends. For small libraries with a single staff member managing the entire electronic resources lifecycle, continuing education and networking opportunities can be critical, even if there does not seem as though there is enough time to allow for it. Finally, electronic resources librarians at any career level will find beneficial content within the *Journal of Electronic Resources Librarianship* and *The Serials Librarian,* references to which can be found throughout this book.

The Role of the Electronic Resources Librarian within the Organization

Electronic resources librarians can be found within public services, technical services, or collection development departments, or they can be found bridging between all three. Given the evolution of the position and its diverse requirements, such varied situations are not surprising. No matter the position in an organization, an electronic resources librarian will need to remain flexible to communicate resource terms of use and be able to troubleshoot access issues with patrons, public services and technical services librarians, and library vendors.

Just as organizational structures vary from one library to the next for electronic resources librarians, so does the actual management of resources. Two general methods of organizational structures for electronic resources management exist within library departments: the first option, centralization, involves a core set of librarians and staff dedicated wholly to electronic resources management; and the second option takes a decentralized approach by integrating librarians and staff from multiple areas—including acquisitions, continuations, and cataloging—who contribute to specific processes throughout the electronic resources lifecycle. Each model has its benefits.

The decentralized model is more focused on library collections and eliminates silos between print and electronic workflows. However, findings from a workflow analysis conducted at Duke University Libraries showed decentralized management can result in staff members having complex responsibilities without a strong understanding of the complete picture.[5] The alternative—centralization—lends itself to strong administrative control over electronic resources but also risks isolating personnel from other library departments and services. No matter the organizational structure, the ever-evolving nature of electronic resources demands that information professionals remain flexible and willing to reevaluate workflows on a regular basis.

With so many structural and management possibilities in electronic resources, librarians and information professionals must remember to focus energy on long-term goals and strategic planning based on user needs and system requirements.

Electronic Resources Lifecycle and Workflows

The electronic resources lifecycle is nonlinear, repetitive, and ongoing. The most basic electronic resource lifecycle will last for a twelve-month period, beginning with an acquisition (purchase or renewal) then moving to activation and setup, and ending with ongoing maintenance and reevaluation for the next renewal period. From this most basic model, the electronic resource lifecycle grows more and more complicated: some lifecycles may span to two-to-five

Electronic Resources in the Modern Library

In the last two decades, the shift from ownership to licensed access has represented a seminal change in how libraries develop and measure the value of their collections. Electronic resources are consuming collection budgets, and collection development practices have become largely focused on assessment using data-driven methods to justify expenditures and ensure valuable acquisitions dollars are spent wisely. Armed with vendor-provided usage statistics, libraries can calculate the exact return on investment for each of their subscription by determining the **cost-per-use (CPU)** for a resource, a data point that helps when deciding if a resource's continued subscription is worth the cost. During the Great Recession of the early 2000s—during which library acquisition budgets were crippled by subscription pricing that rose higher than the rate of inflation, combined with harsh reductions in library funding—libraries questioned the sustainability of both standard subscriptions as well as large package deals. Although packages like the **Big Deal** open up a large amount of content to library users at a huge discount from **list price**, typically the majority of usage in these packages is driven by a small portion of titles, despite the significant access and financial commitment. Publishers have responded to libraries' changing collection needs by developing alternative business models, which still provide users with access to large amounts of content at a reasonable cost to libraries. These models, such as **Pay-Per-View (PPV)** and **Demand Driven Acquisitions (DDA)**, require the library to pay for the content that is used and represent a shift from collecting "just-in-case" to collecting "just-in-time," in which emphasis is placed on providing access *right now,* rather than acquiring content in perpetuity. It is important to note, however, that as of 2016 these new models have not been adopted as the norm and are still being evaluated in the scholarly literature for Library and Information Science (LIS).

Just as libraries are adjusting to changes in the market, publishers are also learning how to manage, price, and sell electronic resources to libraries. **eBooks** are particularly complex and pose more challenges than their electronic **journal** counterparts. Publishers have tried to maintain administrative control over ebooks by implementing **Digital Rights Management (DRM)**, a practice that determines how ebook content can be used, such as the number of users that can gain access at a single time as well as the ability to print, save, and download book sections. For instance, if an ebook allows only one simultaneous user—which functions like a print book loan with a ratio of one book to one reader—then a library will need to acquire multiple copies of that ebook so multiple users can access it at once. There is heated debate whether DRM protects a publisher's copyright or if it is simply a means for publishers to increase revenue. To make matters worse, because different publishers enforce different DRM restrictions, an ebook hosted on one platform may have different functionalities than an ebook hosted on another. Users are unlikely to recognize the cause and will instead become confused and frustrated. And who wouldn't be?

DRM also makes a large impact on a library's ability to participate in resource sharing, or **Interlibrary Loan (ILL)**. In theory, ebooks should be available anytime and anywhere, much like electronic journal articles. eBook publishers, however, have been slow to allow the lending of ebooks although such practices are standard in licensing for electronic journals. These restrictions severely limit a library's ability to fulfill requests in a standard, business-as-usual way.

Keep Calm

By keeping a clear focus and a drive for information, technology, and service, anyone can excel in this field. Communication is an essential skill for a successful electronic resources librarian. That, and keeping up to date with the latest trends in the field! For more information on the responsibilities of an electronic resources librarian, take a look at NASIG's *Core Competencies for Electronic Resources Librarians*.

Libraries are invested in increasing access to resources by making resources more discoverable. Many libraries have implemented **discovery layers** that enable users to more easily locate most of a library's materials. A discovery layer is essentially a tool that sits on top of the library's other access points—the OPAC, databases, research guides, open access collections, archival material, and institutional repositories—to funnel content into a single-search option, similar to a Google experience. The functionality of a discovery layer brings greater emphasis on accurate metadata and effective linking, which is required to have the content discoverable through the discovery layer's central index. NISO's *Open Discovery Initiative,* published in 2014, works to promote the effective and consistent sharing of metadata among content providers and discovery service vendors to prevent biased linking and indexing of content. This trend in metadata sharing is essential as libraries focus energy on making information more discoverable to library users. To learn more about metadata for discovery, see chapter 6.

Libraries have also focused attention toward **Open Access (OA)** initiatives to supplement library subscriptions. Open Access resources are scholarly electronic journals and ebooks that are made freely available online without restrictions on access or use. Material becomes Open Access when authors self-archive their work or when work is published in an Open Access publication. Because all Open Access resources are electronic, the ability to use and access Open Access material is of growing importance for electronic resources librarians. Many libraries have chosen to make large sets of Open Access resources discoverable in library systems, and an increasing number of libraries implement **institutional repositories**, encourage faculty to create and adopt **Open Educational Resources (OERs)**, and promote the importance of Open Access during national Open Access Week each year. To learn more about Open Access, see chapter 4.

Wrap-Up and Where to Go Next

Electronic resources have come a long way in the past two decades. As electronic resources become more and more pervasive, librarians in all areas have begun to increase their focus on user experience. Whether a formal job responsibility of an electronic resources librarian or not, user experience is also at the heart of electronic resources management: access, discovery, and use are all elements of great concern to electronic resources librarians. In fact, it would be very difficult to identify an area of librarianship that does not touch on electronic resources in some way. Due to the evolutionary nature of the format, electronic resources librarians need to be aware of the many diverse functions of other library departments, just as other departments should keep up to date with the concerns of electronic resources management.

NOTES

1. Alexandra Hamlett and Michael Waldman, "Electronic Quicksand: Rethinking Workflows for the Digital Librarian" (presentation at the 2015 Electronic Resources and Libraries Conference, Austin, Texas, February 22, 2015).

2. Karen Jensen, "Managing Library Electronic Resources Using Google Sites," *Journal of Electronic Resources Librarianship* 25, no. 2 (2013): 115–23. doi: 10.1080/1941126X.2013.785289; Andrea Imre, Eric Hartnett, and C. Derrik Hiatt, "CORAL: Implementing an Open-Source ERM System," *The Serials Librarian* 64, no. 1–4 (2013): 224–234; and Kevin Stranack, "CUFTS: An Open Source Alternative for Serials Management," *The Serials Librarian* 51, no. 2 (2006): 29–39.

3. Rebecca S. Albitz and Wendy Allen Shelburne, "Marian through the Looking Glass," *Collection Management* 32, no. 1–2 (2007): 15–30, doi: 10.1300/ J105v32n01_03.

4. NASIG, *Core Competencies for Electronic Resources Librarians,* 2013, www .nasig.org/site, page.cfm?pk_association_webpage_menu=310&pk_association _webpage=1225.

5. Beverly Dowdy and Rosalyn Raeford, "Electronic Resources Workflow: Design, Analysis and Technologies for an Overdue Solution," *Serials Review* 40, no. 3 (2014): 175–87, doi: 10.1080/00987913.2014.950040.

6. Oliver Pesch, "Library Standards and e-Resource Management: A Survey of Current Initiatives and Standards Efforts," *Serials Librarian* 55, no. 3 (2008): 482, doi:10.1080/03615260802059965.

7. Emery, Jill, and Graham Stone. "TERMS: Techniques for Electronic Resource Management." https://library3.hud.ac.uk/blogs/terms/.

FURTHER READINGS

Chamberlain, Clint, and Derek Reece. "Library Reorganization, Chaos, and Using the Core Competencies as a Guide." *Serials Librarian* 66, no. 1–4 (2014): 248–52. doi: 10.1080/0361526X.2014.881162.

Dollar, Daniel M., John Gallagher, Janice Glover, Regina Kenny Marone, and Cynthia Crooker. "Realizing What's Essential: A Case Study on Integrating Electronic Journal Management into a Print-Centric Technical Services Department." *Journal of the Medical Library Association* 95, no. 2 (2014): 147–55. doi: 10.3163/1536-5050.95.2.147.

Duranceau, Ellen Finnie, and Cindy Hepfer. "Staffing for Electronic Resource Management: The Results of a Survey." *Serials Review* 28, no. 4 (2002): 316–20. doi: 10.1016/S0098-7913(02)00224-1.

Elguindi, Anne, and Kari Schmidt. *Electronic Resource Management: Practical Perspectives in a New Technical Services Model.* Elsevier, 2012.

England, Lenore, and Kelly Shipp. "ERM Ideas and Innovations: Flexible Workflows for Constantly Changing ERM Environments." *Journal of Electronic Resources Librarianship* 25, no. 3 (2013): 218–25. doi: 10.1080/1941126X.2013.813312.

England, Mark, and Phill Jones. "Diversification of Access Pathways and the Role of Demand-Driven Acquisition: A Case Study at the University of Utah."

Serials Librarian 66, no. 1–4 (2014): 96–105. doi: 10.1080/0361526X
.2014.879012.

Grogg, Jill E. "The Resilience of the Electronic Resources Librarian." *Serials Review*
41, no. 2 (2015): 57.

Hartnett, Eric. "NASIG's Core Competencies for Electronic Resources Librarians
Revisited: An Analysis of Job Advertisement Trends, 2000–2012." *Journal of
Academic Librarianship* 40, no. 3–4 (2014): 247–58. doi: 10.1016/
j.acalib.2014.03.013.

Hsiung, Lai-Ying. "Expanding the Role of the Electronic Resources (ER) Librarian in
the Hybrid Library." *Collection Management* 32, no. 1–2 (2008): 31–47. doi:
10.1300/J105v32n01_04.

Koury, Regina. "Coping with Economic Issues and a Paradigm Shift in Collections."
In *Managing Electronic Resources: A LITA Guide,* edited by Ryan O. Weir, 17–36.
Chicago: American Library Association, 2012.

National Information Standards Organization. *Open Discovery Initiative.* 2014. www
.niso.org/workrooms/odi/.

Weir, Ryan O. "Learning the Basics of Electronic Resource Management." In
Managing Electronic Resources: A LITA Guide, edited by Ryan O. Weir, 1–16.
Chicago: American Library Association, 2012.

Yu, Holly, ed. *Electronic Resource Management in Libraries: Research and Practice.*
Hershey, PA: IGI Global, 2008.

Ways to Pay

Understanding Electronic Resources Purchase Models

Electronic resources are acquired directly from publishers and from third party providers with business models that range from individual subscriptions, subject-collection, and current copyright year bundles, and pay-per-view options, to name a few. Different business models come with varying levels of access rights and fees based on the level of subscription and licensing rights granted. The vast number of acquisitions options available provides libraries with flexibility to build electronic collections to fit their needs, but careful consideration must be given to the chosen method, as there are benefits and drawbacks associated with each model. This chapter will discuss the business models available for electronic resources acquisitions and access, and will discuss their potential impact on library budget and collection development. Due to the complexities of the business models associated with each electronic resource, it is essential to have a strong understanding of the current market offerings as well as an awareness of how content is licensed, how robust management systems keep track of it all, and how the market is evolving.

The two most basic acquisition models to understand for electronic resources are 1) subscriptions and 2) purchases.

ACRONYMS AND JARGON DEFINED
Big Deal

The **Big Deal** refers to a package-based business model that provides libraries with an extremely large number of journal titles for a price significantly lower than the cost of each individual journal at its list price. Big Deal packages are licensed over multiple years, with fixed price increases for each year.

For more acronyms and jargon defined, see the glossary.

Subscriptions versus Purchases

Subscriptions provide libraries with access to material during a given period. The terms of subscription access are determined by a **license agreement**, which defines contract terms such as the start and end dates of the subscription, the price and percentage increase over time, and when applicable, the conditions for how patrons can use and share the material, as well as **perpetual access** rights. The most basic subscription will last for a period of one year, at which point it will need to be renewed or cancelled. A purchase, just like it sounds, represents a one-time payment and will generally include more flexible access and perpetual access rights. That is not to say, however, that purchased resources do not also require a license agreement to determine rights. For more information on licensing for electronic resources, see chapter 5.

Although the basic access models for subscriptions and purchases may be simple enough, it is important to be aware of why particular options are

FIGURE 2.1

Subscriptions According to Resource Type

JOURNALS	*Individual Subscription*	Libraries subscribe to a single journal; generally a subscription to a single journal will provide perpetual access rights to the year subscribed.
	Collection	Libraries subscribe to a group of journals. Collections can be organized by subject, publisher, copyright year, or a mix of all three.
	"Big Deal"	A term that refers to a journal collection that encompasses all, or most, of a publisher's offerings available at a discounted rate.
DATABASES	*Subscription*	Most databases are available through yearly subscriptions. It would be rare to see a database available for a perpetual access purchase.
EBOOKS	*Individual Purchase*	Some eBooks are available for individual purchase, which grants perpetual access to the material.
	Individual Subscription	eBook subscriptions that require yearly renewal are most often seen with reference works, or content available from content aggregators such as EBSCO eBooks and eBook Central.
	Collection	Similar to the journal collection described above, ebook collections are typically curated by subject and/or copyright year and are licensed for perpetual access.
	Package	eBooks are also available in much larger packages, not unlike big deals. A publisher can make its entire ebook offerings available in a single product.
STREAMING MEDIA	*Individual Purchase*	Single purchase of a film or other type of streaming media with perpetual access rights.
	Individual License	Libraries purchase a license to a single streaming video.
	Collection Subscription	Just like their electronic journal and ebook counterparts, streaming media is also available as a collection subscription. Streaming media collections are usually curated by subject, a particular film maker, or distributor.
	Collection Purchase	Due to complexities in streaming video rights, collection purchases for streaming video content is more rare, but it does occur. Collection purchases for streaming video may indicate that a certain percentage of content can be removed due to copyright.

available, and in which cases options will be limited, and not determined by local collection development decisions. Not all electronic resources will be eligible for both subscription and purchase options, and many times the format itself will dictate the specific access model available. Libraries do not always have the opportunity to select the access model that best fits their needs and budget. In fact, resource type may be the biggest factor in dictating the access model. Figure 2.1 describes the current models available based on resource type.

Subscriptions are more commonly available for individual electronic journals, electronic journal packages and collections, **aggregator databases**, and **streaming video** collections, while purchases are more common for journal **backfiles**, individual **ebooks** and ebook collections, and reference works. The formats that provide purchase options do so because the content is considered to be complete as-is, and therefore will not change over time due to additional issues or volumes published.

The biggest difference between subscriptions and purchases is continuing payment versus one-time payment. However, it is important to keep in mind that purchased resources often require a nominal annual fee—often referred to as a maintenance fee or hosting fee—that covers the on-going cost of hosting the content on a database or publisher platform. License agreements for purchased content should always reference any annual fees, so be sure to read closely and be aware of any ongoing commitments before signing, as any on-going commitment, such as a subscription cost, annual fee, and rate increase, will have a major impact on both budget as well as resource access. An outstanding hosting fee may result in a loss of access.

The Concept of a Database

The concept of a database raises one of the greatest philosophical questions of electronic resources management. What one library considers to be a "database"—for inclusion on its Database A–Z list, for instance—may be very different from what another library considers to be a database. A "database" can be defined strictly and be limited to only aggregator databases, or it can be defined more liberally and extend to include any online resource that contains sets of information, such as publisher platforms, archival collections, and government document websites. For the strictest sense of a database—aggregators and **Abstract and Index (A&I) databases**—the business model is quite simple: databases are acquired as subscriptions. This model is decidedly unlike those available for electronic journals and ebooks, where content providers offer various acquisition options based on price points and perpetual access availability. For instance, publishers sell individual ebooks to libraries as one-time purchases because the content of the book will not change. Likewise, publishers sell electronic journal and newspaper archives as one-time purchases because the content is also fixed. Databases are entirely different, however, because the content is in flux due to third-party vendors adding and removing content based on their own agreements with the actual publishers. To complicate the matter, aggregator databases also contain electronic journal and ebook titles that can be subscribed to individually by a library, but again, when made available through an aggregated database they are subject to both change and **embargoes** that affect their overall stability. A&I databases may also change over time as content is newly indexed and as abstracts are added to the database. The fluid nature of a true "database" means that they likely will never be made available to purchase outright.

Subscription Agents: How They Change the Game

Subscription agents manage subscriptions for libraries, and serve as an intermediary between content providers and libraries. The most common services provided by subscription agents include:

- assistance acquiring new subscriptions
- authorization for renewals and cancellations
- support for licensing and negotiation
- communication regarding changes in journals, publishers, and platforms
- providing price **quotations**
- support for claims and access issues
- consolidated invoicing
- maintaining reports on current and historical subscriptions

Although subscription agents have been in business for years, there is increased demand for efficient mediation and subscription support due to the dominance of electronic journal subscriptions, the plethora of access models, and the constant flux in titles, platforms, and publishers. Subscription agents take on the work of keeping the proverbial ducks in a row for a library's subscriptions. For instance, subscription agents are especially help-ful for libraries with subscriptions from smaller publishers, as a subscription agent will have the capacity to be more responsive and provide more assis-tance than the staff available at a small publisher. With subscription agents adding value to subscription management, librarians can focus their time and energy on higher-order functions, such as license negotiation, advocacy, and usage data analysis.

Because subscription agents are intended to add value to the manage-ment of subscriptions, their fees are far from inexpensive. Libraries must weigh their local needs against the benefits of working through subscription agents, versus the option of working directly with publishers. Likewise, sub-scription agents may not be worth the added expense if they fail to meet expectations or if they do not add enough value to the experience. Libraries need to be clear in communicating management expectations, while also tak-ing into consideration which tasks are best done by subscription agent and which tasks can be handled by a librarian or by publisher staff directly.

For instance, many **consortia** manage vendor offers and pricing for their affiliated libraries, and though there is often a fee associated with consor-tium membership, consortia are generally given hefty discounts for group acquisitions. Options to pay for these types of arrangements generally range from being invoiced through the consortium, through a subscription agent, or directly from the publisher. In such a situation, the benefits associated with a subscription agent might be negated by the centralized management already handled by the consortium. With that said, a benefit of continuing to work through a subscription agent includes more streamlined invoicing across the board. The best option in these situations will be determined by the local needs of the library: is management or cost-savings more important?

Now that the basics of subscription and purchase models have been dis-cussed, it is time to build on that knowledge and discuss complex acquisition models. These complex models are, in part, the result of libraries and pub-lishers working to find sustainable and affordable subscription options that benefit both parties. When considering more complex options, keep in mind local needs and recognize that although one model may be a good fit for one library, the same model may not work well in another, due to scope, cost, and sustainability.

What's the Big Deal?

The term Big Deal describes large journal packages that are offered by publishers as multi-year subscriptions. The Big Deal is so named because the contents of the journal packages include all, or nearly all, of the journal titles from individual publisher at a greatly discounted price. As an industry standard Big Deal license agreements provide libraries with perpetual access rights to the active copyright years of the subscription, with **access only** rights to earlier copyright years, generally going back to 1996 or 1997 at the earliest, when available. For example, if a library has an active subscription to a Big Deal from 2016 through 2018, the available content access for the term of the subscription will range from approximately 1996/1997 to 2016, and will progress by one year until the subscription ends in 2018. When the Big Deal subscription expires perpetual access will only be retained for the direct subscription copyright years, 2016 through 2018. In order to maintain access to **complementary** backfiles, the Big Deal will need to be renewed for another term. Complimentary access and subscription duration will be determined by publisher acquisition models and will always be negotiated locally. The model described here can be thought of as a starting point for what is currently available in the market.

Big Deal subscriptions offer the benefits associated with buying in bulk: libraries gain access to a large number of journals at a lower cost than possible through individual subscriptions to the same content. Due to the extreme volume of content included, many libraries may find that not all of the content will be a good fit for the collection. This concept is similar to buying in bulk at a warehouse store. However, when looking to build a journal collection to meet the research needs of a diverse community, the Big Deal can be a quick and cost-effective solution.

One of the biggest criticisms of Big Deal subscriptions is the very thing that distinguishes them from other models—their size. Gaining blanket access to all of a publisher's journals relieves the burden of selecting which individual titles to acquire. Quite often, though, the selection process can be essential. If a library cannot afford the cost of the Big Deal, then the benefit of having extra content and streamlined fees can do more harm to the library's collection than good. Furthermore, Big Deal subscriptions do not just affect collections decisions and patron access. They also impact library workflows: when a library gains access to a large amount of content from a single publisher, the time it takes to maintain individual subscriptions is greatly reduced. But at the same time, staff resources need to be reallocated to meet the demands of ensuring that access remains stable for the entirety of the Big Deal subscription and that the contents of the collection are monitored and kept up to date year after year. Big Deal subscriptions are just as susceptible to access errors, content migrations, and transfer and ceased titles as anything else. For more information on maintaining access to electronic resources, see chapter 6.

Subscription Journal Packages and Collections

Outside of the Big Deal, there are many other options to acquire groups of journals in a single acquisition. Publishers offer smaller journal package subscriptions containing fewer titles than Big Deal subscriptions, which are often grouped by subject. Such smaller bundles are generally more flexible and may provide options to swap titles in and out during the course of a subscription. A standard caveat for swap options is that titles have a list-price value equal to or less than the title being swapped out. Further, for smaller journal package subscriptions, title-level cancellations can be prohibited, because their **license agreements** will often mandate a commitment of a certain dollar amount, or threshold, that must be maintained during the subscription.

When considering any subscription journal collection, a variety of factors should be weighed, such as:

> Is the collection in question an effective means of providing
>> journal content access to users?
> Is the title list aligned with current information needs?
> What is the perceived future use?
> Do usage statistics, if available, demonstrate demand?
> Are there any multi-year fees, and are they reasonable?

Funding Subscription Journal Collections

Funding subscription journal packages of any size can be quite an endeavor. When debating whether to pick up or cancel any journal package, it is important to evaluate the short and long-term financial commitment. Subscription journal packages generally require multi-year commitments, so it is important to remain aware of not only the annual subscription cost, but also the yearly increase and whether it will be a fixed percentage year after year or be subject to change. Compounding costs can cripple a library budget over the long term and, as a result, a library may decide to reject package options with variable price tags as viable options.

When libraries are faced with budget shortfalls the best option may be to cancel journal package subscriptions, especially if they are not demonstrating good usage or if they have low **cost-per-use (CPU)**. If a package subscription does not include an opt-out option, or if it includes a hefty penalty for cancellation, the next option may be to cancel other, less expensive content in order to balance the fees of more expensive packages. Even though Big Deal packages as a whole are cost-effective, many libraries cannot sustain such financial and collection inflexibility.[1] Data-driven, thoughtful assessment is critical toward making these decisions. For more information on the metrics used to evaluate resources, see chapter 3.

Unbundling Bundles

If the cost-effectiveness of a subscription package—whether a small journal collection or a Big Deal—proves to be poor, it might be time to consider unbundling the deal, which involves cancelling a package in favor of individual title subscriptions. As if deciding to cancel a Big Deal package was not hard enough, selecting which titles to retain can be even more challenging.

Unbundling packages requires a great deal of research into various factors, including cost, title-level usage analysis, the availability of perpetual access rights, and whether titles overlap with database aggregators. Traditionally, library collections reflect the "80/20" rule proposed by the Pareto Principle: the idea that 20 percent of the collection generates 80 percent of the usage. With this rule in play, the process of unbundling will make it simpler—although, not easy—to identify the most highly used titles in a package. The 80/20 rule dictates that most titles within package subscriptions will not be used heavily, and therefore titles with low cost-per-use (CPU) will be clear candidates for individual subscriptions.

Thoughtful and transparent decision-making will help make the entire process of breaking up package subscriptions go more smoothly, and will minimize the impact on library collections, budgets, and services. Before moving forward with unbundling, it will be important to communicate clearly the cause for the change to the content provider, and also to inquire whether a different package would better meet the library's needs (after all, cancellations can create an opportunity for negotiation and relationship-building). Within the library, faculty and staff should also be notified of access changes. It can be helpful to develop talking points for library staff to use if and when they are questioned about changes in access to resources. Depending on the user community and library culture, these conversations may be more successful when accompanied by the usage and pricing data that illustrates why a particular decision was made.

"Just-in-Time" Models for Journals

The landscape of electronic resources and serials has shifted dramatically since the Big Deal was first introduced in 1996 as a response to the serials crisis of the 1990s, when yearly percentage increases averaged 10 percent. As a result of budget shortfalls and changes in the publishing industry and scholarly communication, libraries today have again begun to collect "just-in-time," which refers to the method of subscribing to a resource to solve an immediate need, rather than collecting "just in case" for the future.

Pay per View (PPV) is a business model for journals that provides an affordable option to the traditional subscription model. With PPV, the library deposits funds with a publisher to be used only when a user triggers a purchase by requesting, or downloading, an article. In this way, the library only pays for the journal articles that are used, rather than paying for an entire journal that might be used. Publishers have partnered with third-party companies, such as the Copyright Clearance Center's Get It Now service and ReadCube, to provide faster access to articles through PPV models than with traditional ILL services. Generally, PPV options will not consume a library's entire collection. Instead, libraries have begun to test the waters of PPV with a hybrid approach, in which PPV is used to complement existing collections by providing access to high cost content or content that is used less frequently but still needed by users.

In the next section, two similar "just-in-time" models will be described for ebooks; these are referred to as **Demand Driven Acquisitions (DDA)** and **Patron Driven Acquisitions (PDA)** interchangeably.

Everything eBook

The market for ebooks has quickly matured as libraries and publishers alike find pricing models and access options that best address user needs. Not unlike the transition from print to electronic journals, libraries and publishers are still working to find common ground on business models that work for ebooks. Librarians are still concerned about long-term affordability, sustainability, and accessibility of ebooks.

Like the business models for journals described earlier in this chapter, ebooks are acquired as either individual purchases or as bundled package subscriptions. Acquiring ebooks à la carte provides more control over the titles added to the library's collection; however, title-by-title selection can be time-consuming and expensive. eBook subscription packages contain a significant number of titles, and although their journal package subscription counterparts are known to be stable for an entire subscription period, ebook packages are more susceptible to mid-cycle additions and deletions, especially if the package subscription is through a third-party provider, such as ProQuest or EBSCO. Librarians have little to no control over how and when ebook package offerings change, which is generally the result of content changing hands between publishers and copyright restrictions. This situation leaves the library in a very precarious position in regard to collection management, especially because ebooks are more likely than journals to be adopted for coursework in an academic setting. In response, ebook providers have begun to standardize how often ebooks are added and removed from packages, providing librarians with clearer expectations. This decrease in the frequency changes is certainly an improvement from what came before, which were nearly monthly changes, but more work still needs to be done to ensure the viability of ebook package subscriptions long-term.

"Just-in-Time" Models for eBooks

As with serials, librarians struggle to find an affordable and effective means to provide ebook content to their patrons. Purchasing ebooks à la carte can be an effective method of collection building but can be time-intensive, less efficient, and costly. In response to these issues, libraries have begun to explore "just-in-time" business models for books, like those for journals in which libraries only pay for content that is used.

Check It Out

Demand-Driven Acquisition (DDA) of Monographs: A Recommended Practice of the National Information Standards Organization (www.niso.org/workrooms/dda), was published by NISO in June 2014.

The most common just-in-time model for ebooks is Demand Driven Acquisitions (DDA), which is sometimes referred to as Patron Driven Acquisitions (PDA), and vice versa. In each of these models, librarians work with their ebook vendors to create a profile—not unlike the traditional print book approval plan profile—to define parameters for which ebooks will be included in the DDA program. A properly established profile will ensure library users only can discover ebooks that fit a library's selection parameters and it will exclude ebooks that are out of scope due to price, subject, reading level, or format type (such as reference materials and government documents). Without a well-crafted profile, libraries risk purchasing ebooks that are irrelevant to their collection or not within their monograph budget.

Discovery records for DDA ebooks are loaded into the library catalog in advance of their purchase for patron discovery and access. A purchase is only triggered once a certain level of ebook activity is reached, which can range from a set number of user requests on a single title, or set number of single-user page views in an individual ebook. The purchasing threshold will also be set in the DDA profile as well,

Thresholds for ebook purchases through DDA can also be mediated by enabling **Short Term Loans (STL)**. Instead of allowing a single user request to trigger a purchase, a profile with STLs enabled allows for purchase only after a predetermined number of short-term loans. The STLs themselves also cost a small fee, which is usually based on a percentage of the ebook list price. STLs have the potential to save the library money in their DDA subscriptions, especially if an ebook is rarely needed, or if unintentionally downloaded by a user. On the other hand, STLs also mean that a library could pay up to twice the list price for an individual ebook.

In recent years, libraries and publishers alike have questioned the sustainability of the STL model. In 2014, a group of publishers sharply increased their STL list price percentage. Prior to the price change, STL rates ranged between 10 and 30 percent of ebook list price, and afterward they rose to 40 to 50 percent. This price hike forced many libraries to reassess the value and sustainability of the model. This situation is an excellent example of the tensions and challenges posed by emerging "just-in-time" business models and the impact of a rapidly changing information marketplace. Libraries and publishers must work together to find models that support both parties, for the benefit of library collections and patrons.

When investigating ebook business models, it is important to consider the impact of the business model on users' research experience as well as the overall user experience of the ebook platform. For instance, some ebook platforms allow users to download content directly, either as PDF or EPUB files, whereas other platforms provide read-only access in a web browser. These options determine how ebooks can be used and transferred to other devices, which greatly influences user experience. Beyond the user experience of an ebook platform, the actual function of ebooks themselves is often predetermined by **Digital Rights Management (DRM)**.

What Is EPUB?

EPUB is the industry standard file format for ebooks. An EPUB ebook is recognizable by its file extension, .epub, and may be used on a dedicated e-reader device or by installing an e-reader app or other software on a computer, smartphone, or tablet. A key feature of the EPUB format is that it is optimized for responsive display, making for a better reading experience no matter the device.

DRM: Digital Rights Management

Digital Rights Management (DRM) is the practice of restricting or limiting how electronic resources are used, put in place to protect intellectual property. DRM is most commonly associated with ebooks, and it comes in a variety of flavors depending on the publisher and content. DRM can range from:

- limitations on the number of simultaneous users allowed to access the content at one time
- controls on the length of time that a resource can be used

- limitations on how much content can be downloaded or printed by a single user
- restrictions on the kinds of devices that can be used to read the content

Users are unlikely to be aware of the concept of DRM, but will nonetheless find its restrictions inhibitive, unintuitive, and confusing. DRM can prevent users from printing and downloading ebook content— it can even cause ebooks to completely disappear from devices without notice if a loan period has expired! Making matters more complicated, ebooks hosted on different platforms will likely have completely different DRM restrictions, which means users can grow even more frustrated when they are able to print and download an ebook from one provider, but not from another. Librarians also struggle to keep up with the differences in DRM restrictions between ebook providers and platforms, which causes problems for both behind-the-scenes management and for library instruction and reference services.

The good news is that *not all* ebooks are bound by DRM, and for the most part purchasing ebooks directly from publishers—instead of purchasing from third parties or via subscriptions to aggregator databases—will result in DRM-free content. Purchase options, of course, are much more expensive than gaining access to ebooks from aggregated resources.

Resource Sharing, DRM, and eBooks

The limitations posed by DRM software and publisher restrictions present a philosophical dilemma for libraries. DRM is an example of how copyright and the **first sale doctrine** have become far more complicated for electronic formats. For print monographs, the first sale doctrine allows libraries to loan material to their own users, as well provide materials to other libraries through **Interlibrary Loan (ILL)** and consortium resource sharing. For electronic resources, the first sale doctrine does not apply, and DRM restrictions can prevent resource sharing altogether, or can make it much more complicated due to file format types, device compatibility, and limitations on simultaneous users. Fortunately for libraries and their patrons, a growing number of publishers provide their ebooks DRM-free or without access restrictions. To date, these publishers include SpringerNature, Project MUSE, and JSTOR, among others. More and more publishers will follow as long as libraries continue to advocate for Interlibrary Loan rights.

For more detail on how licensing and contract law affects electronic resources, see chapter 5.

Streaming Media

In recent years, **streaming media** subscriptions have grown in popularity. As library collections in film and music transition from physical tapes and discs to electronic format, they too have followed the patterns established by electronic journals and ebooks. In fact, the acquisition models available for streaming media will be quite similar to those described earlier in this chapter.

In the early stages of streaming media, content was sold in large packages or bundled as subject collections. These options granted libraries access to a large amount of content from a variety of distributors on a single platform and worked well for users as it mimicked the browsing experience to which they were already accustomed from media on the Open Web. Librarians appreciated the convenience of these models as well, despite their inability to select which titles would be included in a package. Additional acquisition options included the ability to purchase or license media individually and then pay a separate hosting fee or host the content on a preexisting platform. These options complemented one another, and when presented with a request for media that was not available in a subscription package, libraries could supplement their holdings by making an à la carte purchase.

More recently streaming media providers have also begun to offer "just-in-time" access models. Kanopy, a streaming video provider with a Netflix-like interface, has led the way in the patron-driven acquisition model for streaming films. In their model, patrons have access to the records for thousands of video titles—ranging from popular movies to documentaries and academic films—and libraries only pay for the content that is actually used. Other industry leaders in streaming media include Alexander Street Press, Naxos, and DocuSeek2, with dozens of other providers in the market offering partial streaming media services incorporated with their other database content. COUNTER Release 4 has kept up with the trend, too, and now includes a report for these services, the Multimedia Report 1 (MR1)—the number of successful multimedia content requests by month and collection—and the Multimedia Report 2 (MR2)—the number of successful multimedia content requests by month, collection, and item type.

More information on usage statistics and COUNTER can be found in chapter 7.

The Financial Side of Access Models

Though numerous acquisition models for electronic resources exist, they can still all be boiled down to two options: licensed subscriptions and one-time purchases. As an ever-growing portion of library budgets are used to support subscription content, libraries are forced to reexamine the structure of their budgets and think carefully about the sustainability of ongoing commitments. Thoughtful budget planning and resource evaluation is critical. Although the majority of electronic resources librarians will not be responsible for balancing a collection budget or allocating dollars to line items, an electronic resources librarian will likely be tasked with analyzing usage statistics and supporting the evaluation of resources. To this end, electronic resources librarians need to evaluate usage statistics and collection analysis within the context of the access model. For instance, high use of a particular journal in an access-only, aggregator database combined low use of the same journal in a direct subscription should be carefully considered, because a cancellation of an individual journal subscription will likely have greater impact on the library's collection. With that said, for libraries with budget constraints access through aggregated databases may be the best economical choice to provide access to as much content as possible for the lowest price.

Conclusion

In the first chapter, electronic resources management was described as full of change and ambiguity. These changes are driven by a variety of reasons, ranging from enrollment shortfalls and changes in higher education, reductions in state and federal funding, and major upheavals in the publishing industry. Further, due to advances in everyday technologies and popular media, library patrons expect anytime, anywhere access to information. Traditional collecting methods no longer align with today's patrons needs, and just-in-case collection strategies have proved unsustainable in the changing library climate. The long-term implications of these fundamental changes in collection building are still unknown, but one thing is certain: the legacy print collections that reflect years of careful selection and cataloging is a relic of the past. The library collections of the future will be dynamic, fluid, and reflective of the demands of their changing environment.

NOTE

1. Trey Lemley and Jie Li, "'Big Deal' Journal Subscription Packages: Are They Worth the Cost?" *Journal of Electronic Resources in Medical Libraries* 12, no. 1 (2015): 1–10, doi: 10.1080/15424065.2015.1001959.

FURTHER READINGS

Boissy, Robert W., Thomas N. Taylor, Christine M. Stamison, Kittie S. Henderson, Ann Okerson, Rob Van Rennes, Jim Dooley, Rebecca Kemp, Geoffrey Little, David C. Fowler, Kimberly Douglas, Lawrence Clemens, and Alexis D. Linoski. "Is the 'Big Deal' Dying?" *Serials Review* 38 (2012): 36–45. doi: 10.1016/j.serrev.2011.12.012.

England, Mark, and Phill Jones. "Diversification of Access Pathways and the Role of Demand-Driven Acquisition: A Case Study at the University of Utah." *Serials Librarian* 66, no. 1–4 (2014): 96–105. doi: 10.1080/0361526X.2014.879012.

Enoch, Todd, and Karen R. Harker. "Planning for the Budget-ocalypse: The Evolution of a Serials/ER Cancellation Methodology." *The Serials Librarian* 68, no. 1–4 (2015): 282–89. doi: 10.1080/0361526X.2015.1025657.

Frazier, Kenneth. "What's the Big Deal?" *The Serials Librarian* 48, no. 1–2 (2005): 49–59. doi: 10.1300/J123v48n01_06.

Glasser, Sarah. "Judging Big Deals: Challenges, Outcomes, and Advice." *Journal of Electronic Resources Librarianship* 25, no. 4 (2013): 263–76. doi: 10.1080/1941126X.2013.847672.

Goedeken, Edward A., and Karen Lawson. "The Past, Present, and Future of Demand-Driven Acquisitions in Academic Libraries." *College and Research Libraries* 76, no. 2 (2015): 205–21. doi: 10.5860/crl.76.2.205.

Grogg, Jill E. "Using a Subscription Agent for eJournal Management." *Journal of Electronic Resources Librarianship* 22, no. 1–2 (2010): 7–10. doi: 10.1080/1941126X.2010.492649.

Hutchens, Chad. "Biz of Acq—Big Deal E-Journals Packages and Third Party Subscription Vendors: Does It Make Sense Anymore?" *Against the Grain* 18, no. 4 (2013): 24.

Kerby, Erin E., and Kelli Trei. "Minding the Gap: eBook Package Purchasing." *Collection Building* 34, no. 4 (2015): 113–18. doi: 10.1108/CB-06-2015-0008.

Lawson, Karen G. *Serials Collection Management in Recessionary Times*. London, New York: Routledge, 2013.

Litsey, Ryan, and Kenny Ketner. "Occam's Reader: The First Library-Developed eBook Interlibrary Loan System." *Collaborative Librarianship* 7, no. 1 (2015): 13–15.

Mischo, William H., Michael A. Norman, Wendy Allen Shelburne, and Mary C. Schlembach. "The Growth of Electronic Journals in Libraries: Access and Management Issues and Solutions." *Science and Technology Libraries* 26, no. 3–4 (2007): 29–59.

Nable, Jonathan, and David C. Fowler. "Leaving the 'Big Deal' . . . Five Years Later." *The Serials Librarian* 69, no. 1 (2015): 20–28. doi: 10.1080/0361526X.2015.1048037.

Pedersen, Wayne A., Janet Arcand, and Mark Forbis. "The Big Deal, Interlibrary Loan, and Building the User-Centered Journal Collection: A Case Study." *Serials Review* 40, no. 4 (2014): 242–50. doi: 10.1080/00987913.2014.975650

Price, Jason. "DDA in Context: Defining a Comprehensive eBook Acquisitions Strategy in an Access-Driven World." *Against the Grain* 27, no. 5 (2015): 20–24.

Rathmel, Angie, Lea Currie, and Todd Enoch. "'Big Deals' and Squeaky Wheels: Taking Stock of Your Stats." *The Serials Librarian* 68, no. 1–4 (2015): 26–37. doi: 10.1080/0361526X.2015.1013754.

Schopfel, Joachim, and Claire Leduc. "Big Deal and the Long Tail: eJournal Usage and Subscriptions." *Library Review* 61, no. 7 (2012): 497–510.

Smulewitz, Gracemary, David Celano, and Jose Luis Andrade. "ROI or Bust: A Glimpse into How Librarians, Publishers, and Agents Create Value for Survival." *The Serials Librarian* 64, no. 1–4 (2013): 216–23. doi: 10.1080/0361526X.2013.761064.

Strieb, Karla L., and Julia C. Blixrud. "Unwrapping the Bundle: An Examination of Research Libraries and the 'Big Deal.'" *Libraries and the Academy* 14, no. 4 (2014): 587–615. doi: 10.1353/pla.2014.0027.

Zhang, Yin, Kay Downey, Cristóbal Urbano, and Tom Klingler. "A Scenario Analysis of Demand-Driven Acquisition (DDA) of E-Books in Libraries." *Library Resources and Technical Services* 59, no. 2 (2015): 84–93.

3

Evaluating Content, Old and New

- Evaluating New Content
- Comparing Two or More Resources
- Perceived Future Use
- Measuring Impact
- Technical Requirements
- Accessibility
- Evaluating Renewals
- Conclusion

Electronic resources librarians have an important voice in the decision-making process for library collections, with effective evaluation being a critical component of the **electronic resources lifecycle**. Decisions about library collections—from new purchases and subscriptions to cancellations—should not be made alone, and should not be made without supporting data, whether quantitative or qualitative. To make collections decisions an electronic resources librarian can gather information from subject and reference librarians, acquisitions librarians and library stakeholders, in addition to a review of any curriculum and accreditation standards along with a standard evaluation of usage data.

With the proper set of tools and a clear eye on purpose, collections decisions can be made collaboratively.

Libraries can expect two basic types of resource evaluation: the first type occurs as a new resource is being evaluated for potential acquisition, and the second type occurs when a resource is up for renewal. Thorough resource evaluations will blend quantitative metrics (**COUNTER** statistics, **link resolver** statistics, **Interlibrary Loan** statistics, and overlap analyses) with qualitative metrics (feedback from stakeholders and the user community). Although the volume of possible metrics can feel overwhelming, remaining attentive to the situation at hand—such as the needs and expectations of library administration—can be an effective way to narrow the scope to only the most necessary or relevant metrics. With that said, metrics for evaluation will vary from one resource to the next, so be mindful to choose appropriate metrics and do not use the same canned, general metric for everything.

The next two sections will take a close look at the specific metrics and processes that can be used when 1) evaluating new content and 2) evaluating renewals.

ACRONYMS AND JARGON DEFINED
Cost-per-Use (CPU)

Cost-per-use (CPU) is a common metric used to measure the continued value of library materials in electronic format. To obtain cost-per-use data, the total cost of a resource is divided by the number of times it was used during a subscription period. Cost-per-use can be calculated for nearly any resource, including individual and package journals and ebooks, streaming video, and aggregator databases.

For more acronyms and jargon defined, see the glossary.

Evaluating New Content

When investigating a new resource for acquisition, the first step should be to assess its overall fit and relevance to the library's mission. For an academic library, the resource should work with the curriculum and/or the research needs of faculty, and it should be supported by the library's collection development policy. Subject librarians, public services staff, and faculty can be helpful resources to consult about the types of resources they need. In fact, in many cases they will come forward to recommend resources for acquisition. For a public library, the resource should benefit the local community of users and should match the library's core mission. Though an electronic resources librarian should have a strong understanding of the library's resource needs, soliciting input from actual stewards and users is crucial. Regardless of method, collaboration and communication are essential when taking the first steps to investigate possible new resources.

New Resource Evaluation Checklist

When reviewing either new acquisitions or renewals, a checklist is a simple but useful tool to ensure due-diligence.

Has the resource been directly requested?

☐ Yes, by _____

☐ No

Has the resource been evaluated by stakeholders or potential users?

☐ Yes, by _____

☐ No

Does the content fit with the curriculum and/or mission of the library?

☐ Yes

☐ No

Is this content duplicated within other library resources?

☐ Yes; if yes, is the duplication necessary? (Y___ N___)

☐ No

Does the content fill a gap or provide a solution for an information need?

☐ Yes

☐ No

Has the vendor made efforts to make the resource accessible; is it ADA compliant?

☐ Yes

☐ No

This chapter will go through the elements of this checklist, because answering each option is not quite as simple as checking a box.

To begin, efficient ways to solicit feedback from library stakeholders and enhance direct resource feedback include 1) resource request forms and 2) trial feedback questionnaires.

Resource Request Forms

Implementing resource request forms can be a simple solution to facilitate input from both stakeholders and users. Request forms generally ask for the requestor to provide: their name, institutional affiliation, the name of the desired resource, why a resource is needed, and a free-text space for specifics to add any qualitative information. Many of these forms are prominently posted to a library's website and the submissions generally go to collection development or acquisitions librarians for review. Often, when users fill out these forms, the requested resources are already available at the library—either due to user error or because resources are not connected fully to the library's discovery systems—or are best delivered through **Interlibrary Loan (ILL)** instead. For these reasons, it is important to have a method to triage these requests in order to reroute requests before they are considered for acquisition.

Trial Feedback Questionnaires

Trial subscriptions are also an effective way to get to know new electronic resources because they provide an opportunity to evaluate both the content and platform. Trials are short subscription periods, usually made available at no cost, that allow librarians to review a resource in advance of a full subscription. Most vendors provide trial access with no future commitment required, and can be as short as one week or as long as six months to a year. Trials can be reviewed by any stakeholder that seems appropriate, because most trials are set up using the same method of authentication as the library's subscription and purchases electronic resources, through **IP authentication**.

Once a trial has been set up staff should be informed of its availability along with any information regarding the active dates as well as how to access the trial. An effective way to ensure librarians both use the trial and submit feedback is to establish an online questionnaire to post alongside the trial

Sample Trial Feedback E-Mail

Dear [Librarian/Library Stakeholder],

The library currently has a trial subscription to [resource name] from [date] to [date]. I encourage you to take a look at this resource given [your past interest/ commitment to the subject/etc.]. After you have a chance to use and review this potential resource, please use the Trial Feedback Form located on the library's website [URL] to provide us with your feedback.

If you have any questions about this trial, or any of the library's other electronic resources, please feel free to contact me.

Sincerely,
[Your Name]
Electronic Resources Librarian

access point. Questions can range from content relevancy and quality, database functionality and user experience, and curriculum and research needs. Keep in mind, however, that as with any survey tool participants are likely to provide quality responses for only a limited number of questions, or only respond when their reaction is highly positive or negative. Again, though it is important for stakeholders to have an opportunity to evaluate and provide their own feedback about new resources, receiving consistent input can be a challenge. To optimize responses, send emails to users throughout the trial period to remind them of the trial and the importance of their response.

After trial feedback has been gathered, the following questions should have clear answers:

> What need will this resource fill?
>
> Who will be the primary users?
>
> How does this resource fit the academic curriculum, collection development policy, library mission statement, and/or criteria set by library administration or board of trustees?

If the answers to these questions determine a positive response—that the resource is indeed desired *and* needed—the next step will be to determine whether the content is available from a single-source or from multiple providers. When researching content availability, the following questions need to be considered:

Is the content duplicated in an existing library resource?

☐ Yes; if yes, is the duplication warranted (due to aggregator access, or preferred platform access)?

☐ No

Is the content made available freely online?

☐ Yes; if yes, is there additional or enhanced content included with a paid subscription?

☐ No

Is there a more competitive price from another vendor?

☐ Yes; if yes, which vendor? _____

☐ No

The next section will identify ways to compare resources objectively, using an overlap analysis.

Comparing Two or More Resources

If there is reason to believe that two or more resources contain overlapping content, an overlap analysis can be conducted to measure the percentage of overlap, both for title-level overlaps and for coverage years. Including holdings years in an overlap analysis is important because two resources can provide overlapping titles but have completely different coverage years. This situation is especially true when current resources also include smatterings of **backfile** years.

Title lists are needed to conduct an overlap analysis. Title lists (in Microsoft Excel or .csv format) can be acquired from vendor websites, from **knowledge base** exports, or can be directly requested from vendor sales representatives. Not all title lists are created equal, and the quality of the data should be checked before any analysis is done. Mandatory fields for an overlap analysis include title, ISSN, and coverage start and end dates. Vendors that advertise **KBART (Knowledge Bases and Related Tools)** compliance have ensured that their title lists include essential metadata fields that are

FIGURE 3.1

Overlap Analysis Example

NAME	TITLE UNIQUE	TOTAL UNIQUE	FULL HOLDING OVERLAP	PARTIAL HOLDING OVERLAP	TOTAL HOLDING OVERLAP	TOTAL	PERCENTAGE FULL OVERLAP	PERCENTAGE UNIQUE
Database A	120	120	73	41	114	234	31.2	51.3
Database B	553	553	47	69	116	669	7.0	82.7

kept up to date. If a KBART title list is available, it should be used by default before any other list is considered.

A basic overlap analysis can be done using Microsoft Excel pivot tables or with formulas such as VLOOKUP. In some cases, an overlap analysis can be automated using a knowledge base. The automated option requires that the library have a subscription to a knowledge base that offers that functionality, and that the packages being evaluated are included, active, and up to date.

The grid in figure 3.1 is an example of the results from a knowledge base overlap analysis, where "Full Holding Overlap" indicates the total overlaps between titles and content years between two resources; "Partial Holding Overlap" indicates the total titles with partial content year overlaps; and "Percentage Unique" is the total unique percentage within each reviewed database.

Perceived Future Use

To determine if a new resource fills an active need or a gap in the library's collection, Interlibrary Loan (ILL) requests can provide data on resources that were actively requested but not available for immediate use in the collection. To use Interlibrary Loan data as a metric, compare the annual subscription price for a resource to the corresponding price paid in ILL borrowing fees. To obtain the ILL borrowing fees, pull data from the ILL Borrowing Reports, which measures the titles requested from library patrons. For instance, if the cost of an annual subscription for "Journal A" is $100 per year, and the ILL Borrowing Report shows that ILL fees for "Journal A" have exceeded that cost each year for the past three years, then a direct subscription to "Journal A" would be a good candidate for an individual subscription. The scenario described above can be considered best practice in regard to budgeting. However, there are both guidelines and, at times, strict rules on how a library can loan subscription content. **CONTU guidelines** strongly suggest that a journal should be subscribed to directly if it has been borrowed through ILL more than five times in a calendar year. Though CONTU is not law, it is widely accepted. Further, license agreements for subscription resources may include language that sets how and when content can be shared through ILL. When a license agreement includes that language it overrides all other guidelines. For more information on licensing for electronic resources, see chapter 5.

Like any metric, ILL data cannot exist on its own. ILL requests will not always be an exact representation of definite future use, because library users can gain access to content through a variety of methods, and at times a patron request will be made for resources already available at the library. For these reasons, it is important to consider the results of an ILL analysis within the scope with the library's full collection. It is also important to communicate with ILL staff about electronic resources holdings, and the difference between the lack of access due to no subscription and an access error. Further, some resources are very important yet hardly used because they appeal to a niche audience and may not demonstrate a high volume of ILL requests. By keeping lines of communication open, an electronic resources librarian can ensure that resource evaluation is kept in context and that metrics are not analyzed in a vacuum.

Measuring Impact

When analyzing the importance of a particular resource, value metrics such as journal impact factors, SCImago rankings, and **altmetrics** can be helpful tools. These metrics provide insight into the value of a journal in its field and allow for journal comparison which can guide the development of a high-quality collection. Tread carefully, however, as the measurements from these ranking resources use distinct data and cannot be directly compared to one another.

Impact factors, published in Journal Citation Reports (JCR) within Web or Science, are available for the sciences and social sciences and use citation counts to determine the significance of a journal. The product SCImago pulls data from Elsevier's Scopus database. Multiple factors are pulled into a

SCImago ranking, such as **H index**, citations, and level of international collaboration, and each citation is weighted based on relative importance. Altmetrics are non-traditional metrics, and measure the item level, versus at the title level seen previously, and measure how content is used and shared in the Open Web and in social media. Altmetrics (plural) is the concept, and resources that supply altmetrics include Altmetric (Digital Science), ImpactStory (National Science Foundation and the Alfred P. Sloan Foundation), and Plum Analytics (EBSCO). In the information and research community there is currently debate about the validity of traditional impact factors and whether altmetrics might be a viable solution. Just like many of the metrics described in this chapter, these rankings are most effective when used in concert with other data and feedback from library constituents.

Technical Requirements

Once qualitative (requests and feedback) and quantitative (statistics and metrics) data has been gathered, further evaluation can focus on technical requirements. During a trial, an electronic resources librarian should evaluate interface design, functionality, and accessibility. Though vendors usually provide information sheets with database platform specifications, testing them in-house is an important step in the evaluation process.

When reviewing technical requirements, questions to consider include:

> How easily can users search, browse, and discover in both keyword
>   and direct citation search queries?
>
> How do search results display?
>
> Are there options to limit and refine search results? Are the options
>   clear and do they surface relevant content?
>
> Is the resource designed to work with the library's existing systems,
>   such as for IP and proxy authentication, the link resolver
>   and knowledge base, citation management software, and the
>   discovery layer?
>
> Does the administration dashboard provide opportunities for library
>   branding?

Keep in mind that a user-friendly interface involves more than just good design, and can be just as important as indexing, relevancy rankings, and filtering options. A resource that lacks a user-friendly interface will impede users' ability to find and access content, which may negatively impact the research experience and may contribute to low use over time.

Accessibility

Accessibility, or the design and functionality of web products for people with disabilities, is an essential factor to include in resource evaluations to ensure that all members of the user community can access digital resources. Section 504 of the Rehabilitation Act as well as the Americans with Disabilities Act (ADA) mandate that people with disabilities have access to public programs and services. Although section 504 and the ADA do not state that electronic resources fall into the category of public programs and services, the United States Department of Justice and the US Office of Civil Rights have stated that ADA accessibility requirements apply to electronic resources. Vendors can self-declare the level of their accessibility compliance by completing a **Voluntary Product Accessibility Template (VPAT)**. Most vendor VPATs are available upon request, and many can also be found in the VPAT Repository (http://uniaccessig.org/lua/vpat-repository/) developed by the group Libraries for Universal Accessibility (LUA), supported by the Association of College & Research Libraries (ACRL). Important to remember with vendor VPATs, however, is that their presence not equate to accessibility compliance. VPATs simply state to what level a vendor is or is not compliant, and having one should not preclude additional research into accessibility or usability testing.

When reviewing a vendors VPAT and overall accessibility, considerations include:

Is the platform compliant with **Web Content Accessibility Guidelines (WCAG)**?

Is the resource compatible with screen readers and voiceover technology?

Is language support (e.g., dictionaries) available?

Can the text size be adjusted?

Are there text tags for non-text items (such as tags for "image" and "video")?

When library resources are not designed to work with assistive technology, users with disabilities will be inherently denied access, even if the user already has assistive technology, such as a JAWS screen reader. Further, if assistive technology is partially available—for example, if an electronic journal in PDF format has been optimized with Optical Character Recognition (OCR) but the platform to discover and download the journal is not compliant—the resource as a whole will still be rendered inaccessible. When investigating platform accessibility, contact the vendor to talk about accessibility features. If it turns out that accessibility features are not yet available but the resource is vital for the library's collection, try to negotiate language into the license agreement that clearly states the current accessibility level with a confirmed time frame for when accessibility will be improved. This kind of documented advocacy not only shows vendors that accessibility is very important, but it also gives the library something to reference when inquiring about accessibility improvements.

The first part of this chapter has provided an overview of essential concerns when evaluating new electronic resources, and reviewed possible methods of evaluation. The next sections will focus on how to evaluate electronic resources for renewal. Keep in mind that, even though this chapter is divided into two distinct sections for new and renewing resources, the concerns and methods for evaluating new resources can also be used to evaluate renewals. With that said, the exact metrics used to evaluate renewals will not be available as metrics for new resources.

Evaluating Renewals

Renewals provide libraries with an opportunity to assess whether their subscription resources have continuing value. If the resource under evaluation has demonstrated use, the assumption is the resource will have continued value for the library. If a resource fails to demonstrate active use, or if the renewal cost is too steep, the renewal period provides an opportunity to end the subscription. Renewal dates are simply the date an invoice is due, but since electronic resource subscriptions can have start dates that begin at any time it is important to be aware of these dates and plan well in advance to conduct a thorough evaluation. The stringency and frequency of renewal evaluations will depend on a library's collection development policy and projected budget. If a library anticipates budget cuts, renewal evaluations might be more stringent than in previous years.

When evaluating renewals, keep the following questions in mind which will help keep metrics in context:

> Has the cost increased by a sustainable amount?
>
> Has the resource proved to be valuable, based on usage statistics?
>
> Will other subscription options be more cost-effective? Does the vendor provide options to modify simultaneous users, the package subscription, or are there PPV or DDA options?
>
> Has access been stable?
>
> Have there been any changes to the platform that might affect accessibility, either positively or negatively?
>
> Has any content been added or removed? Do the changes affect the overall quality of the resource?

The results of these questions may vary, and particular answers may hold more weight than others. Think through these options with colleagues, and with the library's budget in mind. Also take into account the time it takes to evaluate an individual resource, and whether that time is warranted based on the subscription price.

Yearly Percentage Increases

Although purchased electronic resources—such as journal and book archives, electronic reference works, and certain streaming video collections—are not affected by increasing annual fees, subscription electronic resources do require an annual subscription fee. Subscription fees typically increase between 4 to 7 percent each year, but some libraries and some resources may see higher or lower percentages. For libraries with flat-lined or level-funded budgets—meaning the budget will not increase, not even for inflation—or for those libraries with reduced budgets, percentage increases can wreak havoc. For this reason, libraries often have distinct collection development policies for subscription electronic resources' yearly percentage increases.

In advance of a renewal invoice, be sure to consult license agreements to check for predetermined percentage increases. Vendor representatives can also supply projected pricing for the upcoming year. Although projected prices are not final, they do give the library a perspective of where its budget stands in terms of allocated monies. In the absence of projected pricing, a renewal price can be estimated using a placeholder, such as 5 percent, until a final renewal invoice is received. Additionally, *Library Journal* publishes an annual Periodical Price Survey, which includes projected inflation rates broken down by discipline and analyzes and predicts the rate of inflation according to previous years.

Regardless of the method used to gauge the yearly percentage increase of electronic resources, determining a ballpark cost is critical to planning next steps, such as whether or not the library will need to prepare for possible cancellations and if so, how much cost savings is needed to balance the budget.

Resource Use

Usage statistics are the standard metric used for evaluating how a resource is used. Most statistics data will come from **COUNTER** reports, and additional data can be gathered from proxy logs, website analytics, and link resolver statistics. COUNTER reports count the number of times a resource is accessed and used. Metrics include counts of article downloads in electronic journals, record reviews and result clicks in databases, and chapter downloads and section requests in ebooks, among many others. Below are some ways in which COUNTER reports can assist in evaluating renewals.

> *Compare a resource against itself.* When looking at a single resource, consider how it performs over time, and how the individual titles perform. Consulting the Reporting Period Total over a period of years will demonstrate if the resource has shown consistent use. Further, when COUNTER reports are viewed in spreadsheet software such as Microsoft Excel, a filter can be applied to the Reporting Period Total values to surface both the highest and lowest use titles. Use this type of basic measurement to determine if the resource as a whole demonstrates enough use to justify the continued subscription.

> *Compare a resource against another similar resource.* COUNTER reports can also be compared against each other. To conduct this kind of analysis for a journal package, for instance, retrieve the

COUNTER Journal Report 1 for two similar content providers for the same reporting period. Be careful to consider two resources that are alike in subject matter and scope, and consider whether the two resources have overlapping content. To compare the use of individual titles between two reports, use something simple like Microsoft Excel's "Find" function, or conduct a more comprehensive comparison using the VLOOKUP formula.

Review link resolver statistics to determine the most popular, or least popular, referring resources. Link resolvers provide users with the ability to easily connect to the full-text of a citation. Therefore, link resolver statistics can show, among many other metrics, which aggregator databases referred users to full text the most. Such a statistic, when combined with a COUNTER Database Report 1 (DB1), can demonstrate which database subscriptions add the most value to the library's direct subscriptions.

Use COUNTER reports to calculate cost-per-use (CPU). Cost-per-use is calculated by dividing resource use—as demonstrated in a COUNTER report—by its cost. COUNTER reports are the gold standard when considering a cost-per-use evaluation, because the metrics in COUNTER reports are vetted and consistent. Resources that demonstrate high cost-per-use—that is, low usage and therefore a high price per use—might require additional investigation. Some institutions set a benchmark value when assessing cost-per-use, such as $11.00 per use, and anything at and above that benchmark will face further review and potential cancellation.

The next section will go in-depth on the cost-per-use calculation. For more information about usage statistics, COUNTER, and how electronic resources are measured, see chapter 7.

Calculating Cost-per-Use

The cost-per-use (CPU) metric is useful when evaluating resources for cost-effectiveness. The cost-per-use calculation can be done at the title, database, or package level, and is calculated by dividing the number of downloads in a single year by the total amount paid. Resources with a high cost-per-use are considered to have a poor return on investment (ROI).

For journal title cost-per-use, the COUNTER Journal Report 1 (JR1) will provide the necessary annual download statistics. The following example demonstrates the process of calculating cost-per-use at the title level:

Journal XYZ

2015 title subscription price:	$950.00
Use from JR1 in 2015:	23 downloads
2015 cost-per-use:	$950 ÷ 23 = $41.30 per use in 2015

Cost-per-download at the package level or database level is calculated by dividing the total annual number of downloads by the annual cost of the package. This calculation will help provide context to journal-level metrics and will provide an overall ROI figure for a package subscription. The example below demonstrates the process of calculating cost-per-use at the package level, which can also be applied to cost-per-use for database subscription assessment:

Journal Package XYZ

2015 package subscription price:	$23,500.00
Use from JR1 in 2015:	975 downloads
2015 cost-per-use:	$23,500 ÷ 975 = $24.10 per use

These metrics are most valuable when calculated over a multi-year period. A variety of factors can influence these numbers, including inflation costs, changes in curriculum and research on campus, and the evolving information needs of the user community. A multi-year analysis will be more likely to reflect usage trends, and will thus be useful to identify sudden changes and outliers.

Evaluation Do's and Don'ts

Do ask for help and input from colleagues, library stakeholders, and vendor representatives.

Don't focus on just one metric.

Do consider metrics in context with the material.

Do inquire with library vendors if data is not clear or not available.

Creating Local Benchmarks

When evaluating whether a resource has been successful, local benchmarks can be established to standardize how low and high usage is perceived. Earlier in this chapter, benchmarks based on ILL Borrowing Reports was discussed for evaluating new resources, and that same threshold concept can be applied to establish benchmarks for renewals. Using benchmarks for renewals can be a simple as ensuring that resource use increases over time, either as a concept or by a certain percentage each year; or benchmarks can be more comprehensive and can establish a minimum cost-per-use (CPU) figure that resources must meet in order to be renewed. A single benchmark for all resources will not be appropriate, but it can be done effectively for selective resources or for selective purchasing areas. To establish benchmarks, calculate the average cost-per-use for as many years as possible, at least three to start. Though the average CPU will be a definitive number, the next steps in benchmarking require a bit of judgement and a lot of collaboration. Talk to colleagues about a cost figure that will act as a benchmark and workshop the figure with test scenarios. Figures should be reasonable and scalable, and should correspond with the library's anticipated budget. Example benchmark figures for single journal titles can range from $5.00 to $30.00 USD depending on the budget and total user population, where any cost-per-use above that dollar amount might be cause for cancellation. Any benchmark also needs to take into consideration the content itself, as some resources will fail a benchmark review due to their specificity but may still be required for subject accreditation.

Resource Coverage

Just as an overlap analysis can be done to evaluate new resources, it can also be done to evaluate resource renewals. Because libraries add and cancel resources on a regular basis and because resources themselves change over time, the results from an overlap analysis can also change. Changes in resources are often caused by additions and deletions from a collection, due to **ceased titles**, **transfer titles**, or content moving **Open Access**. Fortunately, conducting an overlap analysis for renewals is the same exact process as conducting one for new resources: title lists from two or more resources can be compared manually using the VLOOKUP formula in Microsoft Excel, or an overlap analysis can be automated within a knowledge base.

Information gathered from the **Transfer Code of Practice** and Ulrichsweb can also be useful to consult when evaluating resource changes (but continuing access is, of course, subject to whether a library decides to continue its subscription for the next year). Though publishers are expected to notify libraries of changes, the Transfer Code of Practice also provides an online title look-up and an option for automatic email reminders. Ulrichsweb is a subscription database of periodical information and a useful source for current and accurate information. A library can use this consolidated information to determine how many titles have moved in and out of a subscription package and whether the subscription contents for the upcoming year still fit within the library's collection expectations.

Qualitative Renewal Evaluation

Once quantitative metrics have been thoroughly reviewed for subscription renewals, it will be important to consider the environment of resource use, especially for newer resources. Resources that have only been available to library users for a year may need more time and promotion before they will demonstrate their value. Other environmental factors to take into consideration are:

- whether access to the resource has been reliable and stable during the last subscription period
- whether the resource is cataloged and set up correctly in the library's discovery systems
- whether resource promotion and marketing occurred
- whether training and documentation was provided to either users or to librarians that support resource

Incorporating these considerations into a renewal evaluation will require a bit of judgment, especially if any of these environmental factors cause a resource on the edge of renewal or cancellation to move solidly into either category. More information on maintaining access to electronic resources can be found in chapter 6, and on marketing in chapter 9.

Conclusion

As decision-makers, electronic resources librarians need to exercise due dili-gence when evaluating resources to make the best possible choices for the library, its users, and the collection. The recommended strategies for effec-tive evaluation involve completing evaluation early and involving colleagues and other constituents in the process. Though evaluation metrics will vary depending on local library needs and policies, the process evaluation is none-theless an essential stage in the electronic resources lifecycle for any library.

FURTHER READINGS

Association of Specialized and Cooperative Library Agencies. "Internet and Web-Based Content Accessibility Checklist." August 2016. www.ala.org/ascla/asclaprotools/thinkaccessible/internetwebguidelines.

Bergstrom, Theodore, C., Paul N. Courant, R. Preston McAfee, and Michael A. Williams. "Evaluating Big Deal Journal Bundles." *Proceedings of the National Academy of Sciences* 111, no. 26 (2014): 9425–30. doi:10.1073/pnas.1403006111.

Blecic, Deborah D., Stephen E. Wiberley Jr., Joan B. Fiscella, Sarah Bahnmaier-Blaszczak, and Rebecca Lowery. "Deal or No Deal? Evaluating Big Deals and Their Journals." *College and Research Libraries* 74, no. 2 (2013): 178–94. doi: 10.5860/crl-300.

Brown, Jeanne M., and Eva D. Stowers. "Use of Data in Collections Work: An Exploratory Survey." *Collection Management* 38, no. 2 (2013): 143–62.

Brown, Meredith. "Is Almetrics an Acceptable Replacement for Citation Counts and the Impact Factor?." *The Serials Librarian* 67, no. 1 (2014): 27–30.

Bucknell, Terry. "Garbage In, Gospel Out: Twelve Reasons Why Librarians Should Not Accept Cost-Per-Download Figures at Face Value." *The Serials Librarian* 63, no. 2 (2012): 192–212.

Bucknall, Tim, Beth Bernhardt, and Amanda Johnson. "Using Cost Per Use to Assess Big Deals." *Serials Review* 40, no. 3 (2014): 194–96.

Crotty, David. "Altmetrics: Finding Meaningful Needles in the Data Haystack." *Serials Review* 40, no. 3 (2014): 141–46.

Emery, Jill, and Graham Stone. "Ongoing Evaluation and Access." *Library Technology Reports* 49, no. 2 (2013), 26–29.

Mulliken, Adina. "Introductory Resources for Web Accessibility." *ALA Connect,* March 25, 2015. http://connect.ala.org/node/79199.

Smulewitz, Gracemary, David Celano, and Jose Luis Andrade. "ROI or Bust: A Glimpse into How Librarians, Publishers, and Agents Create Value for Survival." *The Serials Librarian* 64, no. 1–4 (2013): 216–23. doi: 10.1080/0361526X .2013.761064.

Strieb, Karla L., and Julia C. Blixrud. "Unwrapping the Bundle: An Examination of Research Libraries and the 'Big Deal.'" *Libraries and the Academy* 14, no. 4 (2014): 587–615. doi: 10.1353/pla.2014.0027.

Torbert, Christina. "Cost-per-Use versus Hours-per-Report: Usage Reporting and the Value of Staff Time." *The Serials Librarian* 68, no. 1–4 (2015): 163–67.

Weicher, Maureen, and Tian Xiao Zhang. "Unbundling the 'Big Deal' with Pay-Per-View of E-Journal Articles." *The Serials Librarian* 63, no. 1 (2012): 28–37. doi: 10.1080/0361526X.2012.688167.

Changing the Rules

Selecting and Managing Open Access Resources

O pen Access refers to electronic resources that are free of licensing and copyright restrictions that can range from scholarly **peer-reviewed** articles, conference proceedings, theses, book chapters, and monographs. Open Access resources are openly available for anyone to access, regardless of institutional affiliation and, as a result, the uptick in interest for Open Access resources is surely noticeable to anyone in the information profession.

The difference between "free" and "Open Access" resources can be difficult for anyone to ascertain, but it is especially difficult for users to distinguish the difference, because all resources available from the Open Web *and* from the library are already "free" to them. Throw **hybrid journals** into the mix and the relationship of Open Access publishing to the more traditional access models becomes even more complicated. Although most electronic resources are made available to users through a library subscription, a growing number of electronic resources are being made available freely online, which ranges from the run-of-the-mill content on the Open Web to complimentary access as a result of a subscription to Open Access and anywhere in between.

Multiple factors have contributed to the increase in Open Access resources, including fundamental changes in scholarly communication practices, reductions in library budgets and spending, and users' growing expectations for free and immediate access to information. As a whole, the traditional model of publishing has proven in many ways to be unsustainable: the serials crisis of the 1990s is far from over, as libraries continue to struggle to keep up with subscription costs while at the same time publishers struggle to remain profitable. Financial realities have motivated libraries to participate in the Open Access movement by supporting Open Access awareness and publishing, as well as by ingesting Open Access resources into their collections. Publishers, too, have become interested in Open Access, and found ways to incorporate it into their business models.

Although chapter 10 highlights much of the philosophical discussion and trends emerging from around Open Access publishing, this chapter will provide practical information about selecting, activating, and managing Open Access resources.

Open Access Publishing

Open Access aims to establish free and legal access to scholarly works, enabling access to scholarly research for all who want it, not just individuals associated with institutions. When people talk about Open Access (OA), it is most often in reference to free electronic journals, but recent years have seen Open Access expand to monographs. When a resource is Open Access, it means that it has been published without restrictions on use or access, and that it is freely available online.

Not all Open Access resources are made available in the same way. Perhaps the greatest source of confusion associated with Open Access is its varying levels of openness, commonly referred to as **Green Open Access** and

What Is Creative Commons?

Creative Commons is an American nonprofit organization that provides a range of free copyright licenses for original works published online. Creative Commons licenses are available for anyone to use, and provide creators with an easy way to communicate how a work can be used or modified, which ranges from:

Attribution Designated with "CC BY": with this license users may distribute, remix, modify, and build on an original work (even commercially) but must give credit to the original author.

Attribution Non Commercial: Designated with "CC BY-NC": with this license users may distribute, remix, modify, and build on an original work, but must give credit to the original author *and* the revised content must be non-commercial.

Attribution ShareAlike: Designated with "CC BY-SA": with this license users can copy, distribute, display, perform, and modify a work (even commercially), but they must publish the modified work using the same terms as the original *and* they must license their new work under identical terms.

Attribution No Derivatives: Designated with "CC BY-ND": with this license users may redistribute the material (even commercially), as long as it remains unchanged and credit is given to the original author.

It is important to note that Creative Commons licenses are not a replacement for copyright; rather, they are built off copyright and designate how content can be reused.

Gold Open Access. For an electronic resources librarian, understanding the different types of Open Access is imperative, because the different types of Open Access determine how and when content is made available. This information becomes especially helpful when troubleshooting, and when communicating information about access availability with both colleagues and end-users.

Green Open Access

Green Open Access (Green OA) provides unrestricted access and use of resources through the process of authors' self-archiving in an Open Access repository, such as arXiv from Cornell University or PubMed Central from the National Institutes of Health. When an author submits an article to an Open Access repository it becomes freely available for anyone to use. The caveat with Green OA journals, however, is that they are generally not in their final version of publication, but are preprints that have been accepted for final publication with a traditional subscription-based publisher. With Green OA the publisher retains the copyrights for the final version, and the copyright for the preprint in the Open Access repository remains with the author. Because of the dual access points involved with Green OA the publisher may require a delay, referred to as an **embargo**, on when articles can be submitted to an Open Access repository. These embargos can range anywhere from six to eighteen months with the exact time frame dependent on the requirements of the publisher.

Sources for Authors to Consult
Before Publishing In An Open Access Publication

SHERPA/RoMEO
(www.sherpa.ac.uk/romeo/index.php)
   Database of the Open Access publishing permissions, based on journal title and publisher.

Eigenfactor Index of Open Access Fees
(www.eigenfactor.org/openaccess)
   An index that measures the impact of Open Access journals, based on Eigenfactor score (a measure of incoming citations and article publication frequency) and publication fees.

Think. Check. Submit.
(Thinkchecksubmit.org)
   A checklist for researchers to use in assessing the validity of Open Access publishers and journals.

Gold Open Access

The second option is to publish **Gold Open Access (Gold OA),** for which there is no embargo period. Although Green OA is made freely available to the public through the process of self-archiving, Gold OA material is made freely available from a traditional publisher, where the cost of publication is supported by **Author Processing Charges (APCs)** instead of through individual or institutional subscriptions. In the event that a publication is the result of research funded by a grant or institutional research fund, an APC can be paid by the author's institution, scholarly society, or government funding organization. Some publishers of Gold OA only publish Open Access, while others publish a mix of both traditional publications and Open Access content. The Public Library of Science (PLoS) is an example of a publisher that only provides Open Access content; SpringerNature and Wiley are examples of publishers that provide both subscription and Open Access content. Figure 4.1 summarizes the distinguishing characteristics of each type of Open Access.

FIGURE 4.1
Types of Open Access

TYPE	CHARACTERISTICS
Green Open Access	• Typically pre- and post-prints • Self-archiving in an open access repository • No fees (APCs or subscription) • Copyright remains with the author • Embargo period may apply
Gold Open Access	• Fees are paid by Author Processing Charges, grants, advertising, or society support • Published by traditional publisher in an Open Access or hybrid journal • No embargo period
Hybrid Open Access	• Published in a subscription journal that contains individual Open Access articles • Fees paid by a mix of Author Processing Charges and subscription fees

Hybrid Open Access

Sometimes referred to as "Paid Open Access," **hybrid journals** are subscription journals that include individual articles that are Open Access. The cost of publication for hybrid journals is paid by a combination of APCs and traditional subscription fees. Most commercial publishers offer a suite of hybrid journals along with their traditional subscription journals. Note that because hybrid journals provide a mix of both traditional articles and open access articles they may still appear in title lists for subscription journal packages and the total cost for the journal will likely be reduced as a result.

Selection and Evaluation of Open Access Resources

Just like any other resource the library makes available for its users, Open Access resources should be evaluated before being incorporated into the library's collection. Evaluation should be based on their quality, relevance to the library's mission and collection development policy, as well as their metadata quality and publication standards. The following questions are worth considering before making an OA resource discoverable and accessible in library systems:

> Does the content support user need and fit within the library's collection development policy?
>
> Who is the publisher, and does it have a good reputation?
>
> Are there reviews that speak to the value and quality of the content?
>
> Are the links to the material stable, and are they available in the knowledge base?
>
> Does the publisher provide a contact for support and troubleshooting?

Though most Open Access resources are peer-reviewed—especially those published under Gold OA—some OA publishers have come under scrutiny for not carefully reviewing manuscripts before submission. In 2013, the magazine *Science* published an article describing a fake scientific article that was submitted to, and accepted by, hundreds of Green OA publishers.[1] The fraudulent article was accepted by 157 publishers—including big name publishers like Sage and Elsevier—and was rejected by only 98—including PloS

Beware the Predatory Publisher

Predatory publishers are the black sheep of the Open Access movement, and are dangerous for two reasons: first, they take advantage of the Gold OA method and charge exploitatively high publication fees; second, content is not peer-reviewed, though it might claim to be. This practice is harmful to not only researchers and funding bodies, but also to the reputation of Open Access publishing.

In 2010, Jeffrey Beall, librarian and researcher at the University of Colorado Denver, created what is known as Beall's List, which up until early 2017 identified potentially predatory Open Access journals. The list is controversial and many members of the information community have questioned the criteria used to identify predatory publishers. Beall's List could be one source to check when researching and evaluating an OA journal, but should definitely not be the only metric used.

ONE.[2] Additionally, in 2009 Philip Davis, a then Cornell graduate student, submitted a fake computer-generated paper to an Open Access journal and it, too, was accepted.[3] Although these two examples are extreme situations that detail problems in the publishing industry as a whole, it is worth noting that careful evaluation is especially important when dealing with not only Open Access journals, but all journals.

A library's collection development policy is the best place to set guidelines and criteria for selecting Open Access resources. Incorporating simple rules for Open Access resources into a larger collection development policy will ensure that resources are selected based on the library's mission and user need, and not simply because they are free. If all Open Access resources were included in a library's collection, they would consume the collection.

A strong collection development policy for Open Access resources will address the following:

- preferred format types (journals, books, reference works) disciplines, and publishers
- designations to which subject selectors will be responsible to evaluate OA resources
- the frequency with which OA resources are evaluated, and how often new resources are added to the collection

Once an Open Access resource has been vetted for its content, it will need to have its technical requirements evaluated, such as:

- whether it has a stable platform and URL
- whether it has a technical support contact, for access and troubleshooting
- whether it can be added and managed within the library's systems (catalog, knowledge base, link resolver, and Database A–Z list)
- whether it has usage statistics available and if they are COUNTER-compliant

Specific criteria within rubrics can also facilitate consistent selection decisions. The University of North Texas Libraries developed a rubric for Open Access resources to use alongside its formal Collection Development Policy for Open Access resources.[4] For the full rubric, see Appendix A.

Discovery and Management of Open Access Resources

Electronic resources librarians must be thoughtful and consistent when making Open Access resources discoverable because the unique characteristics that distinguish Open Access resources from their subscription counterparts can also be those that complicate their management. One option is to activate Open Access resources in the **knowledge base**, side by side with the library's other subscription electronic resources. Alternatively, a subset of top-level Open Access repositories can be created within the library's Database A–Z list, or librarians can include Open Access resources in their research guides. For each of these options, there are an array of checks and balances.

Open Access resources are not purposefully subscribed to or licensed, and therefore a library's claim on them is not guaranteed. If bad links and metadata errors are pushed out to users as a result of knowledge base activations, the library does not have much power to request corrections. In fact, many technical services departments do not pursue access errors or metadata enhancements related to Open Access content, preferring to focus management and maintenance efforts on subscription resources. Therefore, planning and implementing an Open Access policy is crucial to managing workflows and setting reasonable expectations for colleagues and end-users.

Activating Open Access Targets in the Knowledge Base

One of the prime challenges associated with activating Open Access resources in a knowledge base is handling metadata inaccuracies, since metadata errors can result in a multitude of problems associated with user discovery and content linking. Though these challenges also exist with subscription resources, the lack of ownership and licensing rights can make resolving Open Access inaccuracies more difficult. (For a comprehensive review of knowledgebase maintenance and access for all kinds of resources, see chapter 6.) When subscription resources experience a metadata or access problem, an electronic resources librarian can contact their vendor for support. Open Access providers do not have the same legal responsibility to maintain their resources for accuracy, and are far less motivated to correct metadata and access problems. Additionally, Open Access repositories are likely to have much smaller staff operations than traditional publishers, and therefore may not have the infrastructure to keep up to date with metadata requirements for accurate discovery and linking.

Open Access resources are also particularly susceptible to errors due to platform migrations. For subscription resources, publishers have a list of subscribers on hand to notify about changes, but Open Access publishers do not have information on subscribers or users and therefore have no effective way to communicate a significant availability change. Although an Open Access publisher could post notification to its homepage, a librarian would have no way of knowing about a change unless by happenstance.

In addition to these primary technical issues with Open Access resources, it is important to check for: advertisements and pop-ups, inaccurate or misleading metadata relating to accessible content years, full-text linking, PDF download availability, and up-to-date contact information for editors and technical support. The following strategies can help when managing access issues with Open Access resources:

> *Focus on known publishers and repositories,* which are more likely to have the infrastructure in place to handle technical issues and maintain stable systems, such as PLoS, PubMed Central, and Gold OA publishers like Springer and Wiley.

> *Give proactive troubleshooting a try!* Though proactive linking checking for Open Access resources is a huge endeavor, a much more

manageable proactive troubleshooting method includes adding access notes to the link resolver menu and catalog records to alert users that the material is subject to change without notice. For more information on troubleshooting methods, see chapter 6.

Turn to the information community for help, where conferences and listservs are great sources of information to learn how other libraries are handling Open Access resources.

Have a policy that presents clear guidelines for how Open Access resources can be included in the library's collection. Share any Open Access policy with colleagues in other departments, because they will need to be aware of potential logistical, theoretical, and technical issues associated with access to Open Access resources.

Sample Open Access Directories, Publishers, and Repositories

arXiv—Open Access resources in physics, mathematics, computer science, quantitative biology, and statistics, from Cornell University

DSpace@MIT—MIT's Institutional Repository

DOAJ—Directory of Open Access Journals

DOAB—Directory of Open Access Books

OpenDOAR—The Directory of Open Access Repositories

PLoS—The Public Library of Science; non-profit, Open Access publisher

PubMed Central—Open resources in medicine, from the National Institutes of Health (NIH)

Zenodo—Open content from all fields of the sciences

The Future of Open Access

Open Access publishing is destined to increase as the demand for freely accessible research grows. The influence of the Open Access movement was noted by the White House where, in 2013, the Obama administration issued a directive from the Office of Science and Technology Policy (OSTP) that requires results of all federally funded research be made freely available to the public after a one-year embargo period. The directive also requires researchers to create data management plans articulating the long-term plans for data storage. The directive has forced researchers to reconsider how their work is published and disseminated to the broader research community and the public.

Industry standards for Open Access are vital because OA resources are playing an increasingly important role in research dissemination and scholarly communication. In 2015, NISO approved a new Recommended Practice, Access License and Indicators (NISO RP-22-2015), which aims to standardize metadata using text labels that indicate whether users can freely access and reuse research material. Before this Recommended Practice was instituted publishers used a variety of inconsistent labels and terms to describe Open Access, which was both confusing to users and to the machines reading the metadata.

Though NISO initiatives have a reach for libraries and beyond, there are also library-specific endeavors underway. TERMS creators Jill Emery and Graham Stone developed **Open Access Workflows in Academic Libraries (OAWAL)**, a community-driven approach to facilitates libraries in their evaluation and management of Open Access resources. Similar in nature to Emery and Stone's **TERMS** project, OAWAL is "an openly accessible wiki/blog site for librarians working on the management of open access workflow within their given institutions."[5] OAWAL is particularly relevant because many librarians are still learning how best to implement effective workflows in support of Open Access, while also staying up to date on the latest trends. To date OAWAL includes resources for advocacy, models and mandates, standards, library scholarly publishing, copyright issues, and discovery. OAWAL is available online, for free of course, at https://library3.hud.ac.uk/blogs/oawal/.

Open Access Advocacy and Awareness-Building on Campus

Though the availability of scholarly resources is a principle close to nearly every librarians heart—especially for electronic resources librarians—advocacy for Open Access looks very different across libraries and institutions. Such variations are caused by local goals, library mission statements, strategic plans, personnel and staffing, and institutional culture. For any electronic resources librarian interested in starting formal advocacy for Open Access, by far the most popular and widely-known event is Open Access Week. Celebrated internationally, Open Access Week (http://openaccessweek.org/) is an opportunity to draw attention to the benefits of Open Access and to inspire wider participation, such as encouraging faculty to publish Open Access, and, when possible, to deposit their work into an **institutional repository**. For libraries with limited staff time, Open Access week does not need to be a huge endeavor. In fact, the Open Access Week website contains ready-made promotional materials and examples of past years' events. A few examples of how college and university libraries have participated in Open Access Week includes:

- hosting panel discussions with faculty, students, administrators, and/or librarians to discuss how to publish Open Access
- inviting guest speakers to give talks on Open Access
- holding informational workshops and presentations on:
    - how to submit a work to the institutional repository
    - how to acquire funding for publishing fees, author rights and copyright, and Open Educational Resources (OERs)
    - how to create research data management plans
    - how to make data openly accessible
    - how to select an Open Access publisher

For many libraries, Open Access advocacy means more than sharing information and building awareness. A growing number of academic institutions are adopting Open Access policies that require their faculty to deposit all research outputs into the institutional repository. The most prominent example of such a policy is the Presidential Open Access Policy at the University of California. Adopted in 2015, the policy not only requires that all University of California employees deposit their research into the institutional repository, but it also allows authors to grant rights to the University before signing a contract with a publisher, which means research can be made available Open Access and still be published in a scholarly journal without violating publisher copyright terms. The University of California is far from the only university making great strides in Open Access. Harvard University, MIT, and Temple University have all also implemented Open Access policies.

The library plays an important role in facilitating the institutional repository submission process, which includes being able to answer questions about copyright, permissions rights, APCs, and any required citation metadata necessary to successfully upload research. If a library employs a scholarly communication librarian, these duties will likely be fulfilled by the person in

Check It Out

For a complete list of policies and mandates by institution, visit the ROARMAP's (Registry of Open Access Repository Mandates and Policies) website at http:// roarmap.eprints.org.

that position, and in which case an electronic resource librarian will play an important role when it comes to collaboration for discovery and troubleshooting. Regardless of organizational structure, all librarians should be aware of whether or not their institution has an Open Access policy, and how Open Access resources are selected, vetted, and enabled in the library's discovery systems. Users are unlikely to distinguish Open Access resources from subscription resources, or an institutional repository from other electronic resources databases, so having a knowledgeable staff to assist is invaluable.

Conclusion

As libraries seek a sustainable model for providing access to scholarly content, many libraries are leveling the field by reallocating funds from traditional subscription resources toward Open Access initiatives. Some libraries have established programs that contribute funds for Author Publication Charges (APCs), while others have opted to contribute to community-driven programs, such as Knowledge Unlatched. To participate in Knowledge Unlatched, funds are pledged toward the cost of publishing an ebook. An ebook becomes "unlatched" when the funding level is reached, meaning that its publication costs have been covered and that it is freely available. Undoubtedly, as the Open Access movement grows, more and more innovative, community-driven solutions to Open Access publishing will emerge. No matter the initiative or project, the financial support of Open Access requires careful decision-making and stakeholder buy-in, just like any other library acquisition.

In July 2016, the Association of College and Research Libraries (ACRL) announced its Policy Statement on Open Access to Scholarship by Academic Librarians, which encourages academic librarians to publish in Open Access journals and deposit works in Open Access repositories. This policy was a big step forward for the profession. As Open Access publishing continues to grow, academic librarians can lead by example by making their own scholarship openly accessible and be at the forefront of supporting access to research and scholarship.

NOTES

1. John Bohannon, "Who's Afraid of Peer Review?" *Science* 342, no. 6154 (2013): 60–65, doi: 10.1126/science.342.6154.60.
2. Ibid.
3. Natasha Gilbert, "Editor Will Quit Over Hoax Paper," *Nature*, June 15, 2009, www.nature.com/news/2009/090615/full/news.2009.571.html.
4. University of North Texas Libraries, "Collection Development Policy for Open Access and Born-Digital Resources," August 22, 2013, www.library.unt.edu/policies/collection-development/oa-collection-development-policy.
5. Jill Emery and Graham Stone, "OAWAL: Open Access Workflows for Academic Librarians," https://library3.hud.ac.uk/blogs/oawal/.

FURTHER READINGS

Anderson, Rick. "Should We Retire the Term 'Predatory Publishing'?" *The Scholarly Kitchen,* May 11, 2015. https://scholarlykitchen.sspnet.org/2015/05/11/should-we-retire-the-term-predatory-publishing.

Basken, Paul. "The U. of California's Open Access Promise Hits a Snag: The Faculty." *The Chronicle of Higher Education*, July 7, 2016.

Beaubien, Sarah, and Max Eckard. "Addressing Faculty Publishing Concerns with Open Access Journal Quality Indicators." *Journal of Librarianship and Scholarly Communication* 2, no. 2 (2014): eP1133. http://dx.doi.org/10.7710/2162-3309.1133.

Bhatt, Anjana. "Management of Open Access Collections: Current Scenario in American Academic Libraries and a Sample Workflow," *LIPS—2016 From Ownership to Access Leveraging the Digital Paradigm Proceedings,* 225–28.

Berger, Monica and Jill Cirasella. "Beyond Beall's List: Better Understanding Predatory Publishers." *College and Research Libraries News* 76, no. 3 (2015): 132–35.

Burns, C. Sean, Amy Lana, and John M. Budd. "Institutional Repositories: Exploration of Cost and Value." *D-Lib Magazine* 19, no. 1/2 (2013). doi: 10.1045/january2013-burns.

Chant, Ian. "Increasing Participation in Your Institutional Repository." *Library Journal* 141, no. 3 (2016): 20–21.

Cochran, Angela. "A Funny Thing Happened on the Way to OA." *The Scholarly Kitchen,* February 25, 2016. https://scholarlykitchen.sspnet.org/2016/02/25/a-funny-thing-happened-on-the-way-to-oa/.

Crotty, David. "The Pay It Forward Project: Confirming What We Already Knew About Open Access." *The Scholarly Kitchen,* August 9, 2016. https://scholarlykitchen.sspnet.org/2016/08/09/the-pay-it-forward-project-confirming-what-we-already-knew-about-open-access/.

Emery, Jill, and Graham Stone. "Introduction to OAWAL: Open Access Workflows for Academic Libraries." *Serials Review* 40 (2014): 83–87. doi: 10.1080/00987913.2014.924307.

Esposito, Joseph. "Sci-Hub and the Four Horsemen of the Internet." *The Scholarly Kitchen,* March 2, 2016. https://scholarlykitchen.sspnet.org/2016/03/02/sci-hub-and-the-four-horsemen-of-the-internet.

Gadd, Elizabeth and Denise Troll Covey. "What Does 'Green' Open Access Mean? Tracking Twelve Years of Changes to Journal Publisher Self-Archiving Policies." *Journal of Librarianship and Information Science* (2016). doi: 10.1177/096100061667406.

Johnson, Richard K. "Institutional Repositories: Partnering with Faculty to Enhance Scholarly Communication." *D-Lib Magazine* 8, no. 11 (2002). doi: 10.1045/november2002-johnson.

Nassi-Calò, Lilian. "How Much Does It Cost to Publish in Open Access?" *SciELO in Perspective,* September 18, 2013. http://blog.scielo.org/en/2013/09/18/how-much-does-it-cost-to-publish-in-open-access.

Senack, Ethan, and Robert Donoghue. "Covering the Cost: Why We Can No Longer Afford to Ignore High Textbook Prices." February 2016. www.studentpirgs.org/sites/student/files/reports/National%20-%20COVERING%20THE%20COST.pdf.

Sheehan, Jerry. "Increasing Access to the Results of Federally Funded Science," February 22, 2016. www.whitehouse.gov/blog/2016/02/22/increasing-access-results-federally-funded-science.

Stebbins, Michael. "Expanding Public Access to the Results of Federally Funded Research," February 22, 2013. www.whitehouse.gov/blog/2013/02/22/expanding-public-access-results-federally-funded-research.

Straumsheim, Carl. "Scaling Up OER." *Inside Higher Ed,* June 22, 2016. www.insidehighered.com/news/2016/06/22/new-university-initiatives-focus-bringing-open-educational-resources-masses.

Suber, Peter. *Open Access.* Cambridge, MA: MIT Press, 2012.

Negotiation and Licensing for Electronic Resources

Licensing refers to the process by which electronic resources are legally acquired by libraries, where a **license agreement** sets legally binding terms for how electronic resources will be paid for and used. Though licensing is an integral aspect of electronic resources management, most electronic resources librarians have not had formal training in handling license agreements and even fewer are legally authorized to sign them. Still, an increasing number of librarians are involved in the negotiation and license review process. It is safe to say that **copyright law** is a more comfortable area for most librarians, but it is critical for any contemporary librarian to have a general understanding of how license agreements govern resource use.

After all, because license agreements determine how electronic resources are used, librarians need to be aware of their terms and how to translate them out to users. Apropos here is the Latin phrase "Ignorantia juris non excusat," meaning "ignorance of law excuses no one."

In this chapter, the structure and language of license agreements will be picked apart, so that when faced with a challenge—whether it be reviewing a new license, interpreting an old license, or answering a patron question about use—identifying key clauses and language will be much less daunting. Although the breakdown of the specific tasks involved in the licensing process will vary from one library to the next, understanding the general principles of license agreements will be beneficial for nearly all information professionals.

But first things first: this chapter is *not* legal advice.

That last sentence is so important it needs to stand on its own. The authors of this text are not lawyers, but rather librarians with experience in academic publishing, library instruction, electronic resource management, and collection development. If faced with a specific licensing conundrum—and licensing conundrums *will* occur—it is best to consult with institutional legal counsel or, at the very least, internal colleagues. The examples found in this chapter are not recommendations; rather, they are anecdotes about the licensing concerns and methods of both libraries and vendors. The best and most basic *non-legal* advice for library licensing is actually very straightforward:

> There is simply no excuse for a library to accept a vendor's "standard" license agreement unless it meets all of the conditions now accepted as "best practices" by the librarians and legal advisors to them who are the leaders in licensing issues today. It must also meet the needs of the users of the library, which must forcefully negotiate the changes necessary to make it a 'win-win' agreement for both library and resource provider (Webb, 1998).[1]

This statement, with its emphasis on licensing as a means of meeting the needs of all participating parties—including the library, vendor, and end user—applies just as much today as it did when it was written in 1998. But that is not to say that the licensing practices in 1998 were anything like today's. If licensing has not yet sounded daunting enough, rest assured that licensing practices are continually changing as librarians and vendors gain more experience and as business models evolve. Despite the multitude of licensing variables, the principles of licensing will likely not change: at its core licensing provides access to resources for end-users, which libraries have been doing for their print materials for centuries. Though license agreements specifically address electronic resources, they should still reflect the specific needs—whether it be materials for education, research, or leisure—of an institution.

Far more is at stake with licensed resources than with print material. A signed contract is an agreement to comply, and if language in the license agreement cannot be reasonably fulfilled then the library stands at financial and legal risk. Such risks are no different than with any other contract, from obtaining a mortgage to a contract for phone or internet service. A well-negotiated license agreement will reflect the intentions and abilities of both the **Licensee** (the library) and the **Licensor** (the vendor or publisher). Such a situation can become difficult if a license agreement includes language that makes the library responsible for the actions of library users, but this topic will be discussed more later.

A Word on Price Negotiation

Before license review can begin to evaluate the legal access rights for electronic resources, there first needs to be a product with an agreed-upon price, because both the product and price will determine which legal rights are needed by both parties, Licensee and Licensor. Negotiation is an essential step in acquiring new resources. However, most librarians are not in the profession to haggle business terms—though, yes, some are very, very good at it—and negotiation can be an anxiety-provoking exercise. Fortunately, a wealth of literature exists on the subject with plenty of information and best practices. The following list of "do's and don'ts" highlights many of the important aspects of negotiation:

> *Do* be prepared
>> In advance of price negotiation, identify desired outcomes and consider a price compromise that could be accepted should an ideal price not be attainable.

> *Do* have evidence
>> COUNTER reports can be good price negotiation tools to demonstrate whether a resource is being used frequently, but also to

demonstrate that a resource is not being used enough (a potential talking point for a lower price!).

Do know your limits

If a resource can only be acquired for a certain price, be clear about what that price is. Do not try to bluff as a means of persuasion (essentially, be honest, it's good business!). However, if a resource is not an absolute necessity and an acceptable price cannot be agreed upon, be prepared to walk away.

Do look for creative solutions

If provider cannot provide an agreeable price based on one set of terms, they may be willing to explore other creative, multi-year agreements to accommodate a library's budgetary constraints.

Don't damage the library/vendor relationship for the sake of a good price

Remain courteous and professional throughout the process. Remember that the library community is small, and that includes library vendors and publishers in the field. Vendor representatives are doing their job, which is to make sales at a profitable price.

Don't enter the negotiation with unrealistic expectations

Negotiation is just that, negotiation, and the process can take time and require a lot of back and forth. The outcome should ultimately result in a compromise for both parties. Do not enter the negotiation expecting to engage in an argument.

Remember that without libraries and librarians there would not be a price to negotiate, or a service or product to sell. Essentially, nobody would be at the table if it weren't for the customer—again, the library—and librarians ultimately have the upper hand.

Although the goal of most library/vendor negotiations is a discounted price or more desirable license terms, library/vendor negotiations are also an opportunity to build relationships and learn about the marketplace. Good negotiation skills come with practice, but successful negotiations are ultimately the result of thoughtful preparation and research. An excellent example of relationship-building negotiation is the California Digital Library's (CDL) negotiations with Elsevier. In 2014, CDL negotiated (for participating University of California consortial campuses) a multi-year subscription with

Learn More About Price Negotiation

"The Librarian's Guide to Negotiation: Winning Strategies for the Digital Age," Catherine Gilbert, *The Australian Library Journal* 62, no. 1 (2013): 73–74.

Getting to Yes: Negotiating Agreement Without Giving In, Roger Fisher and William Ury, Penguin, 3rd Edition, 2011.

"Gateway to Good Negotiation: From Computer Mediated Communication to Playing Hardball," Jill Grogg, Sara E. Morris, and Beth Ashmore, *The Serials Librarian* 62, no. 1–4 (2012): 183–88.

"Principles of Negotiation," C. Derrik Hiatt, Lesley Jackson, and Katherine Hill, *Serials Review* 41, no. 3 (2015): 180–83.

minimal annual price increases for ScienceDirect, a purchase of the 2014 ebook frontlist, and a one-year trial to Scopus. This negotiation success was the result of long-term discussions and planning by both parties.

The Distinct Role of Licensing

A license agreement is a legal document that determines the right to use electronic resources under a specific set of conditions (such as price, access method, and users) within a set period of time. Licensed electronic resources—which can range from databases and electronic journal packages, to ebooks and streaming media, to name a few—are distinct from their print counterparts in that they are not owned. Ownership of electronic resources always remains with the provider, and even if electronic resources are purchased for **perpetual access**. In this way, electronic resources diverge from copyright law and the **first sale doctrine** that is familiar to librarians. Where the Copyright Clearance Center once reigned over the use and sharing of print materials, electronic resources rely on contract law, and contract law actually overrides copyright law. A license agreement, however, does not mean that electronic resources are wholly without the benefits from copyright law. In fact, a well-negotiated license agreement can include even more beneficial terms than copyright law, because even copyright law on its own cannot represent *how* electronic resources are used. Therefore, a license agreement actually goes a step further than copyright, setting the rules for important things like who can use a resource (**"authorized users"**), how resources can be shared ("resource sharing"), and how a resource can be maintained long-term ("archival rights"). The specifics about these terms, and more, will be discussed later in this chapter. In recent years, libraries have worked to increase the deliverables within license agreements, and such trends have made the clauses in license agreements even more favorable for end-users, bringing an upswing in the availability of license clauses that determine vendor compliance with the Americans with Disabilities Act.

When reviewing a license agreement, it is important to keep in mind that an agreement for one resource at one institution can vary greatly from one at another institution for the same exact resource. Not only can the price vary, but so can the terms. Therefore, the best source of information about how electronic resources can be used lives within a library's own license agreements. With so many variables in place, it is no surprise that licensing horror stories abound in library circles: unresponsive publishers, tedious legal jargon, confusing **amendments**, filing cabinets filled with paper licenses dating from the mid-1990s, unclear signing authorities, missing licenses—the list can go on and on. The process of licensing is complex, and the agreements themselves lengthy and abundant. Staying current and keeping organized are the best defenses against becoming overwhelmed.

A traditional license is composed of three parts: **Terms and Conditions**, or the **boilerplate**; the business terms; and the description of the resource being acquired, which often arrives the form of a license amendment, purchase order, or invoice. Depending on the business practices of an individual vendor, the pieces of a license agreement can be presented as sections of one complete document, or as multiple distinct documents. As an answer to the complexities and delays of licensing electronic resources, the NISO **Shared E-Resource Understanding (SERU)** working group was formed in 2006 to allow libraries and publishers to forgo license agreements in favor of 1) statements of common understandings, and 2) copyright law. SERU simplifies the licensing process by documenting *only* the business terms, which then become uniform for all participating vendors and libraries. The license review process can be skipped if a vendor and a library both participate in SERU, because the terms have already been mutually agreed upon by

Check It Out

"SERU: A Shared Electronic Resource Understanding," National Information Standards Organization, May 2012, www.niso.org/publications/rp/RP-7-2012_SERU.pdf.

accepting SERU. Although SERU's primary focus is on copyright law, it also includes some of the built-in business terms that are critically important for libraries, including definitions of authorized users, appropriate use, confidentiality and privacy, vendor service, and archival and perpetual access. With the preset terms of SERU licensing, the licensing process can be expedited so that a library can move forward to invoice and activate content, thereby expediting access to users.

The License Review and Negotiation Process

When SERU is not a viable alternative for both parties the full licensing process will be required. The licensing process begins with a request to review a vendor's boilerplate license agreement. The boilerplate license agreement is generally a digital file sent over email. It can also come in the form of a click-through agreement on a vendor's website. **Click-through license** agreements require passive acceptance, which many libraries, especially those that are part of state or government institutions, cannot provide. In these situations, it is acceptable to request an alternate version in an editable format, such as in the form of Microsoft Word document. Vendors that frequently work with libraries will have received such requests countless other times.

With the boilerplate license agreement in hand, the review process can begin. The most important thing to keep in mind when reviewing a boilerplate agreement is that it has been drafted specifically to satisfy the needs of the resource provider. Although boilerplate agreements can, and often do, include clauses that are also beneficial for libraries, they will likely not include *all* the language and clauses required by a library to truly fulfill institutional need. The needs and expectations of the library *and* the institution are the most important priorities to remember when conducting a license review. The library's mission statement will be a useful resource when reviewing license clauses. A well-negotiated license agreement will correspond with the mission of the library and the institution. By working with a library's internal legal counsel to develop library-specific template language, or a **model license agreement**, the process of comparing the provider's boilerplate version to the library's ideal language becomes much easier. For example, if a library's mission statement specifically addresses distance education, a model license can set specific language to address remote access for all users, which can then be copied and inserted into the provider's boilerplate agreement.

When a library submits modification requests, the vendor will have the opportunity to review and respond. This part of the process is similar to price negotiation. Responses can range from full acceptance, requests for additional modifications, or follow-up questions. Depending on the extent of changes requested by both parties, the modification and review process can be time-consuming and result in delayed acquisitions and access. Defining and communicating the needs and expectations of the library will allow the vendor to have a better understanding of why certain terms must be included. Clear and open communication between the library and the vendor can go a long way towards creating a stress-free process, while also ensuring that the library maintains a good relationship with the vendor. In extreme cases—when mutual terms cannot be agreed upon between the library and the vendor—the license review process can completely stall, or even prevent, an acquisition. When a negotiation is successful and the document is acceptable by both parties it will be time to have it signed by both the Licensee and the Licensor. Once the signatory process is complete it is considered to be fully executed and binding.

It cannot be reiterated enough that (most) librarians are not lawyers, and the workflows to review and approve license language can be complex. There is good news, however! Libraries have been licensing electronic resources for over twenty years, and there exists a vast community of librarians with licensing experience and advice. It will be extremely rare for an electronic resources librarian to have to start a license review workflow from the ground up.

But What Does It Mean?
Sample Clauses and Descriptions

Whether conducting license review for the first time or the hundredth time, questions will always arise about legal jargon and the relevancy and purpose of license clauses. Inevitably, some license clauses will be written with such complexity that their purpose will be confounding. Because license agreements vary in content and organizational structure among vendors and products, there will always be clauses that require a second review or consultation, even for a seasoned license reviewer. Both newbies and those experienced with license review can benefit from model license agreements, checklists, and colleagues who are willing to do a second or even third review.

The next two sections of this chapter will outline the most common clauses found in license agreements: "Part 1: Terms and Conditions", and "Part 2: Content License and Business Terms". Each sample clause below includes language from actual license agreements, which range from model licenses from library **consortia** and advocacy groups to vendor boilerplate license agreements. When going through these sample clauses, consider how language could be changed, where problems could arise, and what information could be added to make the language more beneficial. Additionally, be sure to check for what is included *and* what is not included. Not every license agreement titles each clause heading in exactly the same way, and not every license agreement will use the same overall terminology. Further, some license agreements might omit entire clauses or include non-standard clauses. Finally, in certain cases it might be advisable to remain silent rather than agree to language that is less than ideal. In some cases less than ideal can put the library at risk. There is a difference between language that is missing and should be included, and language that both parties have deliberately omitted in order to come to agreeable terms.

The license clauses described and explained in the next sections mirror the sample license review checklist provided in appendix B. The checklist is intended to be a learning tool to facilitate understanding the review of license agreements.

PART 1 Terms and Conditions

LICENSE PARTIES

> This License Agreement (the "Agreement") is made effective as of *[date]*
> (the "Effective Date") between *[Provider Name, Address, State, Country,*
> *Postal Code]* (the "Licensor") and *[Institution Name, Address, State,*
> *Country, Postal Code]*, on behalf of *[Library Name, Address, State,*
> *Country, Postal Code]* ("Licensee").

Though the participating parties of a license agreement may seem straightforward, both parties should be clearly defined early on in the license agreement in order to remove any ambiguity about the names of the vendor and library or institution, contact persons, and billing addresses. The parties of a license agreement are commonly referred to as the Licensor and Licensee, where the Licensor will always be the party providing the content, whether it be a third-party vendor or publisher; and the Licensee is the library or the institution acquiring the content. A librarian involved in the licensing process works *on behalf* of the Licensee, and this point is very important to remember: anything agreed upon in a license is agreed upon for the institution as a whole, and not for the individual doing the license review. And the same goes for the Licensor: the party providing the content should have the legal right to do so. These two points can be quickly forgotten, especially as the license review process becomes routine.

Authorized users should probably not be a party to the license, because most institutions will not want to take responsibility for the actions of their individual users. If the preamble of a license agreement includes any phrase such as "the Licensee and its authorize users," consider the implications of end-users being party to the license agreement.

DEFINITIONS

When reading through license clauses it can be easy to assume that key phrases and words are being used in their most widely understood definitions. However, what might be considered a valid definition for "**Interlibrary Loan**" to a vendor might be quite different from a librarian's understanding or an institution's needs. And the same goes for other common phrases, such as "Scholarly Sharing," "Authorized Users," "Course Reserves," and "**Course**

Packs," to name only a few. If a license agreement includes a section titled "Definitions," any included words or phrases should be considered license-specific and non-standard, and therefore should be reviewed just as carefully as the rest of the license agreement. Similarly, if a definitions section is not included in a boilerplate license, it may be advisable to include one. In such circumstances, preapproved model license language can simply be copied into a boilerplate license agreement.

Keep in mind any capitalized, underlined, quoted, or italicized word that has also been predefined by the Licensor—especially if that word or phrase is not capitalized in everyday speech—and should be understood as described by the license definitions rather than under any commonly understood definition.

JURISDICTION AND GOVERNING LAW

> The License Agreement and the rights and obligations of the parties hereto shall be construed, interpreted and determined in accordance with the laws of the State of New York without reference to the choice-of-law principles of this state or any other jurisdiction and without the aid of any rule, custom or canon requiring construction or interpretation of the License Agreement against the draftsmen.
>
> Terms and Conditions for Online Products of Springer[2]

A library's local state laws should be applied to a license agreement. It would not be feasible to agree to a license that cites outside jurisdiction, which would require an understanding of, potentially, many different laws in a variety of different vendor locations. Further, for state institutions the governing law might be predetermined by policy or statute. If jurisdiction becomes a sticking point in the negotiation process, consult with any available internal General Counsel, as there may be an alternate location that could be more favorable to both parties.

INDEMNIFICATION

> The Licensor shall indemnify, and hold Licensee and Authorized Users harmless for any losses, claims, damages, awards, penalties, or injuries incurred, including reasonable attorney's fees, which arise from any claim by any third party of an alleged infringement of any copyright or any

> other proprietary right arising out of the use of the Licensed Materials by the Licensee or any Authorized User. NO LIMITATION OF LIABILITY SET FORTH ELSEWHERE IN THIS AGREEMENT IS APPLICABLE TO THIS INDEMNIFICATION. Each party shall indemnify and hold the other harmless for any losses, claims, damages, awards, penalties, or injuries incurred, including reasonable attorney's fees, which arise from any alleged breach of such indemnifying party's representations and warranties made under this Agreement, provided that the indemnifying party is promptly notified of any such claims. The indemnifying party shall have the right to defend such claims at its own expense. The other party shall provide assistance in investigating and defending such claims as the indemnifying party may reasonably request and have the right to participate in the defense at its own expense.
>
> CDL License Agreement Checklist[3]

Boilerplate licenses will almost always include indemnification clauses. Ideally, a license agreement should mutually indemnify both the Licensee and the Licensor. If nothing else, it should have the Licensor indemnify and hold the Licensee harmless from any claim of infringement with the license on any patent, copyright, trademark, or trade secret of any third party. However, many libraries cannot agree to indemnify the vendor at all. If an indemnification clause is present, consult with colleagues or any available internal General Counsel on whether the language can be modified.

FORCE MAJEURE

> Neither party shall be liable in damages or have the right to terminate this Agreement for any delay or default in performing hereunder if such delay or default is caused by conditions beyond its control, including Acts of God, Government restrictions (including the denial or cancellation of any export or other necessary license), wars, insurrections, labor strikes, and/or any other cause beyond the reasonable control of the party whose performance is affected.
>
> Liblicense Model License Agreement[4]

Force Majeure, from the French which translates to "superior force," is a common contract clause that frees both parties of liability under extreme circumstances, such as acts of war and acts of God (hurricanes, earthquakes, etc.). If a Force Majeure clause is included in a license agreement, an ideal version of such a clause will represent both parties. If the clause only references Force Majeure rights for one party, consider amending the clause to reference both parties.

TERMINATION OF ACCESS/SECURITY BREACH

> Either party may terminate this license for material breach of the agreement by the other with written notice in paper or electronic form (with verified receipt). Prior to termination, the offending party will have thirty (30) days to cure the breach. If the Licensor is the breaching party and the License is subsequently terminated, Licensor shall make a pro rata refund of the Fee to the Licensee, taking into account the remaining unexpired portion of the Subscription Period.
>
> Florida Virtual Campus Guidelines for E-Resource License Agreements[5]

Although license agreements have a preset term during which they will remain in effect, a termination clause outlines the circumstances by which either the Licensee or the Licensor can end the contract. A Licensor should have the right to terminate a license agreement if the Licensee has been found to be in breach of contract, however, it is not ideal to grant the Licensor the unilateral right to terminate without adequate notice or verification from the Licensee. For instance, a suspected security breach can be grounds for termination, but both parties should be given adequate time to address and resolve the issue. Termination clauses will generally have language to provide the Licensee with refunds for any portion of the subscription period that was not fulfilled.

NOTICE OF CLICK-THROUGH LICENSE

> In the event that Licensor requires Authorized Users to agree to additional terms relating to the use of the Licensed Materials (commonly referred to as "click-through" or "clickwrap" licenses), or otherwise attempts to impose terms on Authorized Users through online terms and conditions invoked by the mere use or viewing of the Licensed Materials, such terms shall not materially differ from the provisions of this Agreement. In the event of any conflict between the click-through terms or online terms

and conditions and this Agreement, the terms of this Agreement shall
prevail. For the avoidance of doubt, Authorized Users are not a party to
this Agreement.

Liblicense Model License Agreement[6]

Patrons may from time to time encounter click-through agreements for **terms
of use** within resource platforms. Because passive agreements are common-
place on the Open Web, for instance within social media and cloud-based
software services, users may ignore such features and accept the terms in
order to pass through to the resource as quickly as possible. Although most
user-focused click-through agreements put the burden of responsibility on
the user, they can be potentially perilous if the language makes the institution liable for their user's actions. Be sure to keep in mind the purpose of a
click-through agreement and to check for matching language and references
to it in the negotiated license agreement. If the language in a click-through
agreement is not favorable, language can be included in a full license agreement that overrides any passive, click-through agreements, which can be
seen above with the inclusion of the phrase "the terms of this Agreement
shall prevail."

AUTHORIZED USERS

All current students, staff and faculty of a Member (whether full or part-
time, permanent, temporary, contract or visiting appointments), and
alumni of a Member, regardless of the physical location of such persons.
For the avoidance of doubt, Authorized Users include those persons who
are granted library user privileges according to the policies of a Member,
including but not limited to retired faculty and staff.

CRKN Model License Agreement[7]

A clause that defines "Authorized Users" can appear in several different
clauses in a license agreement, ranging from "Definitions" to a separate clause
of its own. The license agreement should describe authorized users exactly
as they are understood at the institution and the library. Some licenses will
include a separate section for walk-in users, emeritus faculty, and remote
users, while at other times a higher fee can be requested for the inclusion of
additional sets of authorized users. For this reason, "Authorized Users" is a
point that should be discussed in advance of license negotiation, preferably

during price negotiation. License agreements might also include a separate section for "*Un*authorized Users," in which case such a clause should be very carefully reviewed and evaluated, as essential users can be legally blocked access. "Authorized Users" should also be permitted to use the library's electronic content within the parameters of any clauses that defines "Authorized Uses" and/or "Permitted Uses."

PERMITTED USES

> Licensee and Authorized Users may make all use of the Licensed Materials as is consistent with the Fair Use Provisions of United States and international law. Nothing in this Agreement shall be interpreted to limit in any way whatsoever Licensee's or Authorized User's rights under the Fair Use provisions of United States or international law to use the Licensed Materials.
>
> NERL Consortium Generic License Agreement for Electronic Resources[8]

A license clause for "Permitted Uses" defines the ways in which the licensed content can be used. The terms outlined here should not negate any other rights granted elsewhere in the contract. When reviewing this clause, consider whether the institution is required to claim responsibility for the actions of users. Although most license agreements require that users be made aware of the terms, taking on responsibility for the direct actions of users is something that should be considered carefully and discussed with internal General Counsel.

AUTHENTICATION

> Springer may control access to the Content through Internet Protocol ("IP") authentication, Shibboleth or **Athens** or another identification method agreed upon by Licensee and Springer.
>
> Terms and Conditions for Online Products of Springer[9]

When reviewing a license agreement, double-check to verify that the authentication method provided matches the authentication method available at the library. Ideally, authentication methods should be discussed during product negotiations, but it is good practice to verify its inclusion in the license agreement in case issues arise during resource setup and maintenance.

INTERLIBRARY LOAN

> Licensee may fulfill requests from other institutions, a practice com-
> monly called Interlibrary Loan. Licensee agrees to fulfill Interlibrary Loan
> requests in compliance with Section 108 of the United States Copyright
> Law (17 USC §108, "Limitations on exclusive rights: Reproduction by
> libraries and archives") and clause 3 of the Guidelines for the Proviso
> of Subsection 108(g)(2) prepared by the National Commission on New
> Technological Uses of Copyrighted Works.
>
> NERL Consortium Generic License Agreement for Electronic Resources[10]

The most important element for an Interlibrary Loan clause is that it should
reference copyright law. For libraries in the United States, Section 108 of the
United States Copyright Law (17 USC §108) will apply. Licenses for electronic journals and multi-user ebooks should ideally include Interlibrary
Loan availability, unless resource sharing does not apply at a particular
library. With that in mind, unless a license expressly prohibits Interlibrary
Loan or any form of content reproduction to a third party, US Copyright Law
permits resource sharing by default. Therefore, if an Interlibrary Loan clause
is excluded from a license agreement, it may still be a viable right for the
library. In such cases of omission, consult with internal General Counsel to
be sure.

COURSE PACKS

> Members and Authorized Users . . . may incorporate parts of the Licensed
> Materials in printed and electronic Course Packs and Electronic Reserve
> collections for the use of Authorized Users in the course of instruction
> . . . hosted on a Secure Network, but not for Commercial Use. Each such
> item shall carry appropriate acknowledgement of the source. Course Packs
> in alternate formats may also be offered to Authorized Users that require
> Accessible Formats.
>
> CRKN Model License Agreement[11]

Course Packs are a collection of resources that are assembled for use by
students during instruction. The inclusion of Course Packs in a license
agreement determines whether a publisher's or provider's content can be
temporarily hosted locally or linked to within a separate system. A specific
clause outlining rights for resource use in Course Packs essentially ensures

that content can be used for instructional purposes, and that duplication and distribution of material is not in breach of the license agreement.

USAGE STATISTICS

> Licensor will provide composite use data on a monthly basis. Use data should be at the level of detail required for objective evaluation of both product performance and satisfaction of user needs, including title-by-title use of journals. Providers should refer to guidelines established by either the International Coalition of Library Consortia (ICOLC) or COUNTER with respect to statistical measures of usage of web-based information resources.
>
> New England Law Library Consortium (NELLCO)
> Standard License Agreement[12]

Because providers are not required to follow COUNTER guidelines—they are, in fact, just guidelines—the inclusion of a clause for usage statistics will clarify whether COUNTER reports are available and it sets the library's expectations of deliverables from the Licensor. In the event that a provider cannot provide COUNTER reports, a usage statistics clause can be used to outline the types of alternate reports that will be made available and whether the publisher or provider has a timeline to become COUNTER-compliant.

MARC RECORDS

The inclusion of a clause regarding **MARC** records will vary depending on whether MARC records are provided for free or at a cost, or if they are provided by the publisher or by OCLC. For any of these options, the license agreement should clearly describe how the records will be provided. If MARC records are provided at a cost, it might be advisable to include the records fees with the schedule for content fees.

PERPETUAL ACCESS

> Continued access, archiving and use of Licensed Materials that survives any termination of the License Agreement and ensures continued access consistent with the then current standards in the publishing industry.
>
> CRKN Model License Agreement[13]

A "Perpetual Access" clause provides an institution with the right to use licensed resources past the expiration of a license agreement, in perpetuity. Because electronic resources represent a significant asset for any institution, a license agreement can include language to indicate a "perpetual license" that will survive any termination or expiration of the agreement. License agreements for ebooks and electronic journals will ideally contain a perpetual access clause; however, license agreements for subscription content, such as access-only journals and database aggregators, will likely not include perpetual access language, because of the nature of the content being distributed by a third-party provider.

A "Perpetual Access" clause should reference whether perpetual access will be made available directly on the publisher's platform, through a third-party provider, or in a form equivalent to the access provided during the active agreement, such as via an external hard drive. If a publisher is unable to provide access on its own platform—for example, if content is removed or if a publisher's operations cease altogether—access could be made available through **LOCKSS**, **CLOCKSS**, or **Portico**.

ARCHIVAL RIGHTS

> Upon request of Licensee, Licensee may receive from Licensor and/or create one (1) copy of the entire set of Licensed Materials to be maintained as a backup or archival copy during the term of this Agreement, or as required to exercise Licensee's rights under section XII, 'Perpetual License,' of this Agreement.
>
> New England Law Library Consortium (NELLCO)
> Standard License Agreement[14]

For preservation purposes, an archival and/or backup copy of electronic resources can be secured by including appropriate language in a license agreement. For **ebooks**, electronic **journals**, data, and digitized materials, adding license language for additional copies of the content can be very straightforward and may even be standard. For other types of electronic resources—such as **streaming media** and **abstract and index databases**—archival or backup copies of the material might not apply or might not be available at all, again, due to the nature of the content. Generally, clauses will use conditional language (e.g., "if"), so that content will only be provided if requested, or under certain circumstances, such as if a Licensor dissolves their company.

SERVER AVAILABILITY

> JSTOR will use reasonable efforts to provide continuous availability of
> the JSTOR Platform subject to periodic unavailability due to mainte-
> nance and/or updates of the server(s) and platform and downtime related
> to equipment or services outside the control of JSTOR ("Maintenance
> Downtime"). If JSTOR fails to provide online availability to the JSTOR
> Platform for more than 72 hours during any period of 30 consecutive
> calendar days Institutional Licensee may, upon written request, (a) be
> granted its choice of a refund or a credit of a prorated portion of its annual
> access fee for each 30-day period so affected or (b) terminate its agree-
> ment by providing written notice to JSTOR. JSTOR will provide support
> to Institutional Licensees and Authorized Users in accordance with the
> terms set forth http://about.jstor.org/support.

JSTOR Terms and Conditions of Use[15]

Just as a library needs to pay invoices promptly and in full, content providers
need to make good on the services they provide. License clauses regarding
server availability ensure that the Licensee has safeguards against excessive
resource downtime. Rarely does a Licensor offer a refund upfront because
of anticipated-downtime; therefore, the presence of such a clause does not
indicate immediate payment, and thus many of these clauses require written
request to enact.

COMPLIANCE WITH AMERICANS WITH DISABILITIES ACT

> Licensor shall make reasonable efforts to comply with the Americans with
> Disabilities Act (ADA) requirements, Section 508 of the Rehabilitation Act
> Amendments, and provide Licensee current completed Voluntary Product
> Accessibility Template (VPAT).

California Digital Libraries Standard License Agreement[16]

In recent years, libraries and publishers alike have engaged in conversations
about the accessibility of electronic resources for users with disabilities. Corresponding clauses in license agreements should either reference the level to
which a vendor complies with the Americans with Disabilities Act, or should
include language that indicates its importance to the library. In the example
above, the phrase "reasonable efforts" provides flexibility for the provider to
implement ADA-compliance while allowing the library to advocate for its

inclusion. The license agreement can also request that the vendor complete its own **Voluntary Product Accessibility Template (VPAT)**, which outlines the degrees to which the resource platform is accessible. Another option for these clauses is to include a timeframe for when the Licensor believes it will become ADA-compliant, and to what level of compliance.

TEXT AND DATA MINING (TDM)

> "Data for Research is a JSTOR program for research activities involving computational analysis rather than for purposes of understanding the intellectual meaning of such content. Data for Research users will be able to (i) search the JSTOR archive using the Data for Research search function; (ii) download chart data to view, use and display as Excel-compatible CSV files; (ii) view document-level data including word frequencies, citations, key terms and ngrams; requesting and downloading datasets containing word frequencies, citations, key terms, or ngrams associated with the Data for Research selected; and (iv) subject to registration with JSTOR, use the REST API for content selection retrieval. For the purpose of clarity, Data for Research is not limited to Licensed Content. Additional use of Data for Research and the REST API are subject to JSTOR's approval. Please see the Data for Research registration page for further information http://dfr.jstor.org/accounts/register/. The Prohibited Uses described in Section 5 above apply also to uses of Data for Research."
>
> JSTOR Terms and Conditions of Use[17]

Another license clause that is becoming increasingly of interest to libraries is **Text and Data Mining (TDM)**. The process of text and data mining might require spiders or web crawlers to retrieve data so that scholars can explore patterns and trends across large amounts of content at once without having to download individual article PDFs. With the increased interest in Digital Humanities, more and more libraries are interested in including TDM clauses in license agreements. Note that TDM clauses are distinct from security breach clauses: the process of TDM is active and part of scholarly work, whereas robots crawling sites to scrape content that can cause security breaches are generally not executed by authorized users and such events need to be investigated and resolved by the subscribing library.

USER PRIVACY

> "The Licensor will not, without the prior written consent of the Member and Authorized Users, or as otherwise permitted by the applicable privacy legislation—such as the Freedom of Information and Protection of Privacy Act—transfer any personal information of any Authorized Users to any third party or use it for any purpose other than as described in this License Agreement."

CRKN Model License Agreement[18]

"User Privacy" is an essential clause to include in license agreements, especially because libraries rely on vendors to provide data on resource use. However, usage data should never be linked to individual users and therefore license clauses that outline user privacy are essential. Although COUNTER statistics are anonymous, non-COUNTER statistics might include the accessing user's IP range, which can then trace the user of the content. User Privacy clauses ensure that any type of user information submitted online is not employed in a manner that violates a user's rights as outlined by the Freedom of Information and Protection of Privacy Act. Further, if a resource platform requires that an individual user set up a personal account, a User Privacy clause ensures that the user's account information is not shared with third parties.

PART 2   Content License and Business Terms

LICENSED CONTENT

The way in which the licensed resource is reference in license agreements will vary depending on the Licensor and the type of license agreement. For instance, it is common for a Licensor to provide only a document for the license Terms and Conditions, which will occur when a Licensor uses a single agreement to cover all of its content, and individual products are added through addendum or included as line-items on invoices. In such cases of a Terms and Conditions-only agreement, the licensed resource will not be directly referenced. The variation in how content is referenced can prove challenging for record keeping, especially after years have passed and it is not clear whether a license agreement, payment record, or invoice should be consulted.

To address this problem, some libraries use their model license agreements to standardize how license agreements are structured and how information is displayed. Another option is to append a business terms chart, or to develop thorough parent-child relationships within an **Electronic Resources Management System (ERMS)** in order to connect the Terms and Conditions to the actual products acquired.

LICENSE FEES

> Licensee shall pay the fees set forth in the License Agreement (the "License Fees"). Late payments shall be subject to interest charges at the current applicable interest rates. All amounts payable by Licensee shall be exclusive of any sales, use, withholding, value added or similar taxes, government fees or levies or other assessments which shall be the sole responsibility of Licensee.
>
> Terms and Conditions for Online Products of Springer[19]

While not the *only* important aspect of licensing, it is extremely important to verify the description of the resource fees. Check to make sure that 1) any fee included in a fee schedule matches the previously agreed-upon quote and 2) that pricing information is broken out in a way that can be clearly interpreted.

License fees can be described within license agreements in a multitude of different manners: some use a fee schedule within the license itself, while others include a fee within a lengthy clause of legal terms, and some Licensors opt for a combination of both options. As a word of advice: including a fee schedule as a chart can be beneficial, especially if a license agreement encompasses multiple institutions within a consortium, and if a license agreement covers multiple products. Having a clear fee schedule will be helpful when a final invoice appears, and it will be helpful when consulting a license agreement in the future, as fee schedules act as a quick reference point. If a fee schedule is present, make sure to check and double-check each line and verify any additions and subtractions that were made. Just as the license review process is manual for librarians, the boilerplate license creation process is manually customized for libraries, and simple mathematical errors can occur.

LICENSE TERM

The license agreement should *always* state the applicable term. A license term is the period of time in which a license agreement remains active. Depending on the content being licensed, a license term can be limited to a specific duration, it can be renewed with annual payments, or it can remain in effect in perpetuity. The first two options are most common for subscription resources; the latter option is less common, and generally only relevant if an electronic archival collection has been purchased outright.

It is important to note that the description of a license term has the possibility to include language that is self-referential and points back to other clauses, appendixes, invoices, or purchase orders, all of which should be double-checked for accuracy. When reviewing the license term, consider whether a person at any point in the future would be able to clearly describe the duration for which the license agreement remained in effect. If the answer is unclear, consider revising.

AUTOMATIC RENEWAL

> This Agreement shall be renewable at the end of the current term for a successive three (3) year term unless either party gives written notice of its intention to cancel thirty (30) days before expiration of the current term. In the event of a price increase for a subsequent term as provided for in Section 2.2, Licensee shall have no less than sixty (60) days from the date of notification of the price increase to notify Licensor of Licensee's intent to cancel or renegotiate.
>
> Liblicense Model License Agreement[20]

Generally, a vendor will monitor approaching license termination dates in order to initiate subscription renewals in advance of their expiration. Such notices are referred to as "renewal notices," which can either trigger requirements for new licensing in advance of renewal, or can trigger an auto-renewal (with a caveat that the Licensee provide notice of non-renewal within a certain time frame). A license agreement that includes "Automatic Renewal" language without Licensor notification can be cause for alarm. With an unwanted auto-renewal clause, there will likely be many surprising renewals and unanticipated invoicing, which puts the Licensee at risk.

EARLY TERMINATION

> "The Licensee may terminate this Agreement without penalty if sufficient content acquisitions funds are not allocated to enable the Licensee, in the exercise of its reasonable administrative discretion, to continue this Agreement. In the event of such financial circumstances, Licensee agrees to notify Licensor of the intent to terminate the Agreement as soon as is reasonably possible, but in any case, no less than [enter a mutually agreeable number of days] prior to next payment date."
>
> Liblicense Model License Agreement[21]

Early termination clauses will only apply for license agreements that span multiple years. If an "Early Termination" clause is present in a single-year license agreement, it might be best to strike the clause completely because it will not apply.

Problematic Language

Find and Replace

Once the primary legal and business concerns within a license agreement have been reviewed and identified, a good next step is to thoroughly consider the implications of the specific language being used. As with all aspects of license review, it is best to consult with any available General Counsel to discuss and identify institutional preferences for specific terminology and language to be included in a license agreement. To identify problematic language, read through a license agreement two or three times, take note of the types of words that appear, and consider their weight and implications. Consider whether a specific word can affect liability, or if a word causes too much ambiguity. However, if language changes are small or cosmetic (such as "the Users" instead of "Authorized Users") it might be better to leave as-is in order to appear flexible and to maintain a good relationship with the vendor.

Keep in mind that although it might seem like a quick and easy method to use the "find and replace" command in a word processor to resolve problematic language, the license should still be read in its entirety at least once more, and manually edited. A global find and replace has the potential to create sentences that no longer make sense!

"Best," "Every," and "All" versus "Reasonable"

Phrases that include extreme adjectives, such as "every effort" and "best efforts," imply that there can be a measurable gauge on how licensed content is managed, and that one party is the definitive source that determines the measurement. An example of common use of these phrases would be: "Licensee shall *use best efforts* to ensure that access and use of the Content is limited to Authorized Users and that all Authorized Users are notified of and comply with the usage restrictions set forth in these Terms and Conditions" (emphasis added).[22] Here, the use of "best efforts" makes it very easy for the Licensor to raise a claim using an extreme definition of "best efforts." By replacing the lead word in the phrase with "reasonable," the language becomes much more agreeable without altering the primary purposing of the clause. Some circumstances may exist in which a Licensor's responsibilities are termed "reasonable efforts," whereas a Licensee's responsibilities are still cited as "best efforts." In such cases, the language could be modified so that one party does not hold more responsibility than the other.

A thorough language evaluation can benefit both the Licensee and the Licensor. In the modified clause below, the use of "reasonable efforts" provides more flexibility for common website maintenance, versus a breach of contract:

> Licensor shall use *reasonable efforts* to provide online availability of the Licensor's Websites and the Content, subject to periodic unavailability due to server and software maintenance and services outside of the Licensor's control, and to restore access to the Content as promptly as possible in the event of an interruption or suspension of access to Licensor's Websites (emphasis added).

"Perpetuity" versus "Permanent" versus "Continuing"

The concept of permanence can be a difficult issue for both the Licensee and the Licensor. In extreme cases, the word "perpetuity" could potentially, and wrongfully, indicate permanence of publisher, platform, and resource after all life ceases to exist (an extreme case, for sure). The word "perpetuity" indicates that services would never end and it would be rare to find a boilerplate license agreement that includes it. Instead, phrases such as "continuing access" and "perpetual access" will be more prominent. These alternatives communicate the same concept without alluding to a world beyond time.

If administrative concerns arise regarding the exclusion of "perpetuity" in relation to rights for purchased electronic content, make sure that other license clauses clearly define options for third-party services (LOCKSS, CLOCKSS, and Portico) and local archiving, as well as a clear statement about hosting fees.

QUICK RECAP

Read the license agreement, at least twice. Ideally more than one person will read any given license agreement, as well as any available General Counsel.

Don't assume all license agreements are the same. The basic elements of a license agreement—such as "Definitions" and topical headings—may appear to be standard from one agreement to the next, but be assured that all licenses are different, even from the same provider from one year to the next.

Build from model license language. Use a model license and model language to piece together modification requests based on specific institutional needs.

Map the license terms to the negotiated quote. If a price quote includes a discount, make sure that information is stated clearly in the license. Inserting a fee schedule table into a license agreement can be an easy way to outline content and pricing at a glance.

License Tracking using Electronic Resources Management Systems

By the end of the negotiation process the following points should be clear:

- who is legally allowed to access materials
- what content has been licensed
- when the content will be available
- where can users access the content online
- how the material can be used

By the time the process is completed, the library should be able to confidently and reasonably abide by the license agreement. If any terms remain that the library cannot reasonably abide by, then the licensing process has not been successful.

One way in which libraries do successfully monitor and maintain their licensing terms is with Electronic Resources Management Systems (ERMS). On the back end, an ERMS manages all information about the acquisitions, licensing, and troubleshooting of electronic resources. An ERMS can be a very useful tool to monitor the status of active subscription licenses, and it can also make it possible to advertise licensing terms to end-users, such as information regarding authorized users, and appropriate and prohibited uses. It can also provide valuable information to resource-sharing librarians by clearly designating which electronic resources can be used for Interlibrary Loan. Because of the general lack of uniformity across business models and licensing terms among publishers and vendors, an ERMS can go a long way to parse and display essential legal terms of use.

Final Thoughts

The licensing process is the first step in providing end-users access to electronic resources. With the proper license in place—one that is reviewed and negotiated with the needs of the library's users in mind—the next steps to set-up resource access and discovery can take place. But as beneficial as it is to have a well-drafted license agreement, it can be just as detrimental when a poorly drafted license is put into place. When a license agreement leaves too much open to interpretation and ambiguity, it can hinder, and even prevent, the use of electronic resources.

When reviewing a license agreement, remember that it is intended to protect both the Licensor *and* the Licensee. Most Licensors will have a boilerplate agreement available for libraries to review and modify, and though the modification process is standard and often expected, maintaining the library/ vendor relationship is just as important. Therefore, be sure to make modifications to license agreements based on the needs of the library and its expectations. Do not make modifications just for the sake of making modifications. Consider the scope of the Licensor: if a Licensor is well-known and established, it may have more flexibility in considering modification requests, whereas less established Licensors—such as society publishers—may have a smaller staff or may not license to libraries frequently, and will therefore not be able to review and accept modification requests as quickly.

Finally, now that the fine details of licensing for electronic resources have been uncovered, one last bit of advice is to watch out for making any unintended agreements. Email acceptance of terms, though seemingly informal, can be considered legally (and thus financially) binding. Similarly, a Letter of Intent (LOI) may give a Licensor a false promise of payment. Though there might seem to be workflow benefits of email acceptance or an LOI, each of these shortcuts can put the library at risk and can potentially harm the library/vendor relationship. When facing an email acceptance of terms or an LOI, check with the rules and regulations of the library and, of course, check in with any available General Counsel. Licensing might sometimes feel tedious for all the checking and re-checking required, but it is important for the longevity and security of intangible electronic resources.

NOTES

1. John Webb, "Managing Licensed Networked Electronic Resources in a University Library," *Information Technology and Libraries* 17, no. 4 (1998): 198.
2. Springer Science+Business Media, "Terms and Conditions for Online Products of Springer," Springer Customer Service Center, LLC, www.springer.com/gp/librarians/terms-and-conditions-for-online-products-of-springer/18520.
3. California Digital Library, "Licensing Toolkit," www.cdlib.org/services/collections/toolkit/.
4. Liblicense, "Liblicense Model License Agreement with Commentary," http:// liblicense.crl.edu/wp-content/uploads/2015/05/modellicensenew 2014revmay2015.pdf.
5. Florida Virtual Campus, "Florida Virtual Campus Guidelines for E-Resource License Agreements," 11 January 2013, https://fclaweb.fcla.edu/uploads/FLVC _Licensing_Guidelines_Version_III_Final.pdf.
6. "Liblicense Model Agreement."
7. Canadian Research Knowledge Network (CRKN), "CRKN Model License Agreement," Canadian Research Knowledge Network, http://crkn.ca/programs/model-license.
8. NorthEast Research Libraries (NERL), "NERL Model License," NorthEast Research Libaries, http://nerl.org/nerl-documents/nerl-model-license.
9. "Terms and Conditions." for Online Products of Springer, www.springer.com/gp/librarians/terms-and-conditions-for-online-products-of-springer/18520.
10. "NERL Model License."
11. "CRKN Model License Agreement."

12. New England Law Library Consortium, "NELLCO Standard License Agreement," New England Law Library Consortium, http://c.ymcdn.com/sites/www.nellco .org/resource/resmgr/Files/nellcolicense_071004_w_perp.pdf.
13. "CRKN Model License Agreement."
14. New England Law Library Consortium, "NELLCO Standard License Agreement."
15. JSTOR, "Terms and Conditions of Use," ITHAKA, http://about.jstor.org/terms.
16. California Digital Library "Licensing Toolkit."
17. JSTOR, "Terms and Conditions of Use."
18. "CRKN Model License Agreement."
19. "Terms and Conditions for Online Products of Springer."
20. "Liblicense Model License Agreement."
21. Ibid.
22. "Terms and Conditions for Online Products of Springer," Springer Customer Service Center, LLC. www.springer.com/gp/librarians/terms-and-conditions-for -online-products-of-springer/18520.

FURTHER READINGS

Anderson, Rick. "NASIGuide: License Negotiation 101." *NASIG Newsletter* 28, no. 6 (2005): 6.

Ball, David. "Signing away our Freedom: The Implications of Electronic Resource Licenses." *The Acquisitions Librarian* 18, no. 35–36 (2005): 7–20.

Brevig, Armand. "7 Things to Know before Signing a License." *Online Searcher* 38, no. 2 (2014): 54–57.

Chadwell, Faye A. "A License to Kill For . . .". In *Managing Electronic Serials*, edited by Pamela M. Bluh, 109–28 (Chicago: American Library Association).

Chamberlain, Clint, Vida Damijonaitis, Selden Durgom Lamoureux, Brett Rubinstein, Lisa Sibert, and Micheline Westfall. "Informing Licensing Stakeholders: Toward a More Effective Negotiation." *The Serials Librarian* 58, no. 1–4 (2010): 127–40.

Dygert, Claire, and Robert Van Rennes. "Building Your Licensing and Negotiation Skills Toolkit." *The Serials Librarian* 68, no. 1–4 (2015): 17–25.

Fisher, Roger, William L. Ury, and Bruce Patton. *Getting to Yes: Negotiating Agreement without Giving In*. Penguin, 2011.

Gilbert, Catherine. "The Librarian's Guide to Negotiation: Winning Strategies for the Digital Age." *The Australian Library Journal* 62, no. 1 (2013).

Grogg, Jill E. "Mapping License Language for Electronic Resource Management." Mile-High Views: Surveying the Serials Vista: NASIG 2006 (2013): 29.

Grogg, Jill, Sara E. Morris, Beth Ashmore, and Jeanne M. Langendorfer. "Gateway to Good Negotiation: From Computer Mediated Communication to Playing Hardball." *The Serials Librarian* 62, no. 1–4 (2012): 183–88.

Halaychik, Corey S. "Finding a Way: Library Master Agreements at the University of Tennessee." *Journal of Electronic Resources Librarianship* 27, no. 3 (2015): 171–81.

Hiatt, C. Derrik, Lesley Jackson, and Katherine Hill. "Principles of Negotiation." *Serials Review* 41, no. 3 (2015).

Lipinski, Tomas A. *The Librarian's Legal Companion for Licensing Information Resources and Services, No. 4.* Chicago: American Library Association, 2013.

Regan, Shannon. "Lassoing the Licensing Beast: How Electronic Resources Librarians Can Build Competency and Advocate for Wrangling Electronic Content Licensing." *The Serials Librarian* 68, no. 1–4 (2015): 318–24.

Smith, Jane, and Eric Hartnett. "The Licensing Lifecycle: From Negotiation to Compliance." *The Serials Librarian* 68, no. 1–4 (2015): 205–14.

Taylor, Liane, and Eugenia Beh. "Model Licenses and License Templates: Present and Future." The Serials Librarian 66, no. 1–4 (2014): 92–95.

Keeping the Lights On
Setting Up and Maintaining Access

Now, pull up your chair and prepare for stories of the black
hole where sold-on titles go, the soul-destroying misery of poor
customer service, the missing (or weakest?) link, the dejá vu of
January–March and the end of grace periods, the lost publicity,
the automatic switch-off, the journal identity crisis, and-fanfare-
reasons to be cheerful.

Louise Cole in *The Serials Librarian*[1]

When a library buys print material—whether it is a monograph or a serial—it is cataloged and placed on a shelf. And while this description is accurate, albeit bare-bones, it is often used as an example of the stark difference between the handling of new print materials and the handling of new electronic resources. It implies that print materials are much easier to maintain, and it oversimplifies the long history of library science, including cataloging, access services, **Interlibrary Loan**, and preservation. In practice, electronic resources require many of the same processes used for print workflows, except that electronic resources also use their own distinct systems, and these unique systems generally require workflows for both the

ACRONYMS AND JARGON DEFINED

KBART

A knowledge base for electronic resources is made up of data that publishers and library vendors provide. **KBART** is a recommended practice from the **National Information Standards Organization (NISO)** for formatting and distributing knowledge base data—in the form of title lists and associated metadata—to enhance data and improve linking. The primary goal of KBART is to improve **OpenURL** linking by addressing the data at its source.

For more acronyms and jargon defined, see the glossary.

library and the external vendor. These duel workflows mean that setting up and maintaining access to electronic resources transforms from a predominantly localized effort in the print environment to a collaborative, ongoing endeavor.

At times, managing electronic resources can feel like an uphill battle. The passage from Louis Cole that opens this chapter is an extreme tongue-in-cheek example of the multitude of things that can go wrong, and the delicate dance that is required when content is sold and hosted by one party and licensed to another. As discussed in chapter 1, electronic resources are managed within a continuous lifecycle, where activation and maintenance plays a significant role. In fact, activation and maintenance can be thought of as the thread that connects each lifecycle phase together (see figure 6.1).

The **electronic resources lifecycle** is not a linear process. Due to the varying subscription start and end dates for individual electronic resources, each phase in the lifecycle overlaps and repeats throughout the year. That is to say, while one resource is being renewed, another might still be in its trial period, while still dozens of other resources will be active subscriptions in need of some form of troubleshooting maintenance. Additionally, as with everything in the world of electronic resources, there are exceptions and variations to lifecycle workflows, determined by library size, organization, or structure. For instance, a large library might have advanced systems in place to monitor and maintain electronic resources subscriptions with intricate workflows across dozens of personnel and departments, whereas a small library might accomplish the same tasks using less staff and more manual, bare-bones methods.

FIGURE 6.1

Jill Emery and Graham Stone's Electronic Resources Life Cycle: 6 TERMS

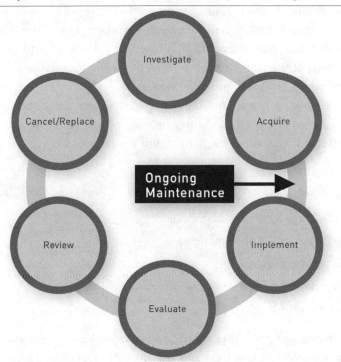

SOURCE: Emery, Jill and Graham Stone, "TERMS: Techniques for Electronic Resource Management." https://library3.hud.ac.uk/blogs/terms/.

The mix of electronic resources systems and workflows can seem infinite. The key to understanding them is to become familiar with different types of systems and how they interact with other systems and incoming data. And though it is also important to become familiar with the names of vendors, companies can merge and names change over time. For instance, at the time of writing this book, Springer Science + Business Media and Nature Publishing became "SpringerNature," ProQuest and Ex Libris merged to "ProQuest, an Ex Libris Company," and an expected merger between LYRASIS and DuraSpace dissolved. So, while remembering vendor and company names is fine and well, remembering the concepts behind the systems, products, and vendors is even better.

Truly, setting up and maintaining access is one of the greatest joys *and* greatest perils of an electronic resources librarian; in order "to be a happy, effective electronic resources librarian, you must enjoy puzzles and must not get frustrated by problems that do not stay fixed."[2] This chapter will provide an overview of how systems work together to provide users with access to electronic resources. It will also provide examples of common access problems and methods of troubleshooting. Use this chapter to gain a better understanding of the standards and protocols at the foundation of electronic resource access, discovery, and maintenance.

Because there are so many moving parts between resource activation, setup, and maintenance, this chapter has been organized into the following seven sections, which are both distinct and interrelated.

1. Authentication

2. Platform administration

3. Knowledge base administration

4. OpenURL and link resolvers

5. Discovery services

6. Proactive and reactive troubleshooting

7. Deactivating resources

As a rule, electronic resources should be set up in library systems only *after* a license agreement is finalized and the invoice is paid (which is why this chapter has come after the licensing chapter). Waiting until the acquisition is finalized ensures that access remains both stable and accurate, two elements that are truly the goals of electronic resources management. For more on licensing for electronic resources, see chapter 5.

Four Types of Authentication

IP Authentication

More often than not, users gain access to electronic resources through **IP authentication**. To set up IP authentication, a vendor needs to be able to identify which IP ranges will include an institution's authorized users, both local and remote. This step is extremely important because authorized users have likely already been defined within a license agreement, and incorrect authentication setup can either enable access to too many users—which would be a breach of the license agreement—or not provide enough access. Registering an **IP address** with a vendor is actually quite simple, and most vendors process the registration via email.

Although it is not necessary to understand the minutiae of how IP addresses work, it is important to identify them and understand their basic function. IP addresses are strings of numbers assigned to a device within a network. IP addresses are written and displayed in numerical notations with 4 octets, for example: 255.255.255.0. An IP range is a set of IP addresses within a given network, written as 192.100.100.0–192.100.100.255. In this example, the first three octets are stable and do not change (192.100.100), while the 4th octet (.255) acts as a variable between 0 and 255. A range with a variable octet can also be represented as 192.100.100.*, where * is the wildcard number.

The IP address examples thus far have been IP version 4 (IPv4) addresses. Due to the finite range of numbers available within the IPv4 structure, the available numeric options are quickly being exhausted and new addresses are being created in IP version 6 (IPv6) format. An IPv6 address is formatted in eight groups of four, such as 2007:0kb5:85k7:0000:0000:8a2v:8670:8872. If an institution has begun to use IPv6 addresses it is essential to register these new ranges with vendors. If new IP addresses are not registered, any user coming from an unregistered IP range will be blocked access to content, since the vendor's systems will not know how to recognize them as associated with a licensed institution. Again, the most important aspect of setting up IP authentication is accuracy, that is, verifying that the list provided to the vendor is error-free, so that access is neither too broad nor too restricted for an institution's licensed, authorized users. It is also important to double-check that a vendor has assigned the IP ranges correctly and to make sure that they are kept up to date. Due to the manual work involved in notifying vendors of updates, changes in IP range add a level of difficulty, especially if an institution regularly updates its IP ranges for security purposes.

Though IP authentication is the most standard method of providing access to electronic resources in the United States, not every vendor has the ability to provide IP authentication, especially so for smaller vendors and for those whose market is not specifically libraries. In such cases, alternate access methods generally require a username and password of some form. Over the years, the number of vendors that cannot provide access via IP authentication has decreased significantly, but there are still a number of resources that may require both username and password access *in addition to* IP authentication. An ebook loan is the most common example of where IP authentication will be required in addition to username and password access. If an ebook is bound by **Digital Rights Management (DRM)** and has limitations on, for instance, the length of time an individual user can borrow the ebook, a user account may be needed in addition to IP authentication in order to manage use rights.

Proxy Authentication

Some institutions use **proxy** authentication—such as **EZproxy** from OCLC or Millennium ILS **Web Access Management (WAM)**—to identify remote authorized users. When a proxy server is in place, the proxy server's IP range will also need to be registered with vendors at the same time that local IP ranges are provided. When a proxy such as EZproxy is enabled, the URL for an electronic resource is dynamically altered to redirect users to the proxy server. The EZproxy server then verifies users with a single sign-on using a library barcode or institutional ID number.

VPN Authentication

A **Virtual Private Network (VPN)** is a method of providing remote access that securely extends a private network over a public network. VPN enables remote users to appear as if they are on a local network (on-campus or in the library) and a user's private IP range will be identified by the vendor's systems as if it was a part of an institution's local IP network. Institutions that use a VPN for remote authentication will not need to register an additional IP range.

Shibboleth Authentication

Shibboleth authentication is a method of remote authentication that requires users to select their institutional affiliation on a resource platform from a drop-down menu. Once the selection has been made, users are redirected to an institutional login and then routed back to the resource. Shibboleth can be labelled in various ways on resource platforms, which can range from "institutional login," "login via your home institution/organization," to "academic sign-in."

Shibboleth can become confusing for users when the login script is featured prominently on a resource platform by default but cannot be suppressed if an institution does not participate in Shibboleth authentication. To help identify Shibboleth inquiries over other login authentication requirements, a good rule of thumb is to replicate the user's steps to find the exact message displayed. Screenshots can be extremely helpful to acquire this information without asking too much of the user. If the login prompt is branded for a particular vendor—such as EBSCOhost—it is likely a Shibboleth prompt. Should that be the case, the next best step would be to replicate the user's steps to identify whether access has been lost to the database completely, or if the user made an error and mistakenly bypassed the standard authentication method. Additional troubleshooting methods will be provided throughout this chapter.

Troubleshooting Tips

When remotely troubleshooting electronic resources, ask users to provide the following information:

- name of the database or platform being accessed
- a full citation
- screenshots of database error messages

BONUS: To identify whether a user is connected to the institution's local network, prompt the user to enter "What's my IP?" into any search engine, and then compare the resulting IP range against the institution's local and/or proxy IP ranges.

Platform Administration

Once an acquisition has been finalized—with a license agreement in place and an invoice paid—most vendors distribute an activation email which includes the active resource URL, along with vendor contact information, marketing material, and a username and password for the administrative

ACTIVATION AND MAINTENANCE CASE STUDY
"University of ABC"

New licensed content: ebooks

Remote access method: EZproxy, from OCLC

Integrated Library System (ILS): Aleph, from Ex Libris

Link resolver and discovery layer: SFX/Primo, from Ex Libris

Database A-Z: LibGuides, from Springshare

The University of ABC is a four-year college with approximately 4,800 FTE. The library recently purchased a collection of ebooks from a new vendor. The electronic resources librarian receives notification of a finalized license agreement and emails the vendor to register local and proxy IP ranges, and then adds the new URL stanza in the EZproxy configuration file. After the vendor notifies the library via email that access is available, a student employee does a spot-check of title-level links. When title-level access is verified, the cataloging department is told that MARC records are ready to batch load into the catalog. At the same time, the electronic resources librarian activates local holdings in SFX and adds the link resolver base URL to the backend administration system. Finally, the electronic resources librarian adds a new top-level database URL to LibGuides to publish on the Database A–Z list.

backend system. It is best-practice to extract the information included in these messages and keep it in a safe place, such as an **Electronic Resource Management System (ERMS)**. Although this aspect of the workflow can seem a bit informal and at times imbalanced (as not all vendors provide an activation message, and there is no guarantee that the activation message will reach the correct staff member) it is a vital part of the access and maintenance process. In fact, the *Core Competencies for Electronic Resources Librarians* cites account management as one of the key supervisory activities necessary for the job; Section 5.6.2 states that an electronic resources librarian should have familiarity with systems administration through "knowledge of best practices for account and data management (e.g., setting user Permissions, performing regular backups, etc.)."[3]

Backend account administration systems, which on database platforms can be identified by labels such as "For Librarians," "Librarian Login," or "Institutional Login," include functions to add or edit IP addresses and add link resolver base URLs, modify default search settings, view the library's electronic entitlements, download usage statistics, and upload institutional branding. Each of these options empower an electronic resources librarian to customize how resources display, which if done well can greatly improve functionality, and if done poorly can lead to further complications and problems. Benefits include the ability to optimize search settings and add link resolver branding, and potential complications include lost access due to IP address registration typos or broken links due to a base URL that is not input correctly.

Knowledge Base Administration

Once access has been verified, the next step is to set up access points in the library's **discovery systems**. Verifying that an electronic resource is accessible *before* a bibliographic record is created ensures that users do not hit a **paywall** or discover content that is not available. Just as a cataloger would not catalog a book that has not arrived, an electronic resource should not have an electronic holding in discovery systems until it is available to access online.

Though activating electronic resources in a **knowledge base** is akin to cataloging because it makes electronic resources discoverable in the library's systems, it is a distinct practice from traditional cataloging. This book is not intended to comprehensively address cataloging practices for electronic resources, because electronic resources librarians generally do not catalog per se. Instead, electronic resources librarians will likely be the recipients of important cataloging notifications from publishers and vendors. Such notifications can include when new content is accessible, directions to updated **MARC** records, and whether MARC records are provided for free or at a cost. It is important to have at least a general understanding of institutional cataloging workflows and standards, because many electronic resources librarians are tasked with communication workflows between acquisitions, licensing, and cataloging—a veritable passing of the baton. For information on cataloging for electronic resources, see the list of further readings at the end of this chapter.

Knowledge Base (KB) Maintenance

A knowledge base is the general term for a repository of structured information. For electronic resources, a Knowledge Base (KB) is the term used to describe the database of information about electronic holdings, which includes data on providers, database platforms, and title names, and holdings years. Data in a knowledge base is kept up to date by the vendor of the knowledge base, such as ProQuest or OCLC, as a result of updates provided by the content provider. For instance, if a title switches platform URLs, a knowledge base will be automatically updated to reflect the change without any action needed by the library to correct the URL.

A knowledge base is organized at the provider level, while activations are made at the database or title level. Therefore, it is impossible to activate the resources provided by an entire provider in a single click. Activations are made for full databases or for individual titles. For example, a full-text **aggregator database** would be activated at the database level, and a group of licensed **journals** would be activated at the database level *and* customized at the title level. In many cases, there are databases and titles available from multiple providers. In order to identify which database or which journal is the correct item, the entry in the knowledge base that corresponds to the correct publisher should be selected for activation.

A good knowledge base should:

- efficiently share information about content
- centralize management
- manage workflows
- enable discovery rights
- inform collection development decisions

Figure 6.2 highlights the features and functionalities of the current top-tier commercial knowledge bases, which are from Ex Libris, ProQuest, EBSCO, and OCLC.[4] Each of these knowledge base options can exist as a stand-alone product or can be bundled with a **link resolver** and an Electronic Resource Management System (ERMS). Although it is possible to mix and match systems from various providers, it will require additional maintenance to mirror the separate systems in order to ensure proper linking based on holdings information. Next-generation **Integrated Library Systems (ILS)**, such as Alma, Intota, and WorldShare Management Services, are poised to improve and streamline both management and discovery. As adoption of next-generation

FIGURE 6.2
Knowledge Base Comparison Chart

NAME	SFX GLOBAL KNOWLEDGEBASE	SERIALS SOLUTIONS KNOWLEDGEWORKS	EBSCO INTEGRATED KNOWLEDGEBASE	WORLDSHARE MANAGEMENT SERVICES (WMS)
Local or Hosted	Software as a Service, Hosted or Local	Hosted (Software as a Service)	Hosted	Hosted (Software as a Service)
Data Availability	Proprietary	Proprietary	Proprietary	Open (CC0)
E-Journal Data	Yes	Yes	Yes	Yes
E-Book Data	Yes	Yes	Yes	Yes
Chapter and Article-Level Data	Supported, but not completely	Supported, but not completely	Yes	Yes
Discovery System	Primo	Summon	EBSCO Discovery Service	WorldCat Local
Link Resolver	SFX Link Resolver	360 Link	LinkSource OpenURL link resolver	With WorldCat Local, but not a standalone service
Electronic Resources Management System	Verde	360 Resource Manager	EBSCONET ERM Essentials	WorldShare License Manager
MARC Record Availability	Optional MARCit! service; CONSER for serials	Optional 360MARC service; CONSER	EBSCO MARC Updates service; CONSER	From WorldCat; CONSER
KBART Compliance	Yes	Yes	Yes	Yes

SOURCE: Breeding, Marshall, "E-Resource Knowledge Bases and Link Resolvers: An Assessment of the Current Products and Emerging Trends," *Insights* 25, no. 2 (2012).

systems increases, more and more libraries may move away from disparate knowledge bases and link resolver systems.

Because a knowledge base is centralized, the total content within a knowledge base—ranging from tens of thousands of individual titles, journal

packages, and database aggregators—is shared by all of its subscribing libraries. A knowledge base becomes unique when a library selects their individual holdings for activation. Think of the activation process as filling
out an online questionnaire, where boxes are checked only if a resource is
subscribed. Further, resources in a knowledge base might be top-level only,
meaning all subscribers receive the same titles, or that the individual titles
are citations only. Holdings to full-text aggregator databases will be uniform across all subscribers and cannot be customized at the title level. To
activate a full-text aggregator database, a library simply needs to select the
resource as a whole. Full-text aggregator databases do not require title-level
customizations and, in fact, any customizations would cause the resource to
fall out of line with the vendor's automatic updates to URLs, content, and/
or access dates. Examples of all-in activations include EBSCO's Academic
Search Premier and LexisNexis Academic. Alternately, title-level activations
will be required for **Big Deal** journal packages or for single ebook titles. For
title-level activations, a library can decide which individual titles to include
or exclude, as well as the specific content years. Title-level activations can
be very time consuming, especially as electronic journal and ebook package
offerings grow larger and larger.

A knowledge base can also provide additional services for resource
discovery such as MARC record loads, in which MARC records are sent in
weekly or monthly file transfers for ingestion into the library catalog.

Although a knowledge base makes the work of electronic resources management easier, even the best knowledge base can be very complicated. The
need for granularity in library customizations makes the work of maintaining
a knowledge base an ongoing effort. One study by Serials Solutions showed
that on average electronic resources staff spends eighty-one hours per week
managing electronic content changes alone.[5] Though changes in a knowledge base are automatic, knowledge base providers rely on metadata feeds
from the thousands of content providers and that metadata can be of varying
quality, which can then affect the accuracy of holdings metadata and trickle
down to affect OpenURL linking. Additional challenges relating to this pro-
vider-supplied metadata include: keeping up with frequency of updates on
the platform itself; inconsistent metadata labelling; and variations in naming
conventions, format types, and title history tracking. So, while a knowledge
base makes the work of electronic resources management easier, a knowledge base cannot go untended, and the data contained within it needs to be

CASE STUDY

Knowledge Base Holdings for the *Journal of Y*

Both Library A and Library B have access to the *Journal of Y* within Database ABC from Common Publishing Company, which is available in Serials Solutions from 1997 to the present. Common Publishing Company provides complimentary access going back to 1997 with an active subscription.

Library A has had a subscription since 2002. Library B has had a subscription since 1998, but cancelled the title in 2010. The *Journal of Y* would be activated in the knowledge base for both libraries, but with customized holdings as follows:

Library A

PROVIDER	DATABASE	TITLE NAME	START DATE	END DATE
Common Publishing Company	Database ABC	*The Journal of Y*	1997	to present

Library B

PROVIDER	DATABASE	TITLE NAME	START DATE	END DATE
Common Publishing Company	Database ABC	*The Journal of Y*	1998	2010

cross-checked and verified on a regular basis. At times these checks will simply trigger a local customization so that the knowledge base reflects accurate content and access years, but at other times checks might uncover a global data error. In the case of global errors, vendors rely on librarians to report data corrections to improve data quality and to allow for global changes.

Overview of Commercial Knowledge Base Vendors

The SFX Global KnowledgeBase from Ex Libris was the original OpenURL link resolver and the key participant in facilitating OpenURL for content linking with the establishment of the NISO standard. In 2012 Ex Libris

released a next-generation library system, Alma, which combined its knowledge base and ERMS systems into one. Serials Solutions KnowledgeWorks
from ProQuest was founded in 2000 by Peter McCracken based on the need
for libraries to maintain lists to keep track of ejournal holdings. Content in
KnowledgeWorks is updated monthly and the system stored completely in
the cloud.

In 2016 ProQuest acquired Ex Libris, and the two companies became
"ProQuest, an Ex Libris Company." Since the merger, development efforts
have focused on improving Alma, which includes the creation of what will
be known as the "New Knowledgebase." When released, the New Knowledgebase promises to change the scope and scale of resource data, including more
bibliographic data and content types, integrating authoritative provider data
based on Ulrichs global serials data as well as controlled vocabularies from
Library of Congress Subject Headings (LCSH), and implementing relational
data using IFLA's Functional Requirements for Bibliographic Records (FRBR).[6]

EBSCO also offers knowledge base and link resolver technology with
its Integrated Knowledge Base. Data in EBSCO's Integrated Knowledge Base
updates dynamically, whereas data within SFX Global KnowledgeBase and
Serials Solutions' KnowledgeWorks is updated on a set schedule. EBSCO
does not offer an API, but knowledge base holdings can be exported and then
imported to other systems.

In 2009 OCLC launched WorldShare Management Services (WMS) and
WorldCat License Manager. The WorldCat knowledge base is a stand-alone
product that drives the OpenURL link resolver within WorldCat Local.
OCLC's partnership with Pubget enables it to automatically harvest the holdings from subscribing libraries to record them in the WorldCat knowledge
base. This approach is notably different from other systems, where activation
relies on active resource selections based on package descriptions.

Emerging Commercial and Cooperative Knowledge Bases

In recent years, so-called "cooperative" knowledge bases have emerged in the
market, marking a shift from vendor-managed data to community-managed data
(hence, cooperative). With a traditional knowledge base, the vendor receives
data from content providers, processes data normalizations, and feeds the data
into the knowledge base, at which point individual libraries make local edits to
customize holdings and submit tickets to correct global data errors.

In a community knowledge base, the data is contributed, edited, and vetted by the users themselves, a concept akin to traditional cooperative cataloging practices. Global data is created as a result of community contributions, and any local data edits move from local to global through a collaborative verification process. As with cooperative cataloging, the open data standards of a cooperative knowledge base improve data accuracy by leveraging the expertise of professionals who are not tied to any one product. In 2008, Ross Singer wrote in the *Journal of Electronic Resources Librarianship* that "by tapping into the power of the entire community—from the beginning of the publishing chain to the end-user—the knowledge base becomes self-sustaining and finds new and interesting uses along the way."[7] Current cooperative knowledge bases include:

> WorldCat Knowledge Base from OCLC
>
> Global Open Knowledgebase (GOKb) from Kuali OLE, Jisc, and the Andrew W. Mellon Foundation
>
> CUFTS Open Knowledgebase led by Simon Fraser University

Cooperative knowledge bases can be used in conjunction with other open source and proprietary knowledge bases and link resolvers. In the case of GOKb and **CUFTS**, the data itself is made freely available to the public under a Creative Commons 0 license. GOKb has the additional ability to track title and package changes over time. For example, GOKb can track if a title has changed names or publishers, or if the title offerings within a Big Deal package have moved in or out. The biggest benefit to all cooperative knowledge bases is that they eliminate duplication of effort. With a traditional knowledge base, any global data error affects each and every library using the same knowledge base, which means that in order to correct an error, each library will need to make the same local edit or submit the same ticket to the provider, whereas in a cooperative knowledge base local edits become global changes after being vetted by the community.

Link Resolvers and OpenURL

A knowledge base maintains the rights management for discovery, but it is not resource discovery on its own. That is to say, knowledge base holdings provide information to a link resolver about *which* resources should be available for full text. A knowledge base on its own does not provide the full text. And while a knowledge base is structured by database and title, a link resolver goes one level deeper, and is article- and chapter-based.

A link resolver attempts to connect users to full text when a catalog or database does not directly provide it. A link resolver connects a **source** to a **target,** where the source is the citation, and the target is the full text. "Source" and "target" are the terminology used in link resolver systems. When a user discovers a resource in an **Abstract and Index (A&I)** database or in a library catalog, a link resolver builds an OpenURL using metadata provided by the knowledge base. It then determines if an electronic resource is available by checking citation information against a library's full-text holdings (see figure 6.3). When a match is made on the source, the link resolver generates a menu of relevant options (the targets) for full text (see figure 6.4). If the citation metadata is robust, the connection can be seamless with a single click directly to the article or chapter requested. If full text is not available, the link resolver might send the user to the next possible level, such as to the

FIGURE 6.3
Link Resolver Diagram

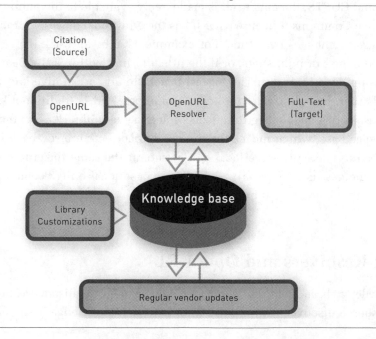

FIGURE 6.4
Links Menu Display

You searched for:					Citation Linker: change or add search criteria	
Article:	Web scale discovery what and why?					
Author:	Vaughan, J					
Journal:	Library technology reports					
ISSN:	0024-2586	Date:	2011			
Volume:	47	Issue:	1		Page:	5

Email ▾ or Export/Save ▾
Always check the citation for accuracy. Click this link for more information.

Content is available via the following links

Links to content		Coverage Range	Resource
Article	Journal	05/01/2002 - present	Academic Search Premier and
Article	Journal	05/01/2002 - present	Education Research Complete

journal or ebook home page or table of contents, or it might provide alternative options to Interlibrary Loan or union catalogs such as WorldCat.

How Resource Linking Works

An OpenURL is composed of two parts: a base URL and citation information. The pieces of the citation are embedded into the URL itself. In the example below, the base URL for the link resolver is in **bold** and the citation information is underlined.

Example OpenURL structure for a book (genre=book):

> **http://resolver.example.edu/abc?**genre=book&isbn=1231234560
> &title=A+Very+Good+Book

Example OpenURL for structure for a journal article (genre=article):

> **http://resolver.example.edu/abc?**genre=article&issn=1234–432X
> &date=2016&spage=300&epage=320&aulast=smith&volume=33
> &issue=5

The base URL notes the location of a library's specific knowledge base, which provides information about the library's electronic holdings to the link resolver. If there is an error with the library's base URL, the link resolver will not be able to identify where full text is available for a specific library. If there is an error in the citation metadata, however, a link resolver will make the best match possible or will provide alternative options. For this reason, it is

Check It Out

The OpenURL is a NISO Framework and is not limited to libraries. It is application-agnostic and can be applied to industries outside of libraries. More information on the OpenURL Framework (ANSI/NISO Z39.88–2004) can be found at www.niso.org.

especially important to check and double-check that the link resolver base URL is inputted correctly into the database administration dashboard.

Failures in OpenURL

Though a link resolver optimizes the discovery of resources, it is not a perfect tool and it will only ever be as good as its metadata. When a link resolver functions correctly it can seem like magic (which, in fact, is the basis of the SFX name which alludes to "special effects"). However, because a link resolver is not a search tool, but rather a linking service, when the linking fails the full text target will display an error message such as "No Results Found" or "Page Not Found," which can be very confusing for a user after having just been told that full text is available. Linking errors occur as much as 30 percent of the time as a result of source URL errors, knowledge base data inaccuracies, and target URL translation errors.[8]

If linking has failed, the first step to determining the cause of the problem is to compare the citation information with the data in the OpenURL. If bad metadata has made it to the OpenURL, linking can occasionally be corrected with a manual edit in the "bad" field. For instance, if the example OpenURL below included the wrong number for the issue, the field "issue=X" could be manually edited to correct, where X represents the correct issue number from the article citation, as follows:

> http://resolver.example.edu/abc?genre=article&issn=1234–432X
> &date=2016&spage=300&epage=320&aulast=smith&volume=33
> &issue=X

Manually editing OpenURL to force a link is a good option in desperate times, such as at the end of the semester if a patron cannot wait for a vendor to correct the issue and if Interlibrary Loan will take too long. With that said, systems vendors should always be notified of errors in order to correct data errors globally as errors will continue to occur each time a user requests the same link.

OpenURL errors can also occur if a provider has labelled citation parts inconsistently. For instance, newspaper databases have numerous ways of labelling article titles, including "source," "title," or "headline." Linking systems can only pick one label to map to the title field, and if the wrong label is chosen linking will fail.

OpenURL errors are also common when citation fields include non-standard data, such as with journal supplements. It is particularly challenging to have a successful OpenURL request for articles within journal supplements because of the different ways supplement metadata is cited among databases. A successful OpenURL request for a supplement journal requires an additional label for "Part," which in an OpenURL query will signify a special subdivision of a journal volume. "Part" can be included in addition to the required OpenURL fields, the metadata for which is often designated with letters or names, such as "B," "S," or "Suppl."

In the two examples below, "Part" is included at the end of the OpenURL string. In the first example, "Part" is distinct, whereas in the second example, "Part" is excluded and instead its metadata is merged with the issue field.

A successful OpenURL structure for a supplement might look like:

> http://resolver.example.edu/abc?genre=article&issn=1234–5678
> &date=2016&epage=200&vol=20&iss=3&part=B

Whereas an *unsuccessful* OpenURL structure merges the "issue" metadata with the "part" metadata:

> http://resolver.example.edu/abc?genre=article&issn=1234–5678
> &date=2016&epage=200&vol=20&iss=3B

Though it is not necessary to know how to create an OpenURL from scratch, having an understanding of how to read them, piece them apart, and identify the cause of errors and failures will go a long way to becoming an expert at troubleshooting electronic resources. Maintaining metadata for electronic resources holdings is a shared responsibility among vendors, publishers, aggregators, and libraries. In fact, vendors rely on libraries to submit error and update requests. After all, librarians are experts in the field and are generally in the front lines of actual content use.

Despite imperfections, "linking is necessary because library and information users today expect to move seamlessly among library content and information on the Internet."[9] The systems that generate linking are invisible to users so any failure to reach full text reflects poorly on the library and its

Overview of Why Linking Fails

The database is missing full-text items that the knowledge base believes to be there (the knowledge base and the database are out of sync).

Target site does not support OpenURL linking at the article or chapter level (only the top-level content will resolve).

Incorrect metadata in the OpenURL (resulting in an error page or the wrong article entirely).

Incorrect date coverage in the knowledge base (custom holdings in the knowledge base advertise content that is not actually available for the institution).

services. Despite the time commitment involved, there is considerable value in improving the performance of link resolvers.

One way that a library can leverage enhancements for both content linking and collections is by consulting link resolver statistics. Link resolver statistics can be used to inform collection development decisions by providing information about which full-text resources users access most frequently. Link resolver statistics can also be used to uncover access issues relating to activation, authentication, and metadata.

For more information on using link resolver statistics, see chapter 7.

Discovery Systems

Since the mid-2000s, there has been a well-documented shift in research behavior whereby users bypass the library's website and OPAC in favor of Google, Wikipedia, and other free online resources. Although Google Scholar can connect users to library resources via OpenURL, only a percentage of a library's resource metadata is available in Google Scholar, and even fewer through Google and Bing.[10] Despite this fact, the simplicity of the Google and Bing interfaces provides users with a very easy way to search. When users are conducting research on an unfamiliar topic, simplicity goes a long way toward improving user experience in what *appears* to be a very comprehensive search. Unfortunately, the same simplicity is not available from traditional library search tools in part because library tools live within so-called "silos"—ranging from the library catalog, databases, serials and ebook holdings, to archival collections—which means users must identify both the content and the resource type in which the information is contained.

Discovery systems provide an alternative to the far too common silos of traditional library systems. Discovery systems such as Summon, EDS, and Primo Central present a single point of entry for users to search across (most of) a library's traditional systems. The goal of a discovery system is to reveal everything possible on a given topic, whether it is a subscription database, streaming video, a print monograph, or an electronic journal article. To do so, a discovery system searches across not only a library's traditional catalog, but also across other subscribed databases and electronic resources using a centralized index. At its most basic level, a discovery system provides an easy-to-use interface and a single search box option. Discovery systems also provide relevancy-based search results, facets that can be selected to narrow results according to specific categories, and tools to identify other similar material.

How it Works

To create a unified searching experience in a discovery system, metadata from each of the library's content sources—the library catalog, databases, serials and ebook holdings, and archival collections—need to be combined into a central index. Keep in mind that a discovery system's central index is different from a federated search. **Federated searching**, also known as "metasearching," simultaneously queries multiple databases, whereas a discovery layer pre-harvests content from its centralized index that improves upon the speed and relevancy of a federated search. A central index also significantly reduces the number of duplicate results that had been a failure of federated search. De-duplicating results also enables more content to be retrieved from a single search query.

Although a discovery system can connect users to a myriad of library materials using a single search, not all of the library's electronic resources have their metadata available for such discovery. Discovery systems may not be able to retrieve material like music scores, manuscripts, archival collections, rare books, and non-English language materials due to their complicated metadata.

Choosing a Discovery System

Discovery systems first appeared on the market when OCLC's WorldCat Local was released in 2007, followed by Serials Solutions' Summon in 2009. In 2010 more systems emerged, most notably EBSCO Discovery Service (EDS) and Ex Libris Primo Central. These discovery systems are described in figure 6.2 alongside their companion knowledge bases. Each system provides the same service, but there is ongoing debate about the strengths and weaknesses of each product. Libraries may spend months or years evaluating discovery systems before deciding which to implement. Some questions to ask when thinking about implementing a discovery system include:

> How does the discovery system work with the library's existing integrated library system (ILS)?
>
> Which databases are included in the central index?
>
> What is the breadth and quality of the metadata in the central index?
>
> How are search results ranked, are they objective, and can local modifications and rules be applied?
>
> Is it necessary to have suggestion features (such as "did you mean . . .") and spelling correction?
>
> Will there be persistent links?
>
> Will there be facets (and will users know how to use them)?
>
> Is mobile access available?
>
> What is the cost?
>
> How many FTE will be required to keep it running?

When evaluating a discovery system, a library might want to consider the volume of systems already in place with a particular vendor. Even though a discovery layer and knowledge base can be bundled together, it may be advisable to opt for a separate system in order to create bibliographic diversity. Discovery providers have agreements in place with content providers that set the terms for how content can be harvested and included in a central index. These agreements can have a significant impact on search results, and for librarians and end-users alike the breadth and depth of indexing can be quite opaque. Evaluating discovery systems, including how content is indexed and how content is surfaced, is a significant task that requires considerable effort.

For a look at other discovery layers and a listing of the libraries that have implemented them, see the list compiled by Marshall Breeding available at http://librarytechnology.org/discovery.

NISO Open Discovery Initiative

To address issues of data transparency, the NISO *Open Discovery Initiative* (NISO RP-19–2014), published in June 2014, provides best-practice recommendations for data exchanges between discovery services and content providers.[11] The recommended practice aims to simplify the data exchange process to ensure that discovery services follow fair and unbiased indexing and linking practices. It also is designed to help librarians better understand how their licensed resources are included and used in discovery services.

One issue that subscribers face with discovery systems is the opacity of the central index, which prevents them from knowing exactly what is included and to what extent. NISO *Open Discovery Initiative* (ODI) addresses this challenge by recommending that content providers make their whole catalog available for indexing. Similarly, ODI recommends that content providers disclose their level of participation in discovery systems. To ensure that data is transferred in a standard and reusable manner, ODI also recommends that discovery services utilize existing standards for data transfers, such as OAI-PMH and **KBART**. ODI includes several recommendations in regard to search result ranking, results display, and full-text linking to avoid bias toward a particular content provider.

A Word on Open Source Discovery

The promise of simplified and streamlined discovery is alluring. In reality, a discovery system will not solve all issues relating to information retrieval. Nor should a discovery layer be used as a means to transition away from information literacy instruction. Within a discovery system, just as in Google, a simple keyword search can return thousands upon thousands of results, a situation which requires users to think critically about both the tool used to bring back results and be critical about the results themselves.

Open source discovery is a recent trend in libraries which aims to improve discovery by using neutral data and result rankings that are not based on content provider. Open source discovery layers provide more opportunities for customization, shared code, and system transparency, but this flexibility comes at the cost of increased development time, implementation, and general system maintenance. Two such open source discovery systems are Blacklight and VuFind. Blacklight, developed at the University of Virginia, features relevance ranking, faceted browsing, a customizable interface, and remixable data. VuFind, developed at Villanova University, includes faceted browsing, enhanced content, social network integration, the ability to index non-MARC records, and content recommendations.

Libraries choosing between commercial and open source options will need to weigh the benefits of open source against the greater requirement for technical expertise and dedicated staff time. As discovery systems and research expectations continue to develop, libraries should also consider whether they are simply playing catch up with technology companies like Google, and whether they can continue to evolve while also serving their core mission.

Proactive and Reactive Troubleshooting

Troubleshooting comes in two basic flavors: proactive, which can include link checking for individual titles and informing public services staff of planned database maintenance; and reactive, which is defined by addressing access issues as they are reported, such as fixing broken links, altering incorrect coverage date ranges in a knowledge base and catalog records, and contacting vendors about missing content and metadata errors. Due to the volume of electronic resources held by libraries it is likely that most troubleshooting efforts will be reactive; nevertheless, the time investment for both proactive and reactive troubleshooting will be substantial.

Proactive Troubleshooting

A good practice related to proactive troubleshooting is verifying that electronic content is, in fact, available before users have an opportunity to discover that it is not. In the print world, this link checking process is akin to serials check-in; it ensures that licensed electronic resources are 1) accessible without a paywall, and 2) complete and not missing any content. Electronic content can be accessed at much more granular levels than print—with chapters and articles individually retrievable versus only whole titles or single issues—so link checking is a time-consuming process, especially as journal packages continue to grow in size.

In addition to checking title-level access, link checking can also be used to verify proper link resolver setup and can ensure that top-level database URLs are active. Although software does exist to identify broken links, such software generally cannot tell the difference between an available web page and an available PDF. For instance, link checking software can determine that a link directs users to a working web page, but will not be able to identify the page as a paywall, which in the world of electronic resources is a considerable error. Further, link checking should include testing PDF availability, which link checking software cannot do.

Good Catch

Link checking for top-level databases can also help to identify whether users will encounter a click-through Terms and Conditions, and if any user registration is required for access. If not previously known or licensed, these two elements can make the library and the institution vulnerable, and should be addressed before full access is made available to users.

For more on click-through license agreements, see chapter 5.

If a systematic link checking process is not feasible, more passive options are available that can still be considered proactive troubleshooting. Alternative proactive options range from reviewing denial usage reports (COUNTER reports JR3, BR3, and BR4), subscription agent notifications, and Electronic Resource Management System (ERMS) notifications.

System Notifications

Electronic resources librarians will often be able to recall, as if instinctively, the subscription or renewal status for the library's biggest resource providers, in part because they are often very expensive and in part because the renewals occur at the same time every year. Although a mental list of resources helps job proficiency, it also evokes "hit-by-a-bus syndrome," a figure of speech that refers to the possibility that at any given moment anyone may not be able to fulfill essential duties. As a rule, if an electronic resource is not paid for or licensed, or if a subscription has expired, access should not be expected. But what about those situations in which a renewal date is approaching or when a renewal invoice has not arrived on time? Renewal season can put electronic resources in a state of limbo. Both vendor and the library share responsibility to ensure invoices arrive on time and are paid in a timely manner. It's just good business.

The **Integrated Library System (ILS)** traditionally played this role, but an ILS is not able to track the nuances of electronic resources, such as non-standard payment schedules, trial periods, and complimentary content. A more effective back-up plan for electronic resources is an Electronic Resources Management System (ERMS), which can track not only content, contacts, and licenses, but can also provide advance notifications regarding individual resource renewals. With a system in place that can anticipate upcoming renewals, proactive troubleshooting can occur before a lapsed renewal—and lost access—becomes a threat.

Ticketing systems can also facilitate proactive troubleshooting. By triaging and categorizing user-reported errors, ticketing systems can be used to resolve issues as they occur and to analyze report data over time, which will benefit electronic resource access overall. At the most basic level, ticketing systems provide a central location for problem reports and facilitate communication between departments, thus allowing more efficient problem resolution. IT software, such as Footprints Service Core (BMC), or survey software, such as Qualtrics, can be implemented as electronic resources ticketing systems. A low-cost option is a generic email address that can be shared by multiple staff members, where users can communicate through a single point of contact but reports are seen by multiple people, ensuring timely response and follow-through.

Reactive Troubleshooting

By becoming familiar with the systems and applications discussed earlier in this chapter—such as IP authentication, remote access, knowledge base maintenance, and link resolver functionality—the process of reactive troubleshooting will become much easier. The value of being able to identify the source of an error and describe it to all relevant parties cannot be understated. Electronic resources librarians must work within their local systems, but also need to be able to explain system functionality to various parties (e.g., vendor technical support, public services staff, and colleagues in technical services) at different levels. The ability to communicate how to resolve problems to outside parties and be clearly understood is a clear sign of system proficiency. Effective communication also requires asking the right question at the right time. Reactive troubleshooting should include a standard set of triage questions, similar in concept to the reference interview, in which sets of questions are asked to identify user research needs. The standard set of questions will help troubleshooters replicate the problem, clarify the source, and determine if an access problem is the result of user error or a global issue. Common user errors include expired remote-authentication sessions and attempts to retrieve content from the Open Web that is not licensed by the library. Pervasive and global errors include proxy configurations, security violations, incorrect holdings, OpenURL metadata and syntax, platform maintenance, missing target content, and subscription and payment errors.

Keep in mind that the terminology used by electronic resources librarians will not be familiar to end-users. Instead, a user may say: "I clicked the link and it didn't work. Other links are working fine." In such cases, additional follow-up questions will be necessary, including identifying link location, where in the process the problem occurred, and which other resources can be accessed successfully. The triage steps below are an example for working with a user to resolve an access issue.

SAMPLE TROUBLESHOOTING TRIAGE

1. Ask the user for screenshots, the resource link, and the citation.

2. Try to replicate the results.

If the problem *cannot* be replicated, proceed to #3–5.
If the problem *can* be replicated, skip to #6.

3. Ask the user to Google "What's my IP" to confirm the IP ranges

4. If the IP range is off-campus, double-check that the user has correctly authenticated for remote access.

5. Ask the user to clear the web browser cookies and cache, or try using another browser.

If the problem *is still not resolved,* proceed to #6.

6. Contact the provider to verify local and remote IP ranges.

7. Describe the issue to the vendor; inquire whether partial or full access has been dropped; provide licensing and/or payment confirmation.

8. Check for platform and content migrations (see Transfer Code of Practice).

If access cannot be restored immediately, or if it's necessary to contact a vendor for resolution, it is good customer service to direct the user to an alternative method for access, such as obtaining a print copy or using Interlibrary Loan. This last step in the triage process is perhaps the most important and bears repeating: if the problem cannot be resolved immediately, refer the user to an alternate method of access. Access problems can impact a user's perception of the library because users do not understand how the library collects and makes electronic resources available; therefore, any link failure is seen as poor service, even if the library was not the source of the problem. When using triage questions to troubleshoot access problems, keep in mind that users are not aware of the minutiae involved in electronic resources management, library science, or metadata. Users need access to fulfill a requirement for a class, apply for a job, or write a thesis. Users also approach electronic resources with varying levels of familiarity, so be sure to keep triage questions as simple as possible, while remaining friendly and helpful. Overall, troubleshooting electronic resources requires a high-level of customer service and patience.

Dropped Access

One of the great troubleshooting conundrums is that access can seem to fade in and out for any number of reasons, or for no reason at all. Systems on both the library and vendor sides are not perfect. The mysteries of access can be very complicated, but illustrate another reason why a good relationship with vendors is important.

When dealing with a situation involving lost access, do not panic! Check the following internal resources before sending an S.O.S. message to the vendor:

- payment records
- subscription dates
- IP ranges on file
- platform migrations and/or Transfer Code of Practice

Renewals and new subscriptions are the most common causes of dropped access, either due to an error in account setup or in submitting the correct resources for access. Most vendors will offer a grace period for lapses in subscription, but not every vendor's grace period is the same, and not every grace period is automatic. A strong relationship with vendors can go a long way toward ensuring transparency and stable access during the renewal process.

Deactivating Resources

At this point, it should not be surprising to learn that properly deactivating electronic resources is just as important as setting them up. Although cancelling a resource may feel definitive and absolute, more works needs to be done to avoid problems down the line! The process of deactivating a resource essentially requires undoing or modifying the work that was done during setup and activation. If resources are not deactivated in library systems at time of cancellation, the resource will still be available and accessible to users. If a user tries to access a cancelled resource, he or she will encounter an error message or paywall; for this exact reason, ILS payment records are included in a standard troubleshooting checklist. Workflows for deactivation require:

- communicating changes to stakeholders
- editing ILS payment records
- confirming perpetual access rights with the vendor
- removing holdings or editing content years in the catalog and knowledge base
- retrieving usage statistics to be saved locally in case the library loses access to the administration portal

The most problematic aspect of the deactivation workflow is also the least technical: communication. Communicating changes in access can become complicated when multiple departments are responsible for decision-making or if a library is part of a consortium. For instance, if the library's collection development department decided to cancel a niche, department-specific resource due to low use, it would be customary to consult the department most impacted by the decision. It would be just as important to notify technical services and/or electronic resources departments of the change so systems can be updated accordingly. Depending on the timing of each of these conversations, however, one party might learn of the change before the other, which would result in either what would appear to be "missing" content, or content that is not accessible to users. Communication regarding changes in electronic resources should also include front line staff, so research guides and finding aids can be updated.

Best practices for communication can be challenging, because information can only be communicated when it is known. Focusing on transparency and teamwork will go a long way in ensuring that information travels and reaches the right ears.

For more tips and tricks on effective communication, see chapter 9.

Conclusion

This chapter provided a high-level overview of the systems and applications available for electronic resource access setup and maintenance. Of course, the systems and methods discussed here were the most relevant at the time of writing. Inevitably, new initiatives, products, and vendors will join the market by the time of publication. Such trends are expected, which illustrates why a broad understanding of how systems work together, as well as flexibility and openness to change, are so important.

When working through any puzzle related to electronic resources access and maintenance, the most important takeaway is to remember that none of us are in it alone: there are huge networks of information professionals working through the same questions and issues every day around the globe. Remember to ask questions on listservs and follow conversations, even if they do not seem relevant at the time. Remember to consult with other partners, such as vendors, peers, and colleagues. Although electronic resources may at times seem to have minds of their own, there is no problem that truly cannot be fixed.

NOTES

1. Louise Cole, "A Journey into E-Resource Administration Hell," *The Serials Librarian* 49, no. 1–2 (2005): 141–54.
2. H. Zuniga, "A Student's Voice," *Colorado Libraries* 34, no. 3 (2008): 55–56.
3. NASIG Executive Board, "Core Competencies for Electronic Resources Librarians," www.nasig.org/site_page.cfm?pk_association_webpage _menu=310&pk_association_webpage=780.
4. Marshall Breeding, "E-resource Knowledge Bases and Link Resolvers: An Assessment of the Current Products and Emerging Trends," *Insights* 25, no. 2 (2012).

5. Jane Burke, "Do you Need a New System? Why," presented at ALIA 2013, www .slideshare.net/proquest/do-youneeda-newsystemalia2013janeburke.

6. Yvette Diven. "What's this I Hear about a New Knowledgebase? Part 1, Why a New KB?". ProQuest Blog, 14 December, 2015. www.proquest.com/blog/ pqblog/2015/Whats-this-I-Hear-about-a-New-Knowledgebase-Part-1-Why-a -New-KB-.html

7. Ross Singer, "The Knowledgebase Kibbutz," *Journal of Electronic Resources Librarianship* 20, no. 2 (2008): 81–85.

8. Cindi Trainor and Jason Price, *Rethinking Library Linking: Breathing New Life into OpenURL*, American Library Association, 2010.

9. John McDonald, and Eric F. Van de Velde, "The Lure of Linking," *Library Journal* (2004), http://lj.libraryjournal.com/2004/04/technology/the-lure-of -linking/#_

10. See Roger C. Schonfeld, and Ross Housewright, "Faculty Survey 2009: Key Strategic Insights For Libraries, Publishers, and Societies," (2010); Anna M. Van Scoyoc, and Caroline Cason, "The Electronic Academic Library: Undergraduate Research Behavior in a Library without Books," *Libraries and the Academy* 6, no. 1 (2006): 47–58.; and Ian Rowlands, David Nicholas, Peter Williams, Paul Huntington, Maggie Fieldhouse, Barrie Gunter, Richard Withey, Hamid R. Jamali, Tom Dobrowolski, and Carol Tenopir, "The Google Generation: The Information Behaviour of the Researcher of the Future," *Aslib Proceedings* 60, no. 4 (2008): 290–310.

11. Open Discovery Initiative Working Group, *Open Discovery Initiative: Promoting Transparency in Discovery*, National Information Standards Organization, April 13, 2016, www.niso.org/apps/group_public/download.php/14820/rp-19-2014 _ODI.pdf.

FURTHER READINGS

Asher, Andrew D., Lynda M. Duke, and Suzanne Wilson. "Paths of Discovery: Comparing the Search Effectiveness of EBSCO Discovery Service, Summon, Google Scholar, and Conventional Library Resources." *College and Research Libraries* (2012): crl-374.

Calarco, Pascal, Lettie Conrad, Rachel Kessler, and Michael Vandenburg. "Metadata Challenges in Library Discovery Systems." (2015), http://docs.lib.purdue.edu/ cgi/viewcontent.cgi?article=1645&context=charleston.

Davis, Susan, Teresa Malinowski, Eve Davis, Dustin MacIver, Tina Currado, and Lisa Spagnolo. "Who Ya Gonna Call? Troubleshooting Strategies for E-Resources Access Problems." *The Serials Librarian* 62, no. 1–4 (2012): 24–32.

Mann, Sanjeet. "Electronic Resource Availability Studies: An Effective Way to Discover Access Errors." *Evidence Based Library and Information Practice* 10, no. 3 (2015): 30–49.

McCracken, Peter, and Kristina Womack. "KBART: Improving Access to Electronic Resources through Better Linking." *The Serials Librarian* 58, no. 1–4 (2010): 232–39.

NASIG Executive Board, *Core Competencies for Electronic Resources Librarians,* www.nasig.org/site_page.cfm?pk_association_webpage_menu=310&pk _association_webpage=780.

Pesch, Oliver. "E-Resource Standards You Should Know About." *The Serials Librarian* 61, no. 2 (2011): 215–30.

Samples, Jacquie, and Ciara Healy. "Making It Look Easy: Maintaining the Magic of Access." *Serials Review* 40, no. 2 (2014): 105–17.

Schonfeld, Roger C. "Rethinking Authentication, Revamping the Business." *The Scholarly Kitchen.* June 22, 2016. https://scholarlykitchen.sspnet.org/ 2016/06/22/rethinking-authentication/.

Schonfeld, Roger C., and Ross Housewright, "Faculty Survey 2009: Key Strategic Insights for Libraries, Publishers, and Societies," (2010), https://cyber.harvard .edu/communia2010/sites/communia2010/images/Faculty_Study_2009.pdf.

Sloat, Rebecca. "The Joys (and Woes) of Electronic Resource Interoperability." *Journal of Electronic Resources Librarianship* 27, no. 2 (2015): 138–41.

Stevenson, Liz, and Chad Hutchens. "KBART—How It Will Benefit Libraries and Users." *Against the Grain* 23, no. 1 (2014): 12.

Stohn, Christine, Sherrard Ewing, Sheri Meares, and Paul Moss. "Building and Maintaining Knowledge Bases for Open URL Link Resolvers—Processes, Procedures, and Challenges." *Against the Grain* 23, no. 1 (2014): 11.

Stowers, Eva, and Cory Tucker. "Using Link Resolver Reports for Collection Management." *Serials Review* 35, no. 1 (2009): 28–34.

Strader, C. Rockelle, Alison C. Roth, and Robert W. Boissy. "eJournal Access: A Collaborative Checklist for Libraries, Subscription Agents, and Publishers." *The Serials Librarian* 55, no. 1–2 (2008): 98–116. doi: 10.1080/03615260801970808.

Stuart, Kenyon, Ken Varnum, and Judith Ahronheim. "Measuring Journal Linking Success from a Discovery Service." *Information Technology and Libraries* 34, no. 1 (2015): 52–76.

Walker, Jenny. "The NISO Open Discovery Initiative: Promoting Transparency in Discovery." *Insights* 28, no. 1 (2015).

7

Making Sense of Electronic Resources Usage Statistics

COUNTER and Beyond

- Usage Statistics Basics: COUNTER Reports
- Analyzing Usage Statistics
- Other Types of Statistics from Link Resolvers, Proxy Logs, and Web Analytics
- Community Advocacy for COUNTER-Compliant Statistics

Libraries can measure the success and value of their services by assessing data on user engagement activities, which can range from gate entry counts, circulation statistics for print materials, **Interlibrary Loan** requests and fulfillments, and research consultations. Similarly, **usage statistics** for electronic resources capture how often users interact with electronic content, which can demonstrate whether or not a resource is relevant to users. Because there are so many diverse formats for electronic resources specific metrics are needed for each type of resource, which is why usage for electronic resources is measured by the resource type first, and then by access method. For example, usage statistics from an **electronic journal** publisher will count the number of full-text downloads from journals within a given time period, and usage statistics from an **ebook** publisher will count the number of downloads from individual chapters during a specific time period. Put simply, the metric for electronic resource usage will always correspond to the format; after all, it certainly would not be useful to see a metric relating to chapter downloads for a **streaming media** collection!

ACRONYMS AND JARGON DEFINED

Standardized Usage Statistics Harvesting Initiative (SUSHI)

SUSHI is a **NISO** protocol that enables the automatic collection of **COUNTER** usage statistics from vendor administrative platforms and import into **Electronic Resources Management Systems (ERMS)**. In late 2015, NISO published a draft technical report for SUSHI—Lite, which is a simplified version of the original protocol.

For more acronyms and jargon defined, see the glossary.

Electronic resources providers make usage statistics available for librarians to use and analyze for renewal decisions or to demonstrate value to stakeholders. When it comes to renewal decisions, usage statistics play a significant role in the **electronic resources lifecycle**. When deciding to renew or cancel a subscription, usage statistics can be used to determine if the cost of a resource is justified.

Usage statistics can be used when:

> *Identifying gaps in a collection:* Journal publishers often track the number of **denials** (or **"turnaways"**) for journals to which the library does not subscribe.

> *Troubleshooting access problems:* Few or zero recorded uses for subscribed or purchased resources could be a sign of an access issue.

> *Demonstrating value to stakeholders:* In addition to providing information about the number of electronic resources to which the

library subscribes or owns, usage statistics can be used to illustrate the value of those resources.

Identifying trends in user behavior: **Link resolver** statistics, web analytics, and **EZproxy** logs can be especially useful in learning how users navigate the library website and access information electronically.

This chapter will discuss the metrics and processes for the topics listed above. It will also explain the process of harvesting and analyzing usage data and will discuss the standards behind usage statistics, COUNTER.

Usage Statistics Basics: COUNTER Reports

COUNTER (Counting Online Usage of NeTworked Electronic Resources) is a non-profit organization that developed the guidelines for usage statistics which is used by libraries and content providers to report on and measure electronic resources. In 2003, COUNTER published Code of Practice Release 1, which outlined how usage statistics for electronic journals and **databases** should be reported. In 2013, COUNTER published Code of Practice Release 4 and the updated guidelines now reflect many of the changes occurring in the publishing industry, including new standards for **Open Access** publishing, archival content, and **discovery systems**. This chapter will focus on the specifics from COUNTER Release 4, but because COUNTER is constantly reviewing and improving its recommendations, readers should consult the COUNTER website (www.projectcounter.org) for the most up-to-date information. In November 2016, COUNTER provided an overview of the draft for Release 5. The updated release aims to address the changing needs in electronic resources while also reducing the complexity of report types and increasing the clarity of the metrics collected.

See figure 7.1 for an overview of the standard COUNTER reports included in Code of Practice 4 as well as format type, counted user activity, and common applications by librarians.

Before COUNTER, the metrics for reporting on electronic resources usage was not standardized, and content providers measured and made usage data available in any number of different ways, with usage reported by hour, by

FIGURE 7.1
Standard COUNTER Reports

RESOURCE TYPE	REPORT NAME	ACTIVITY RECORDED	COMMON APPLICATIONS
Journals	Journal Report 1 (JR1)	Number of Successful Full-Text Article Requests by Month and Journal	Journal subscription renewals
	Journal Report 1 Gold Open Access (JR1 GOA)	Number of Successful Gold Open Access Full-Text Article Requests by Month and Journal	Identify usage from Gold Open Access journals, which can be useful information for libraries promoting Open Access publishing to constituents.
	Journal Report 2 (JR2)	Access Denied to Full-Text Articles by Month, Journal and Category	1) For Collection Development to identify non-subscribed journal titles in high demand, but that patrons have been unable to access 2) Troubleshooting, to identify subscribed journal titles to which library users cannot access because of technical error
	Journal Report 5 (JR5)	Number of Successful Full-Text Article Requests by Year-of-Publication (YOP) and Journal	Learn which journal content is the most valued by users according to date of publication
Databases	Database Report 1 (DB1)	Total Searches, Result Clicks and Record Views by Month and Database	Database subscription renewal
	Database Report 2 (DB2)	Access Denied by Month, Database and Category	1) For Collection Development to identify non-subscribed resources in high demand 2) Troubleshooting, to identify subscribed resources to which library users cannot access because of technical error
	Platform Report 1 (PR1)	Total Searches, Result Clicks and Record Views by Month and Platform	Database subscription renewal by platform or vendor

RESOURCE TYPE	REPORT NAME	ACTIVITY RECORDED	COMMON APPLICATIONS
eBooks	Book Report 1 (BR1)	Number of Successful Title Requests by Month and Title	eBook subscription renewal
	Book Report 2 (BR2)	Number of Successful Section Requests by Month and Title	1) For ebook subscription renewals 2) Learn more about user behavior and whether or not users are successfully finding information, beyond the title level
	Book Report 3 (BR3)	Access Denied to Content Items by Month, Title and Category	1) For Collection Development to identify non-subscribed resources in high demand 2) Troubleshooting, to Identify subscribed resources to which library users cannot access because of technical error
	Book Report 4 (BR4)	Access Denied to Content items by Month, Platform and Category	For troubleshooting, to identify subscribed resources and platforms to which library users cannot access because of technical error
	Book Report 5 (BR5)	Total Searches by Month and Title	1) For ebook subscription renewals 2) Especially useful when paired with Book Report 1 and 2 to learn if users are finding the information they need
Streaming Media	Multimedia Report 1 (MR1)	Number of Successful Full Multimedia Content Unit Requests by Month and Collection	Streaming media license renewal

Check It Out

COUNTER's glossary of terms is an incredibly useful resource when examining COUNTER reports and understanding the context of the usage statistics. See www.projectcounter.org.

day, or by week, with reports available as images pasted in emails to view-only HTML web pages. These variations made consistent gathering and analysis of statistics nearly impossible. Consider how difficult it might be to compare one report where the metric recorded downloads by hour, to another report where the metric recorded downloads by month! Today, COUNTER-compliant vendors provide usage statistics in a consistent way, with the data organized by resource type, time periods based on both month and year, and standard file types for user-friendly downloads. Most major publishers and vendors follow the guidelines developed by COUNTER, but not all. For vendors that have not become COUNTER-compliant the type and quality of their usage statistics can still run the gamut. For this reason, it is important that all electronic resources librarians continue to advocate for COUNTER and the overall importance of standardized reports. Community advocacy will be discussed later in this chapter.

Accessing and Reading COUNTER Reports

COUNTER's Code of Practice requires that content providers make usage statistics available as either comma separated values (.csv) or tab-delimited (.tsv) files, which can then be manipulated and analyzed in spreadsheet software such as Microsoft Excel. All COUNTER reports are self-service downloads from within administration backend systems, which is another reason why it is so important to maintain records for account details like username and passwords.

COUNTER standards also require usage statistics be made available within four weeks *after* the last day of the reporting period (e.g., usage counted for the month of February, should be available by the end of March). COUNTER reports are broken down at the title level, whether it be a journal title or database title, and include a total for the complete reporting period ("Reporting Period Total"), as well as an option for monthly breakdown of

COUNTER Statistics and User Privacy

Section 7.4.1 of the COUNTER Code of Practice Release 4 forbids vendors from sharing user data. Usage statistics that are COUNTER-compliant should never contain data that can identify a specific user. COUNTER-compliant vendors do not track individual users, accounts, or search history!

usage. With this in mind, it should not be surprising that the date range is the most important field to customize in a COUNTER report because it will determine the range for the Reporting Period Total, which has the biggest impact on **cost-per-use (CPU)** calculations. For instance, if a library tracks its budget based on **fiscal year**, the COUNTER report date range selected should reflect the fiscal year versus the full calendar year. In general, accuracy and consistency is the most important consideration when preparing COUNTER reports for analysis.

All COUNTER reports are formatted in a standard way. The visual appearance of all COUNTER reports, no matter the report type, is distinguished by uniform headers, spacing, and column and row names. Figure 7.2, a Database Report 1 (DB1) from ProQuest, will be used as an example for the next sections of this chapter.

The header of a COUNTER report will always be presented in the same way. In figure 7.2, the header constitutes Section A and B, where Section A describes the report type, COUNTER Code of Practice version, with the institution name and a brief description of the user activity recorded in the report; and Section B describes the Period Covered by Report and Date Run. The information within the header can provide a quick cross-check after downloading a report, when analyzing multiple reports, when comparing calculations across multiple years, and for quality control over time. Next, the column headings seen in Section C of figure 7.2 describe the content. For instance, in a Database Report 1 (DB1, Section C includes descriptions for Database, Publisher, and Platform.

Database reports are unique from other types of COUNTER reports in that they count multiple types of user behavior, whereas other reports, such as the Journal Report 1 (JR1) and the Book Report 2 (BR2), record only one type of user behavior: successful downloads. Section D of figure 7.2 highlights the four types of User Activity found in a Database Report 1 (DB1):

FIGURE 7.2

Sample Database 1 Report (DB1) in Microsoft Excel

Database	Publisher	Platform	User Activity	Reporting Period Total	Jan-14	Feb-14	Mar-14	Apr-14	May-14	Jun-14
Database Report 1 (R4)	Total Searches, Result Clicks and Record Views by Month and Database									
INSTITUTION NAME										
Period covered by Report:										
2014-01-01 to 2014-12-31										
Date Run:										
2/6/2015										
ABI/INFORM Dateline	ProQuest	ProQuest	Regular Searches	25063	1349	2640	3330	3942	1394	883
ABI/INFORM Dateline	ProQuest	ProQuest	Searches-federated and automated	0	0	0	0	0	0	0
ABI/INFORM Dateline	ProQuest	ProQuest	Result Clicks	16	0	5	4	1	0	0
ABI/INFORM Dateline	ProQuest	ProQuest	Record Views	12	0	2	8	0	0	0
ABI/INFORM Global	ProQuest	ProQuest	Regular Searches	30526	1616	2983	4762	4352	1605	1025
ABI/INFORM Global	ProQuest	ProQuest	Searches-federated and automated	0	0	0	0	0	0	0
ABI/INFORM Global	ProQuest	ProQuest	Result Clicks	5743	321	352	1329	505	189	130
ABI/INFORM Global	ProQuest	ProQuest	Record Views	3572	283	313	683	424	118	78
ABI/INFORM Trade & Industry	ProQuest	ProQuest	Regular Searches	25113	1349	2640	3330	3942	1394	886
ABI/INFORM Trade & Industry	ProQuest	ProQuest	Searches-federated and automated	0	0	0	0	0	0	0
ABI/INFORM Trade & Industry	ProQuest	ProQuest	Result Clicks	81	3	2	3	6	2	2
ABI/INFORM Trade & Industry	ProQuest	ProQuest	Record Views	35	0	3	2	2	2	0
Accounting & Tax	ProQuest	ProQuest	Regular Searches	25075	1349	2639	3328	3938	1394	882
Accounting & Tax	ProQuest	ProQuest	Searches-federated and automated	0	0	0	0	0	0	0
Accounting & Tax	ProQuest	ProQuest	Result Clicks	21	5	0	0	3	0	0
Accounting & Tax	ProQuest	ProQuest	Record Views	17	3	0	2	0	0	0
Alt-PressWatch	ProQuest	ProQuest	Regular Searches	25528	1353	2844	3386	3903	1412	835

Regular Searches: A search query, typically equated to submitting the search form of the online service to the server.

Searches—Federated: A federated search program allows users to search multiple databases owned by the same or different vendors simultaneously with a single query from a single user interface. The end user is not responsible for selecting the database being searched.

Searches—Automated: A search from a **discovery layer** or similar technology where multiple databases are searched simultaneously with a single query from the user interface. The end user is not responsible for selecting which databases are being searched.

Result Clicks: A user-click on an item in a set of search results.

Record Views: A successful request for an item record that originated from the set of search results, from browsing the database, or from a click on another database record.

A preliminary review of figure 7.2 shows that all databases experienced a higher number of Regular Searches than Result Clicks and Record Views, which means users searched the database more frequently than they clicked through to an abstract or full-text article. Keep in mind that though the COUNTER Code of Practice Release 4 records Searches-federated and Searches-automated, these metrics will almost always be zero because few databases still use federated search. Any use seen within these metrics may be the result of citation software such as EndNote pinging the resource.

Finally, in Section E, the Reporting Period Total refers to the total number of uses during the Period Covered by the Report from Section A. The Reporting Period Total is the sum of the individual months from Section F.

As a rule, academic libraries will see usage decrease during the summer months and usage increase in the months leading up to the end of each semester. Figure 7.3 provides a visual example of the ebb and flow of standard journal usage during an academic year, where high-usage can be seen in both April and October over a two-year period, and where usage drops when classes are not in session in the winter and summer.

Although the Reporting Period Total alone is a very important metric, usage breakdown by month is incredibly useful when isolating usage patterns and outliers. For example, if a specific database or title experiences unusually high-usage for a full reporting period, usage within individual months

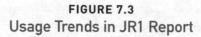

FIGURE 7.3
Usage Trends in JR1 Report

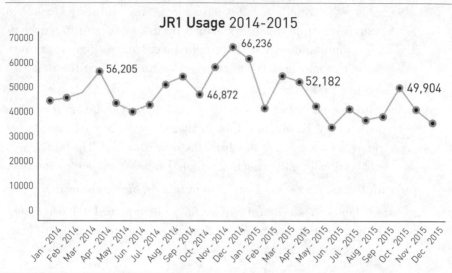

can help identify when usage occurred. A sudden, isolated spike in usage for a single resource in one month can be an indicator of a security breach or **Text and Data Mining (TDM).** In figure 7.3, the 66,236 downloads from December 2014 might be considered uncharacteristically high-compared to other months. If unusually high-usage is identified for an individual title, it is best to report the issue to the vendor to further investigate a possible security breach.

Non-COUNTER Statistics

Although the majority of electronic resources vendors provide COUNTER-compliant statistics, some do not. The causes for noncompliance varies: some publishers manage small operations with limited staff and resources so adapting to COUNTER guidelines could be too costly, and some resources report usage information that is not conducive to the existing COUNTER Codes of Practice. For example, specialized electronic resources, such as datasets, do not always align well with the existing metrics used for COUNTER statistics. Collecting non-COUNTER statistics requires modified workflows.

When determining whether a provider is COUNTER-compliant or not, COUNTER's overview of participating providers is a sure bet. Although

Check It Out

The Mitchell Dunkley's Friendly Guide series are online guides for librarians that provide a helpful explanation of COUNTER usage reports.

Friendly Guide to COUNTER Book Reports: A Guide for Librarians

Friendly Guide to COUNTER Database Reports: A Guide for Librarians

Friendly Guide to COUNTER Journal Reports: A Guide for Librarians

Find these guides and more at www.projectcounter.org.

COUNTER statistics are formatted uniformly, judging whether or not a report is COUNTER-compliant on appearance alone can be misleading since non-COUNTER statistics sometimes use similar terminology as COUNTER statistics, such as "searches," "page views," and "result clicks." It is important to remember that COUNTER does not simply assign names to its metrics, but instead standardizes how metrics are counted as well.

ICOLC

In addition to COUNTER and non-COUNTER usage statistics, there is a third category of usage statistics from ICOLC, the International Coalition of Library Consortia. Created in 1997, ICOLC is a global network of libraries and library consortia. First published in 1998, ICOLC's *Guidelines for Statistical Measures of Usage of Web-Based Information Resources* predate COUNTER's Code of Practice. ICOLC Guidelines set rules and expectations for vendors with many of the same goals we recognize today: ensuring usage statistics are accessible, reliable, and consistent across content providers. The Guidelines were the library community's first major step forward in establishing and communicating expectations for usage statistics to vendors. In March of 2003, ICOLC issued a statement of support for COUNTER.

Usage statistics that follow ICOLC Guidelines are not terribly common these days. Although ICOLC usage statistics will be standardized in a consistent manner and comparable to other ICOLC statistics, they should not be compared to COUNTER statistics. Similar steps should be taken when analyzing ICOLC usage statistics as with all non-COUNTER compliant statistics.

Best Practices for Handling
Non-COUNTER Compliant Statistics

When reviewing non-COUNTER statistics, take caution not to make a direct comparison with COUNTER statistics. The absence of standardization in non-COUNTER statistics can wreak havoc on the most well-intentioned usage analysis. Similarly, non-COUNTER statistics from one provider should not be compared to the non-COUNTER statistics from another provider, as any resulting analysis will be just as misleading. Comparing usage across resources or across providers will simply not work because the user activity is not measured in the same way.

Look for Trends

When analyzing non-COUNTER statistics, comparing data and looking for trends across resources can lead to misleading results. For any non-COUNTER statistics, it is best to compare a single resource against itself year after year. By doing so, a resource is not inappropriately compared, and at best, it will show whether usage has decreased, remained consistent, or increased over time.

Ask for Help

Due diligence is a must when analyzing non-COUNTER statistics. Leverage relationships with library vendors and ask an account manager or technical support specialist to define the usage metric and describe how the metric is collected. Such information will provide more insight into non-COUNTER statistics and can provide more context for decision-making.

ERMS and SUSHI

Manually downloading COUNTER statistics from administration dashboards is a process that requires a substantial time commitment. For years, electronic resources librarians have sought more efficient and automated means of gathering and compiling statistics. To solve this problem, components within an Electronic Resources Management Systems (ERMS) can automatically harvest usage statistics from vendors that offer the SUSHI (Standardized Usage Statistics Initiative) protocol. The SUSHI protocol is a NISO standard that automates the collection of usage statistics reports from SUSHI-compliant vendors.

In late 2015, the NISO SUSHI working group published a draft technical report for SUSHI-Lite. This new report is designed to deliver "snippets of usage" as well as complete usage reports using a protocol for web services. SUSHI-Lite is a simplified version of the full SUSHI protocol, but not a replacement for SUSHI. SUSHI-Lite is an excellent example of NISO's efforts to improve existing procedures and expand the access to and efficiency of COUNTER reports.

ERMS and SUSHI improve efficiency for COUNTER usage statistics, but automated systems are not without their flaws. Automated systems require time to set up, and because harvesting usage statistics requires a username and password, administration information must still be kept up to date manually. Additional time commitments include the maintenance of any usage reports that are not available for SUSHI harvesting, and keeping current on the availability of the SUSHI protocol. Librarians continue to express frustration when harvesting non-COUNTER compliant reports or when troubleshooting scenarios in which SUSHI has failed to collect COUNTER reports. As mentioned in chapter 1, some libraries have addressed this problem by creating their own local ERMS or by modifying an existing open source ERMS. Despite its imperfections, the SUSHI Protocol has allowed libraries to make great strides in harvesting usage statistics and SUSHI-Lite promises to further increase efficiency.

Analyzing Usage Statistics

When librarians talk about their on-going need for usage statistics, it is usually because statistics are needed to evaluate renewals or to demonstrate resource value to stakeholders. Usage statistics should be analyzed at least annually so that informed renewal decisions can be made.

When evaluating usage, keep the following in mind:

1. *Needs of the users*

High use can indicate that a resource is aligned with the information needs of the institution; low use can indicate that the content contained in the resource is not needed by users or that the need is being fulfilled by another resource.

2. Resource accessibility

High use can indicate that a resource is easily accessible from the library website, discovery layer, and/or catalog; low use can indicate that a resource is difficult to locate or that the interface is challenging to navigate.

3. Resource relevance

A high number of searches, but low number of downloads indicate that users search the resource frequently, but do not find the information they need. A high number of searches can also be a sign of inflation caused by platform or discovery layer searches in which each database is searched regardless of access point.

4. Inconsistent usage

Low use during high-traffic periods can be a sign of an access issue; therefore, library systems should be checked to ensure that the resource is set up correctly.

Reports to Use When Analyzing Usage for eJournals

As described at the start of this chapter, resource type will dictate the metric used to count user activity and the associated COUNTER report. Accordingly, resource type will also determine the most appropriate type of usage analysis. The standard COUNTER reports for journals—Journal Report 1 (JR1), Journal Report 1 Gold Open Access (JR1 GOA), and Journal Report 5 (JR5)—count full-text article downloads. Most commonly, libraries calculate the cost-per-use (CPU) for subscriptions by dividing the annual number of downloads by annual cost of the subscription (see chapter 3 for an example of this calculation). This calculation works well because the user activity for journals is always the same: full-text downloads. Depending on local needs, the usage analysis may stop after calculating CPU or further, in-depth analysis may be necessary.

While most usage statistics count how many times a resource is successfully retrieved, some provide information on when resources are not retrieved. The Journal Report 2 (JR2) counts the number of times users have been denied access to a journal because of an access issue or because the journal is not licensed by the library. Though a JR2 counts essentially the opposite of JR1, it can also assist electronic resources librarians in identifying journals in high demand The data in a JR2 can be helpful in making swaps between low-usage subscribed titles and high-demand unsubscribed titles. For instance, a journal with a high number of **denials** (or **turnaways**) is one worth considering for acquisition because the numbers indicate that the resource is needed, but unattainable.

Usage can also be examined according to copyright year. In situations where the library separately licenses the most recent copyright years and back issues, distinguishing the usage between the two can be useful in evaluating renewals. The Journal Report 1a (JR1a) counts the number of full-text article downloads from an **archive**.

The Journal Report 5 (JR5) counts the number of full-text article downloads by journal and year of publication. Depending on research interests and information needs of the user community, currency of content can be a major factor. Based on data found in a JR5, the library may opt to increase or decrease access to current or archival content.

Although the majority of usage analysis is for renewal decision-making, the library can glean additional meaningful information from COUNTER reports. The Journal Report 1 Gold Open Access (JR1 GOA) counts the number of full-text article downloads from **Gold OA** journals. This data can be useful if the library is considering financially supporting a Gold OA publisher or an author publishing in a Gold OA journal. When selecting which publisher or author to support, the library may focus funds on journals and publishers that are widely used by the user community. Alternatively, the library may look to Gold OA journal usage statistics as part of the selection process for ingesting Open Access resources in the library catalog and knowledge base.

Finally, the Journal Report 3 (JR3) report is an optional COUNTER report which counts the number of full-text downloads from mobile devices. Although this data would most likely not impact a renewal decision, it may inform web design and help the library better understand how users are accessing electronic resources using mobile devices.

Analyzing Usage for Databases

In some ways, analyzing and evaluating usage statistics for databases can be more complicated than for journals. The primary reason for the added complication is COUNTER for databases records more than one user activity. As mentioned above, COUNTER counts a single user activity for journals: downloads. But for databases, COUNTER records Regular Searches;

Searches–Federated; Searches–Automated; Result Clicks; and Page Views. Though the Database Report 1 (DB1) certainly adds value to Journal Reports, and vice versa, when analyzing usage statistics and making comparisons between resources, it is imperative to compare metrics like-with-like. For instance, a comparison of Regular Searches of a single database with the Results Clicks of another database will result in a misconstrued analysis.

Complicating matters further, databases vary greatly in content and scope. One can expect the overall usage from **A&I databases**—which do not provide full-text article access—to be lower than **aggregator databases**, which do provide full text. Databases that contain statistical data, images, or other types of information cannot be compared to the usage experienced by their article database counterparts, because these resources are used differently and will therefore have distinct metrics. Instead, it will be more advisable to compare databases according to type or content.

Perhaps the most accurate analysis for databases—and, in fact, for all resources—is to examine usage across time. If usage is available for multiple years with the same metric, an electronic resources librarian can evaluate whether usage has remained consistent or if it increased or decreased, and can begin to identify trends and note red flags that indicate a need for further evaluation.

Analyzing Usage for eBooks

COUNTER records multiple user activities for ebooks: title and section downloads, denials, and searches. In Release 4 of the COUNTER Code of Practice, Book Report 1 (BR1) counts the number of times an ebook was downloaded, and Book Report 2 (BR2) counts the number of times a section or chapter of an ebook was downloaded. The BR2 is most useful when analyzing usage for a single ebook, whereas the BR1 is helpful when analyzing usage for a bundle or package of ebooks.

In addition to providing data on ebook downloads, the Book Report 5 (BR5) provides a means of analyzing how often ebooks are searched. Such information may be the most useful for analyzing usage of an electronic reference work, such as an encyclopedia or dictionary, within which users may search heavily but download content less frequently. Similar to analyzing usage for databases (in which awareness of content and type of database is important), it is also valuable to be aware of how ebooks are accessed and used. The fact that a given ebook is an encyclopedia or part of a multivolume set, or that an ebook is licensed as part of a package and not an individual license, will all impact the type and level of usage analysis.

Finally, COUNTER also provides Book Report 3 (BR3) and Book Report 4 (BR4). Not unlike Journal Report 2 (JR2)—which counts the number of times users tried to access journal articles but were denied access—BR3 and BR4 count the number of times users tried to access an ebook but were denied. This data can be used to troubleshoot access issues if users are denied access to content to which they should have access, or to inform collection development decisions by identifying high-demand titles that should be considered for acquisition.

Basic Principles for Managing Usage Statistics

Document Workflows
Maintaining consistency can be a challenge and documentation is critical. Documentation will keep workflows relevant, dynamic, and consistent over time. This is especially helpful for libraries that only harvest usage statistics once a year.

Do Not Delay
COUNTER only requires that vendors keep a minimum twenty-four months of historic statistics on file. Although many vendors keep more than just twenty-four months of data, it is a good idea to collect all the necessary statistics when they become available to avoid later discovering that necessary data is missing.

Customize the Reporting Period
The Reporting Period is the one element of the COUNTER report that can be customized. Some libraries harvest data according to fiscal year to align usage with annual cost, other libraries align usage with exact subscription start and end dates, and still others analyze data according to calendar year. Decide which set of dates makes the most sense for local needs and then make sure that reports are continually collected over time for the same reporting period.

Investigate the Details
If a given resource is reporting uncharacteristically/or low usage, be sure to investigate as soon as a potential problem is identified. Vendor-provided statistics can include errors, database administration dashboards can malfunction, or there could be a security breach that needs to be addressed.

Other Types of Statistics from Link Resolvers, Proxy Logs, and Web Analytics

In addition to usage statistics provided by publishers and vendors, data can also be harvested from the library's link resolver, EZproxy logs, and website. These additional sources of statistics can provide insight into user behavior beyond clicks and downloads in database platforms as well as users' starting and ending points when navigating to find resources.

Link resolver statistics count how often users click-through to full-text content and also track whether or not full-text content was available when requested from citation-only databases. Link resolver statistics also record which full-text **targets** are most often selected from link resolver options within an A&I database and which options did not result in full text or a failed connection. Used alongside COUNTER statistics, link resolver statistics can be used to evaluate journal renewals by indicating if access via an aggregator database is sufficient or if a full-text subscription is needed. Link resolver statistics can also support collection development by counting the number of times full-text content was not available and users opted for Interlibrary Loan, because link resolvers will often direct users to Interlibrary Loan when full text is not available.

The actual report names and report types for link resolver statistics will vary depending on the provider. The following basic reports, however, are typical across providers:

> Type of resource (journal, book, article), the number of times it was requested, and how frequently the user clicked through to the resource
>
> Number of requests and click-throughs by service type (full-text online, print, Interlibrary Loan)
>
> Most popular titles by target
>
> Unsuccessful requests for the full text

Proxy logs are another alternative source for statistics. Proxy logs illustrate the number of times users have logged into a particular resource. If vendor-supplied statistics are not available, proxy logs can provide a ballpark number of uses. Likewise, website analytics are another source of alternate usage data that can help determine how often users are entering a specific resource. Data gathered from website analytics include clicks and page views and demonstrate how users navigate from the library website to electronic resources.

Community Advocacy for COUNTER-Compliant Statistics

As libraries build larger electronic collections and rely more heavily on usage statistics, it is imperative that electronic resources librarians monitor COUNTER-compliance from their vendors, especially if reports fall short of the Code of Practice guidelines. Further, non-compliant vendors complicate and negatively impact a library's ability to analyze data effectively. However, since COUNTER is a Code of Practice and not a law or requirement, there are zero repercussions for the vendors that do not provide COUNTER statistics. In 2014 **Usus** was formed in response to these issues. Usus, a community advocacy website managed by a supervisory board of librarians, publishers, and vendors, is an outlet for librarians to discuss and advocate for much-needed standardized and reliable usage statistics, as well as report known inaccuracies in vendor data. Usus is the first step towards addressing short-falls in usage statistics reporting and creating a place for the library community to share one voice.

FURTHER READINGS

Cohen, Rachael A. and Angie Thorpe. "Discovering User Behavior: Applying Usage Statistics to Shape Frontline Services." *The Serials Librarian* 69, no. 1 (2015): 29–46. doi: 10.1080/0361526X.2015.1040194.

De Groote, Sandra L., Deborah D. Blecic, and Kristin Martin. "Measures of Health Sciences Journal Use: A Comparison of Vendor, Link-Resolver, and Local Citation Statistics." *Journal of the Medical Library Association* 101, no. 2 (2013): 110–19. doi: 10.3163/1536-5050.101.2.006.

Emery, Jill, and Graham Stone. "Annual Review" TERMS: Techniques for Electronic Resource Management. https://library3.hud.ac.uk/blogs/terms/terms/annual-review/.

Emery, Jill, and Graham Stone. "Ongoing Evaluation and Access" TERMS: Techniques for Electronic Resource Management. https://library3.hud.ac.uk/blogs/terms/terms/ongoing-evaluation-and-access/.

Feather, Celeste. "The International Coalition of Library Consortia: Origins, Contribution, and Path Forward." *Insights* 28, no. 3 (2015): 89–93. doi: http://doi.org/10.1629/uksg.260.

ICOLC. "Guidelines for Statistical Measures of Usage of Web-Based Information Resources." Published October 4, 2006. http://icolc.net/statement/guidelines-statistical-measures-usage-web-based-information-resources-1998-revised-2001–0.

Lamothe, Alain R. "The Importance of Identifying and Accommodating E-Resource Usage Data for the Presence of Outliers." *Information Technology and Libraries* 33, no. 2 (2014): 31–44.

National Information Standards Organization. "SUSHI-Lite: A Technical Report of the National Information Standards Organization." www.niso.org/apps/group_public/document.php?document_id=15331&wg_abbrev=sushi_lite_trwg.

National Information Standards Organization. "The Standardized Usage Statistics Harvesting Initiative (SUSHI) Protocol," January 6, 2015. www.niso.org/apps/group_public/project/details.php?project_id=120

Pesch, Oliver. "Implementing SUSHI and COUNTER: A Primer for Librarians." *The Serials Librarian* 69, no. 2 (2015): 107–125. doi: 10.1080/0361526X.2015.1063029

Pesch, Oliver. "Usus: A Community Website for those Interested in the Usage of Online Content." *The Serials Librarian* 69, no. 3–4 (2015): 223–32. doi: 10.1080/0361526X.2015.1116334

Timms, Geoffrey. "Gathering, Evaluating, and Communicating Statistical Usage Information for Electronic Resources." In *Managing Electronic Resources: A LITA Guide,* edited by Ryan O. Weir, 87–120, Chicago: American Library Association, 2012.

Tucker, Cory. "Benchmarking Usage Statistics in Collection Management for Serials." *Journal of Electronic Resources Librarianship* 21, no. 1 (2009): 48–61. doi: 10.1080/19411260902858581.

8

What You Might Want to Ask a Library Vendor
(*But Never Thought You Could*)

Libraries traditionally form long relationships with their vendor
suppliers. A clear perception, by both parties, of the mutual benefit
inherent in the relationship will insure the smooth and unbroken
flow of information service that marks good library operations.

—Barbara Quint[1]

- Business Ethics
- Perception, Perception, Perception
- Get to Know Your Library Vendor
- Questions to Avoid
- Build a Partnership
- In-Person Visits
- Post-Sales Relationships
- Conclusion

"Account Executive," "Licensing Manager," "Director of Inside Sales," "Library Representative," and "Account Specialist" are just a few job titles of the people who conduct business with librarians; these are the library's vendor representatives. Library and vendor business can range from ordering and paying for library resources, negotiating pricing, and securing license agreements to leasing and purchasing furniture and equipment. The business of libraries is truly learned on the job and, because most librarians have not had formal business training, librarians often fall back on trial and error, as well as basic common sense, when navigating the waters of business relationships.

Other parts of this book have provided a broad overview of the role of an electronic resources librarian. This chapter will provide insight into business with the other side: the library vendor. The current book market is rife with information on how to "make it" in sales. This chapter is not one of those; rather, it will provide insight into the work of both the vendor and the librarian, why the library's relationship with vendors is so important, and advice on building and maintaining a healthy business relationship. A successful relationship requires strong communication skills and a clear understanding of the shared goal, as well as diplomacy, discretion, and a little bit of compassion. This chapter introduces sample questions that can be used or adapted to facilitate conversations with library vendors, to strengthen business relationships, and better understand the role of the library vendor.

Business Ethics

All librarians involved in external communications and/or purchasing decisions need to have a firm grasp of both business ethics in general—from conflicts of interest and vendor relations to intellectual freedom and privacy—as well as specific institutional ethical guidelines. Experienced electronic resources or acquisition librarians may have already established business relationships with vendor representatives which, through common interests and friendships, may develop over time. But even the most friendly and favorable business relationships require thoughtful attention to ethical behavior.

The ethics of business is defined by the American Library Association (ALA), the American Association of Law Libraries (AALL), and the Association for Library Collections & Technical Services (ALCTS). ALA's Code of Ethics, Article VI, states "we do not advance private interests at the expense of library users, colleagues, or our employing institutions;" and the AALL Code of Ethics states that librarians "must avoid any possibility of personal financial gain at the expense of the employing institution." ALA's Association for Library Collections & Technical Services (ALCTS) has twelve Principles & Standards of Acquisitions Practice that addresses issues surrounding business relationships. The ALCTS principles range from:

- striving to obtain the maximum ultimate value of each dollar of expenditure
- granting all competing vendors equal consideration and regarding each transaction on its own merits

Three Simple Ways Librarians Can Practice Good Ethics

1. Do business objectively; do not make a deal because of a friendship, gift, or a free lunch.
2. Attend a vendor's social event if invited, but do not attend if there are feelings of animosity.
3. Pay invoices on time.

Three Simple Ways Vendor Representatives Can Practice Good Ethics

1. Do not assume what the library needs; ask questions and do research.
2. Work with appropriate contacts; do not go over anyone's head in order to make a sale.
3. Schedule meetings in advance.

- subscribing to and working for honesty, truth, and fairness in buying and selling, and denouncing all forms and manifestations of bribery
- declining personal gifts and gratuities, and
- fostering and promoting fair, ethical, and legal trade practices

In addition to professional codes, institutions and libraries generally have ethics statements that address conflicts of interest, professional responsibilities, and workplace cultures. Such statements will cover job responsibilities, reflect the best interests of the institution, and may require that employees disclose potential conflicts of financial interests and legal commitments. These can include stock ownership, additional employment, revenue earned during paid time off, board memberships, and consulting relationships. For any librarian in a decision-making role—as electronic resources and acquisitions librarians often are—it is important to be aware of local institutional policies on ethics and conflicts of interest and to disclose and resolve conflicts in an appropriate and professional manner.

Perception, Perception, Perception

The information community relies on content creators, vendors, intermediaries, and librarians working together for content to be made accessible to users. Although there are many players in the supply chain, a library's initial point of interaction with new content is through a vendor's sales representative. Libraries and vendors are fundamentally different—simply stated, one is for-profit and the other is often not—but without books, reference materials, journals, DVDs, and databases, the library is simply a quiet building with a security guard and a water cooler. Vendors provide content that is needed and used by library patrons. Vendors and libraries are, therefore, partners providing users with the best possible resources.

The best business relationships between libraries and vendors will be built on expertise and honesty. Relationships can be built by working toward a common goal, or can break down when one side sees as an opportunity that the other does not. For the library, business should be done in a manner that addresses the library's organizational and functional needs. For a library vendor, good business will fulfill a direct need. Vendors have something libraries want, libraries have something vendors want, and both parties need to set reasonable expectations to achieve mutual success.

Although libraries and vendors need each other to succeed, common misconceptions exist on both sides. In libraries, there tends to be a perception that vendors hold all the cash, with large profit margins and overly compensated personnel. These days, however, vendors (especially small publishers) are not necessarily making the huge profits that they once did. Although it is true that in the 1990s, when print was still the primary source of capital, vendors saw revenues averaging 13 percent. However, since the uptick in electronic resources this revenue has shrunk to about 5 percent.[2]

Conversely, vendors might perceive that libraries move too slowly, that budget cuts are grossly exaggerated, or that librarians simply are not trying hard enough to uncover additional funds. No matter the perception, both parties must understand that there are elements in every business relationship that may not be fully understood by both parties. The adage about "walking a mile in another person's shoes" truly applies when managing perceptions about an institution's internal operations.

Librarians and vendors see each other in person at occasional library site visits, but most frequently at conferences. Considering just how many conferences happen every year, and how many librarians attend each one of these conferences, vendor representatives spend a good percentage of their time in front of customers and must travel a great deal to do so. Preview any job advertisement for a library vendor and it will likely specify 50 to 80 percent of time will involve travel. That's just one of the challenges faced by the business partners of the library.

Additional challenges for the vendor representative include:

- working in an industry where profit matters, whose customers are primarily nonprofit institutions
- facing uncertainties from business mergers
- pressure to compete
- learning about the library field, which is likely not a representative's primary background
- having a defined sales territory with an assigned value
- meeting quarterly goals, which are seldom in sync with a library's fiscal year
- maintaining both existing customers while developing new business

Vendor representatives face challenges, just as librarians must deal with their own. One challenge both libraries and vendors face in their business dealings with each other is that each side has its own marker of success, and those markers often do not align. Success, more often than not, comes down to money: libraries need to save it and vendors need to acquire it. Immediately, money strains the library/vendor relationship. With that said, libraries and vendors do share challenges; one is the need to keep current with the complex array of electronic products and services. To do so, librarians and vendor representatives participate in the same conferences, collaborate on journal articles and white papers, and communicate on the same listservs. Both librarians and vendor representatives are in the same field, and each side strives to keep up to date with the latest terminology, initiatives, and emerging trends.

Get to Know Your Library Vendor

A good first step in building a healthy business relationship with vendor representatives is to simply get to know them. Some representatives stay at the same company for their entire careers, whereas others seem to be constantly playing a game of musical chairs. Taking the time to get to know a vendor representative—whether a newbie or someone the library has worked with for a long time—is an excellent first step toward building a strong business relationship.

To close the gap between libraries and vendors, librarians can ask:

1. *"What is your typical day like?" or "How often do you travel?"*

> Workflows for electronic resources rely heavily on the internal workflows of vendors. Talking to vendors about their schedules can be extremely helpful to develop expectations about the frequency of communication. The answer to a question such as "What is your typical day like?" will vary depending on the type of vendor representative: help desk or systems personnel are more likely to be in the office and handle a high volume of email correspondence, whereas dedicated sales representatives may have strict travel schedules, work remotely, and be at times unable to access email. Having an open conversation about scheduling will give both sides more reasonable expectations for communication and follow-up. As a follow-up to a scheduling conversation, consider whether it is appropriate to ask about personal interests. If a vendor representative has a heavy travel schedule, inquire about their favorite city, library, or place to stay. A little camaraderie goes a long way!

2. *"Could you tell me about your sales territory?"*

> A question about a representative's sales territory can be especially helpful to get a better understanding of the types of libraries with which the representative works. Territories for vendor representatives can be based on state, region, institution size, and product. If the question reveals that a representative is assigned to a specific product, region, or library type, it can indicate how often and in what context they will be reaching out or visiting the library.
>
> This question can also reveal whether mutual library contacts exist (i.e., a "name game" of sorts) within a representative's sales territory, which provides another opportunity for relationship-building. Asking about territory is a good reminder that library vendors work with libraries and librarians all day, every day.

3. *"What are other libraries our size talking to you about?"*

> A question about a representative's work with other libraries is perfectly valid with one caveat: because license agreements can include confidentiality clauses it is best to not pry into what other

libraries are buying, how much they're paying, or the specific terms of their agreements. This more general type of question can, however, provide insight into how comfortable a certain representative is when "talking libraries." Representatives' responses can demonstrate the degree to which they are comfortable discussing library theories, trends, workflows, and systems, which can be helpful when considering how much jargon and detail to include in correspondence. For instance, if representatives respond that they work with libraries predominantly on product sales, it might be best to stick to high-level sales and pricing conversations. Should this be the case, it is a good idea to inquire whether there is a specific contact for troubleshooting and development inquiries for post-sales.

Every electronic resources librarian dreams of finding a vendor representative who can wear many hats and answer questions about price models, content updates, systems operations, and more. In reality, such a person is seldom encountered. Across the board in the information industry, employees of libraries and vendors alike are being asked to do more with less. Ask questions to get a feel for a vendor representative's knowledge and interests in the field, but do not automatically assume that the person is a wiz in library science. With that said, a growing number of vendor representatives hold advanced degrees in Library and Information Science; if so, a good ice-breaker question might be, "Where did you go to library school?" which, as every librarian knows, is the ultimate ice-breaker.

4. *"Who is your biggest competitor?"*

For librarians, the concept of keeping up with or even surpassing competition is a distant notion, unless they work in a library system where tenure and promotion is considered a competitive sport. Business, on the other hand, is full of competition, which is a reality for vendors, whether or not it is openly discussed with librarians. A conversation about competition in the market as a whole can help maintain transparency and honesty.

Before embarking on a conversation about competition, do a little homework first. It is best to start a conversation about the state of the market with as much information at hand so that a discussion doesn't feel like an interrogation. Direct competitors will at times be obvious (consider Tom and Jerry, Apple and Microsoft, or SpringerNature and Elsevier), and at other times less so. Conversations about competition can also provide useful information about a vendor's priorities and development initiatives. Such a discussion can also provide the library with an opportunity to discuss features and functionalities offered by other vendors. Essentially, this type of conversation allows both sides to discuss the state of the market and share priorities, likes, and dislikes. *One caution:* when discussing competition, both sides should use appropriate amounts of discretion and honesty. It's the right thing to do, and it's only fair.

Build a Partnership

The world of libraries is small, and that includes the businesses that work with libraries. As people move to new job roles and different companies, former colleagues and vendor representatives will likely make an unexpected appearance sometime in the future. After a few years in the field, everyone shuffles around. Personnel turnover can be a result of career advancement, or may be the result of two or more companies merging.

Thinking about business with vendors as a partnership can result in good business relationships today and tomorrow—not just with one specific vendor but with all. For instance, if a business relationship is healthy with a certain representative at one vendor who later leaves to work at another vendor, the healthy relationship should endure as long as mutual business still exists. Similarly, if a relationship is sour, poor feelings can spread from one company to the next as personnel move around.

The most effective partnerships between libraries and vendors are built on communication and transparency. Good business requires both sides to be well-informed, ask questions, and be considerate of the needs of the other party's and their own institutions. Of course, the other side of good business is bad business. A classic example of bad business between libraries and vendors is the "hard sell," or when a vendor submits an offer simply to make a sale without considering the needs of its customer. Bad business is not just something that happens on the vendor side. Libraries can also engage in it, for example, if content is pursued without a true interest in acquisition. In

Questions to Avoid

BAD QUESTION #1

"Will you still be our representative when the companies merge?"

REASON: Companies are constantly merging, incorporating each other, and being bought and sold. These transitions can be tumultuous for both vendors and the libraries that are trying to make sense of it all. Up-to-date records and contacts are important, especially when vendors experience organizational change, but hesitate before asking a question that relates to organizational structures in times of mergers. For the most part, representatives are good at keeping customers up to date, and information regarding organizational change will likely be released as it is available.

BAD QUESTION #2

"I heard another library received a bigger discount.
Why weren't we offered the same price?"

REASON: Content and systems offered to libraries have a list price. A list price is the market value for the product. A sales price can vary greatly from the list price depending on discounts related to library and institution size, Carnegie classification, discounts related to the volume of products and services acquired, and good old-fashioned negotiation. If information is shared by another library regarding a specific price or discount received from a vendor, it is *not* good business to use it as leverage in negotiations. Doing so can jeopardize business relationships and damage trust. As a rule, the offer and negotiation process is unique for each institution.

BAD QUESTION #3

"Will you be expensing lunch?"

REASON: Just as accepting a lunch invitation from a vendor representative does not equal the promise of a sale, asking for a free lunch is not the way to make friends and garner influence. Although a meal might occasionally be offered, one should never be expected, demanded, or required. Further, because many vendor representatives travel for work, their per diems might cover their own meals, but nothing more. Some librarians may think that the simple act of accepting a meal or a drink from a vendor automatically compromises the integrity of the business relationship, but policies on gifts and meals will vary depending on library structure and culture. If there is not an institutional policy in place regarding gifts, use good judgment and never ask for a freebie if one is not offered.

The Business of an RFP

In the United States, some states require a formal approach to reviewing a vendor's product and service through a **Request for Proposal (RFP)**. An RFP provides a means to evaluate vendor products objectively, from price, service, content, and system requirements. Although an RFP certainly helps a library to stay well-informed, it is important to remember that it requires a considerable amount of work: the library needs to draft an RFP to articulate its needs and a vendor needs to respond. During the response phase, good practice would include providing the vendor with access to key library decision-makers. Access and transparency also helps the vendor ensure its response to the RFP will be competitive.

On average, a vendor can expect to spend anywhere from $5,000 to $10,000 to answer a large RFP due to the labor involved. An RFP is no small undertaking, and the library should make every effort to accommodate and assist vendors who are submitting them.[3]

short, good business will always be mutually beneficial and bad business will waste everyone's time. Partnership-building questions to ask a vendor representative include:

1. *"How do you see this product fitting into my library?"*

   Although vendors need to get their products into libraries, not all vendor products are appropriate for every library. An effective sales representative will take the time to understand the needs and issues of a library. As mentioned previously, vendors must compete with market competitors while also working to maintain internal revenue and quarterly sales benchmarks. Most electronic resources are supported through annual subscription payments and when resources demonstrate high use—therefore deemed successful—they will generally be renewed. Libraries are more likely to explore new resources from vendors that have already demonstrated success. Vendor representatives should, therefore, try to learn which products the library already licenses as well as the programs and user population served by the library.

At times it may seem that vendor representatives are only interested in making a sale and are uninterested in the library's needs. This type of situation can be caused by a number of factors, but effective representatives will take the time to understand their accounts. When meeting with a representative, an electronic resources librarian can proactively ask how the product or content will benefit the library to avoid getting caught in the hard sell. By posing such a question in advance, an electronic resources librarian can address an issue before it develops. The answer will either provide the opportunity to gracefully deny the offer, or can facilitate the next steps to understanding the offer.

2. *"What is the long-term plan for this product or service?"*

Inquiring about long-terms plans for a product or service demonstrates an investment in the library/vendor partnership, and the response to such a question gives a representative the opportunity to go beyond the standard sales pitch. If a representative is not aware of long-term plans for a product, do not become discouraged. Instead, use the opportunity to start a conversation about alternate contacts for information and services beyond sales.

Understanding the long-term plans of a vendor's resources can also help inform licensing decisions. For instance, if product enhancements or additional content are expected in the future, it should be clear whether they will be included automatically or added at an additional cost. The license agreement should also clearly reflect which option applies. For more on licensing for electronic resources, see chapter 5.

Similarly, when a vendor presents a new offer for a product or service, questions about the development status can help inform whether the product will go to market complete, or if it will be phased in over time. Further, because librarians are the primary customers for many publishers, new products often need "real world" testers. By inquiring about the current status of a product and its future, an electronic resources librarian may find an opportunity to become part of the development and feedback process. Electronic resources librarians have a vested interest in vendor products, so the opportunity to weigh in is invaluable!

3. *"My library needs some time to research the product and evaluate the offer. How long will the current quote be valid?"*

> This type of question is an example of a *useful* "holding message." Holding messages let another party know that a message has been received, and work is underway to complete a response. In this case, the holding message buys time to research and gather information. It also addresses the importance of timelines for both the library and the vendor. For instance, if purchasing decisions are made by committee, let the vendor representative know the date the committee is meeting to discuss the offer.
>
> For the most part, vendor representatives involved in sales are focused on closing sales pipelines and meeting company revenue goals. Vendors may want to work quickly to close a sale, however, they are at odds with the slow pace of libraries as well as the cyclical nature of electronic resources. For these reasons, librarians often find it difficult to provide representatives with advance notice or handshake agreements. Most deals for electronic resources are not truly set until the moment a license agreement is signed. An electronic resources librarian can ease the purchasing process by sharing information regarding the library's budget cycle and how and when new offers are considered. For instance, a library might not consider new products until all renewals have been processed and remaining end-of-the-year money has been identified.
>
> When using a holding message of any kind, be sure not to use it as a stalling tactic or as a means of rejecting or ignoring an offer. Just as a library has goals for its own renewals, a representative has goals for renewals and new sales opportunities. Don't string along a vendor representative to appear nice or accommodating. A healthy relationship with a vendor means maintaining honesty, even if that honesty involves delivering bad news.

4. *"Who can I contact when I need to escalate certain issues?"*

> In the library/vendor relationship, each party has unique needs, goals, and responsibilities. Clarifying the distinct responsibilities of each party helps prevent unrealistic expectations. Questions regarding the other party's organizational structure will

ensure that the correct level of assistance is given at the correct time. Inquiring about an alternate vendor contact does, however, have the potential to appear passive-aggressive. Consider framing such a question with additional details, such as, "If I receive your out of office message on an urgent inquiry, whom should I contact?" or "If my library has an urgent issue, is it best to contact you or go directly to help desk support?" Ideally, ask these questions at the very beginning of a business relationship to avoid potential confusion or conflict.

With that said, libraries should try to investigate possible problems before contacting a vendor. It is so easy to fall into a pattern of turning immediately to a vendor representative to report every problem or to answer every question. Before contacting vendor representatives, consider whether they work as point of contact or are associated with a specific product or sales specialty. At times, a single vendor representative acts as the point of contact to triage all library inquiries. This type of representative often fields many requests each day, in which case it is especially important to be mindful of correspondence frequency. A little prework on the library's part can go a long way towards resolving problems efficiently, maintaining the library's credibility, and providing the vendor representative with the best possible description of a problem. Prep work on the library's side is simply due diligence and good business practice.

In-Person Visits

In-person meetings can be used to meet stakeholders, gather information, brainstorm, and develop plans. In-person meetings also help facilitate a healthy post-sale relationship, for continued contact with the representative and/or continued support and training. Both librarians and vendor representatives have a shared responsibility to keep up-to-date with the latest technologies, content, and trends in the field, and so in-person meetings will not be limited to on-site library visits, but also take place at library conferences. If a meeting occurred at any point before a library conference, another bonus to in-person visits is seeing a familiar face in a large exhibit hall. In such instances, even if there is no direct mutual business to discuss, a simple friendly interaction or a "hello" will reinforce a good business relationship.

There are many possible motives for in-person meetings, so be sure to ask preliminary questions before scheduling a meeting or accepting an invitation. For librarians, this process is very much like the reference interview. When presented with a meeting invitation, ask follow-up questions to clarify the purpose of the meeting to determine if it's business or social. Preparing questions before a meeting ensures that both sides are prepared and able to address the proper issues.

When accepting an invitation to or preparing for a meeting, possible questions to ask a vendor representative include:

1. *"What would you like to accomplish while visiting our library?"*

    A lot of ground can be covered during on-site meetings, whereas email and phone communication can only effectively cover one topic at a time. These meetings are an opportunity for vendor representatives to demonstrate how their products and content can be used in the library and where opportunities may exist for additional resources, which means meetings can quickly turn into sales pitches. To determine whether an on-site meeting will be related to sales, marketing, usage, or training–just ask! The vendor's answer provides the librarian an opportunity to advocate for the inclusion of library needs in the meeting agenda and that the right people attend.

    For instance, if a vendor representative wants to discuss renewals or new business in person, make sure that stakeholders in acquisitions and collection development are invited to the meeting. If a vendor representative offers or agrees to discuss marketing and training opportunities, such topics and demonstrations are appropriate for a diverse audience. Keep in mind that vendor representatives with set territory regions might send meeting requests simply because they plan to be in the area. Should a meeting invitation be extended because of situational timing, consider if the meeting is actually necessary. A meeting for the sake of a meeting is not a good use of staff time, and in such cases it is perfectly acceptable to decline.

2. *"Do you have any plans to visit our area in the next six months?"*

One way to counteract situational meetings that are the result of a vendor representative's travel schedule is to plan ahead. Because electronic resources librarians work with so many vendors and their products on a daily basis, they often have a long list of non-urgent topics for vendor representatives. If there is a particular vendor for whom you have a growing list of questions, reach out to representatives to ask about their upcoming travel. If a representative does not have travel planned in the library's region, sending questions can plant a seed that the library wants to meet.

3. *"Are you planning an end-user presentation for a large group, or do you want to meet in a smaller group to discuss a specific offer?"*

A question regarding the appropriate size and audience for an in-person meeting conveys respect for a representative's time and specific duties. As a liaison between library staff and vendor representatives, it is important to prepare for on-site meetings by making sure that the right people attend the meeting. At the same time, it is just as important to make sure that representatives are not bombarded by off-topic questions or questions that do not fit within a representative's expertise.

One way to facilitate smaller meetings is to inform library staff of the meeting and allow them to submit topics to be addressed so that those who are not in attendance will have an opportunity to voice concerns and pose questions. In the message, state that a library vendor representative will be on campus to meet with a small group, then solicit questions, comments, or concerns from staff and ask that they be submitted a few days before the meeting. Review staff submissions carefully and send them to the representative in advance. In this way, questions can be addressed either at the meeting, or separately as a follow-up afterwards.

Sample Pre-Meeting Announcement and Call for Questions

Dear colleagues,

A vendor representative from [COMPANY NAME] will be at the library on June 18th to meet with acquisitions and electronic resources departments to discuss upcoming renewals. Because this is one of the library's largest vendors and everyone here has a stake in its resources, please send me any questions, comments, or concerns that you would like to have addressed in advance of or during this meeting. I will submit your responses to our representative, and I will do my best to have them addressed.

Sincerely,

[YOUR NAME]

4. *"Are you going to this conference, and if so would you like to arrange a meeting?"*

Conference attendance can be a good opportunity to schedule a meeting with vendor representatives. Requesting a meeting during a conference will signal to the representative that there are important issues, concerns, or questions that need to be addressed.

At national conferences, vendor representation can range from sales and marketing people to vice presidents and board members, so a meeting might include multiple representatives and some new faces. When entering an exhibit hall at a conference, there is a stark difference between the appearance of librarians and the appearance of vendor representatives. This is simply a byproduct of work cultures, which vary drastically among vendors and libraries. Very few libraries require a suit and tie, while it is common to wear a suit to a vendor board meeting. If the number or appearance of vendor representatives seems intimidating, remember that if it were not for libraries and librarians, vendors would not be at the conference. Meetings occur because librarians are customers, and therefore librarians hold more power than it might sometimes seem.

Unlike formal meetings at conferences, events such as receptions and lunches are social occasions and should not necessarily be used for negotiations or to air lists of grievances. As mentioned previously, an aspect of the library/vendor relationship is social. If social activities do not violate a code of ethics or cause a conflict of interest, it is generally acceptable to attend a social gathering hosted by a vendor.

Post-Sales Relationships

A library's first point of contact for new content is a sales representative, but just because a sale has closed does not mean the relationship ends. Depending on organizational structure, vendors may have distinct pre- and post-sales contacts, or distinct contacts for renewals, technical support, and marketing. Understanding whom to contact and when will not only ensure that issues and questions are addressed in a timely manner, but it will also ensure that work is distributed evenly and appropriately. Post-sales communication also provides excellent opportunities to continue exploring a vendor's offerings and explore future business avenues. Questions to facilitate a good post-sales relationship include:

1. *"Could you provide the name of our post-sales contact?"*

Good project planning and relationship building require setting sights toward the future. An electronic resources librarian should not assume vendor representatives can wear many different types of hats, or that they have all the answers regarding every aspect of their company. Ask sales representatives if they will continue to be the post-sales contact. If the sale has already been completed and it is not immediately obvious who will be your future contact, send a message to the library's primary contact with a caveat—something along the lines of: "My library is working through a question regarding platform functionality. Would you be able to assist with this question, or do you know the name of another contact who could assist?" This type of question actively recognizes that vendor representatives have specific duties, which conveys courtesy and respect for their work.

2. "Do you have any marketing materials that my library can use or adapt?"

During the sales conversation, a plethora of materials marketing the product will be shared. These materials are generally not appropriate for end-users or instruction. Because they want to see their products succeed post-sales, vendors often provide a second set of marketing materials targeted to the end user. Such marketing material is often customizable, either via simple text fields to insert the name of the library or the ability to include the library's logo. At times, the request for marketing material might produce a bounty of vendor-swag in the mail, from branded pens and brochures to stress balls and mints.

When inquiring about post-sales marketing material, be sure to pose the question as "if it is available, we'll take it!" rather than approaching it as something you expect. Depending on the size of the vendor, such material might be lavish, more bare-bones, or not available at all. Either way, it is certainly worth the inquiry!

3. "Are there any opportunities for on-site training?"

If nothing else, do not hesitate to ask about what the library needs now or may need in the future. A successful sale will lead to a satisfied customer and more opportunities for the vendor in the future. Buy-in from library staff is an important aspect of a successful sale, because they will be responsible for fielding questions from users. Because electronic resources are constantly changing, new products and services can be intimidating. Formal on-site staff training can help combat feelings of intimidation, and training done by vendors provides a sense of solidarity. If vendor representatives have gone out of their way to visit the library post-sale, they must be invested in the library and the future of the account. Such an impression diminishes the notion that vendors are the "bad guys" and instead promotes the common goal.

In general, inquiries regarding physical marketing material or in-person trainings can end in one of two ways: yes or no. If the request is made in a respectful manner, it certainly does not hurt to ask, because it also demonstrates to the vendor that the library is invested in the company and a continued relationship.

4. *"Would you be interested in collaborating on a conference presentation/article together?"*

The ultimate sign of a good relationship is collaboration. Collaboration can come in multiple forms: negotiations and troubleshooting, or in something more formal, such as the creation of a white paper, conference presentation, or journal article. Formal collaborations through academic endeavors are especially likely if a vendor representative has a background in library science or once worked in a library, as a growing number of library vendor representatives do. When attending conferences, vendor representatives are not always simply scheduling meetings and working the exhibit hall. Many representatives actively seek opportunities to give presentations at conferences and speak on panels.

Vendors certainly benefit from formal collaborations with libraries, which advertises the favorable business relationship and the success of their product to a wide audience. Libraries also benefit from collaborating with vendors, because the collaboration can provide insight into the vendor's operations and future plans, as well as the personal interests of the vendor representative.

Conclusion

At times, electronic resources librarians can feel as though they need to be experts in both the resources themselves and the companies that provide them. The ability to move between both worlds seamlessly and effectively is a skill that comes with time and experience. Understanding vendors, their representatives, sales techniques, and marketing strategies is complicated and crucial. One way to make the process easier is to remain conscious of the library/vendor relationship and to proactively work toward improving it. When conducting business with vendor representatives, do not simply ask questions—be engaged, inquisitive, thoughtful, and considerate.

In the process of trying to figure it all out, do not forget that the person on the other end of the business relationship is an ally who is invested in

essentially the same field as libraries: information. Treating vendor representatives as allies can lead to productive and healthy business relationships.

NOTES

1. Barbara Quint, "Six Rules of Engagement: Negotiating Deals with Vendors,"
   The Bottom Line 10, no. 1 (1997): 4–10.
2. Christine Stamison, Bob Persing, Chris Beckett, and Chris Brady, "What They
   Never Told You About Vendors in Library School," *The Serials Librarian* 56,
   no. 1–4 (2009): 139–45.
3. Ibid, 141.

FURTHER READINGS

Association for Library Collections and Technical Services. "Statement on Principles
     and Standards of Acquisitions Practice." www.ala.org/advocacy/proethics/
     explanatory/acquisitions.

Brooks, Sam. "Introduction: The Importance of Open Communication Between
     Libraries and Vendors." *Journal of Library Administration* 44, no. 3–4 (2006):
     1–4.

Collins, Maria, Mary Somerville, Nicole Pelsinsky, and Aaron Wood. "Working
     Better Together: Library, Publisher, and Vendor Perspectives." In the *Charleston
     Library Conference Proceedings 2013* (West Lafayette: Purdue University, 2014),
     312–318.

Courtney, Keith. "Library/Vendor Relations: An Academic Publisher's Perspective."
     Journal of Library Administration 44, no. 3–4 (2006): 57–68.

Fisher, William. "A Brief History of Library-Vendor Relations since 1950." *Library
     Acquisitions: Practice and Theory 17,* no. 1 (1993): 61–69.

Fries, James R., and John R. James. "Library Advisory Boards: A Survey of Current
     Practice among Selected Publishers and Vendors." *Journal of Library
     Administration* 44, no. 3–4 (2006): 85–93.

Gagnon, Ronald A. "Library/Vendor Relations from a Public Library Perspective."
     Journal of Library Administration 44, no. 3–4 (2006): 95–111.

Ginanni, Katy, Anne McKee, Jenni Wilson. "Yer Doin it Wrong: How NOT to Interact
     with Vendors, Publishers, or Librarians." Presentation at NASIG Annual
     Conference in Fort Worth, Texas on May 3, 2014.

Harris, Pat. "Library-Vendor Relations in the World of Information Standards."
     Journal of Library Administration 44, no. 3–4 (2006): 127–36. doi: 10.1300/
     J111v44n03_11.

Marks, Kenneth E. "Vendor/Library Collaboration—An Opportunity for Sharing."
     Resource Sharing and Information Networks 18, no. 1–2 (2005): 203–14.

Nagel, Lawrence. "Biz of Acq—What Color Is Your Hat? Ethics in Library-Vendor Relations." *Against the Grain* 14, no. 1 (2013): 27.

Raley, Sarah, and Jean Smith. "Community College Library/Vendor Relations: You Can't Always Get What You Want . . . or Can You?" *Journal of Library Administration* 44, no. 3–4 (2006): 187–202.

Sugnet, Chris. "The Vendors' Corner—The Request for Proposal." *Library Hi Tech* 5, no. 1 (1987): 87–97.

Tenopir, Carol. "Working for a Vendor." *Library Journal* 130, no. 12 (2005): 29.

9

Techniques and Tools for Marketing Electronic Resources

- Why Market E-Resources?
- Developing a Marketing Plan
- Tips and Tricks to Maximize Resources
- Opportunities for Marketing Collaboration
- Conclusion

The American Marketing Association defines marketing as "the process of planning and executing the conception, pricing, promotion and distribution of ideas, goods and services to create exchanges that satisfy individual and organizational objectives."[1] When libraries engage in marketing activities, it is with a services-centered approach, in a less profit-driven manner. Take the similar definition of marketing from the Association of Research Libraries, which states:

> Marketing is the organized process of planning and executing the conception, pricing, promotion, and distribution of ideas, goods, and services to create exchanges and will (if applicable)

satisfy individual and organizational objectives. Marketing collects and uses demographic, geographic, behavioral, and psychological information. Marketing also fulfills the organization's mission and, like public relations, inspires public awareness and educates.[2]

Even though both definitions begin with the same core element—planning, an essential aspect of marketing that will be discussed in depth in this chapter—marketing in libraries diverges from general marketing in that it "inspires public awareness and educates," which divorces it from marketing as a means to increase profit. In fact, engaging in marketing has always been an integral aspect of the library profession. Evidence of library marketing dates to the 1880s where, again, the focus was primarily public relations.[3] Today the idea of marketing as public relations still prevails, and includes outreach activities within the profession, scholarly writing and conference presentations, and developing teaching and learning activities for end-users.

Why Market E-Resources?

In recent years, libraries have focused marketing efforts on electronic resources for two basic reasons: 1) year after year, a high proportion of library funds are devoted to electronic resources, and 2) because they do not have a physical presence in the library, electronic resources require more guided strategies to make users aware of them. Essentially, simply acquiring an electronic resource and making it available does not guarantee its use, and additional promotional efforts are often needed to generate awareness and interest, and to increase use of the resource. Academic library users enter and exit the user community every four to five years, which means marketing should not only occur when resources and services are first acquired, but instead on a cycle to keep current users informed.

The idea of marketing specifically to an electronic format, such as **ebooks** or an individual electronic resource such as ScienceDirect, requires careful consideration of the product's purpose, user need, and resource availability. A marketing message must be well planned and consider the user's point of view and current level of ability and knowledge. Simply advertising that the library has electronic resources may be marketing-like, but may not prove to be successful. An essential part of the planning process is deciding whether marketing is best directed toward end users to increase return on investment

(ROI), or if marketing would be better focused toward library stakeholders to demonstrate the added value of libraries and the need for continued funding. Although marketing for libraries as a concept is removed from the profit-seeking behaviors of business marketing, libraries are a business in and of themselves. In the current dismal economic climate, marketing as proof of value for continued funding is more important than ever.

Keep Current with Marketing

The following journals are good sources of information to keep up to date on current trends in marketing:

> *American Marketing Journal*
> *Journal of Marketing Management*
> *Marketing Research*

The following business databases are good sources for marketing research:

> *ABI/INFORM*
> *Business Source Premier*
> *eMarketer*

Additionally, 2015 saw the debut of the Library Marketing and Communications Conference, a new library-specific marketing conference, that is designed for library employees who are involved in marketing, public relations, and outreach in academic, public, and special libraries.

Because search engines such as Google and Bing are often the first stop when beginning research users are less likely to be familiar with the specific names of resources, and are even less likely to be familiar with resource terminology. All types of resources—even scholarly ones—simply become part of "the Internet," a particularly challenging situation for information literacy. When resources such as Google Scholar retrieve both popular resources and licensed library content through **OpenURL**, it is challenging for the novice researcher to determine how the resource is made available and its originating database. The distinction between content on the Open Web and scholarly resources available at the library is also a challenge for library advocacy. If libraries are going to meet users where they are *and* compete for their attention, libraries need to effectively demonstrate that their resources are more comprehensive than those available on the Open Web.

Furthermore, marketing for electronic resources can extend into outreach for the library's **discovery layer** and to advertise research assistance. Marketing is a process and its goals can build over time. When marketing electronic resources, it might be advisable to begin generally by marketing search strategies, research assistance, and chat reference, and then focus on specific resources as demand increases.

Because the concept of marketing is associated with the business world, perceptions can exist that marketing and libraries should not mix and that marketing clashes with the idea of library collections as a service. For this reason, marketing does require compromise, so the credibility of the library is balanced with increased user awareness, information users actually need, and realistic marketing goals and techniques. Electronic resources librarians understand particularly well both the joys and frustrations of marketing, because electronic resources librarians are typically the recipients of the marketing efforts from library vendors: at times vendor email campaigns are useful and benefit the library, and at other times email campaigns are best filtered into junk mail. Similarly, library users will want to receive information that might be of value to them, but not want to feel pressured to use a service or resource that is not right for them. Library marketing should provide the right information at the right time.

The planning involved in marketing can feel overwhelming, but there are definite benefits to taking a slow and deliberate approach! This chapter will discuss methods to market electronic resources efficiently, including developing a marketing plan, finding internal and external collaborators, and tips and tricks on how to use freely available digital tools.

Developing a Marketing Plan

Marketing differs from promotion in that marketing involves advance planning and evaluation of results. Marketing involves finding out what an audience wants, developing a method of providing it, and evaluating its success. Before taking the time to market the library or a particular resource, an electronic resources librarian should give substantial thought to the big picture: the purpose of the project, who will be involved, how it will be implemented, how much time and money will be required, and methods to assess

Sample Marketing Narrative to Increase Awareness and Use of Electronic Journals

EXECUTIVE SUMMARY The Common Library is a four-year academic library that serves a population of 12,500 FTE, approximately 4,000 FTE of whom are enrolled in a distance-education program for business. The library provides products and services that include print and **electronic journals,** electronic books, reference material, **databases**, an online catalog and a discovery layer. Resources are made available in person and through the library's website, with proxy access available for remote users. Although the library experiences moderate-to-high use overall, the use of electronic resources is low and ejournals in business display the lowest **cost-per-use** value at $12.67 on average. These journals are essential for accreditation of the business program and thus cannot be cancelled despite their overall high cost. The ultimate goal of this marketing plan is to *increase* the usage of electronic resources for distance business students, and if marketing is successful to adopt the plan for other user groups and subject areas.

PURPOSE The Common Library has a large population of distance business students who need access to electronic resources. The library would like to expand the breadth of awareness of relevant resources to this community, as evidence shows low awareness and low use of essential electronic resources. The long-term goal is to increase the use of electronic journals in the subject of business, as demonstrated by a decrease in the overall cost-per-use of these resources within a year's time. Due to the distance-learning factor, the library will need to increase its online presence in order to reach remote students. To this end, the library has selected to use email and social media as low-cost platforms for yearly marketing campaigns.

MARKETING PLAN The library can better serve a specific community of users through marketing electronic resources to them, due to the nature of their studies and their remote location. The foundation is already in place to provide resources to this user group with strong marketing opportunities to expand the breadth of access to this community. To this end, the library will leverage resources and services already available, embedding links to the electronic journals within email newsletters and social media outreach. At the end of the fall and spring semesters COUNTER JR1 reports will be analyzed compared to the same time in the previous year, with the goal of decreasing the overall cost-per-use by $1.00 each semester. Evidence that the marketing has succeeded will also be evidence of the library's impact on the coursework and research of this specific user population.

successes and failures. The big picture should involve the library's mission and a consideration of the user population before putting any official plan into place.

When developing a marketing plan, it is advisable to have something written down. A written marketing plan does not need to be lengthy, but it should include an executive summary, a purpose statement, and a description of the marketing plan. An example of a written narrative for a plan to market electronic journals is provided in the text box on page 177.

A written marketing plan should be deliberate and thorough, covering five basic parts:

1. The general user population
2. The target audience
3. Goals and evaluation methods
4. The medium to carry the message
5. A budget

The next five sections of this chapter will cover each of these areas with sample charts and lists, which can be used as worksheets to create building blocks toward a written marketing plan like the one above. The example of the marketing plan for electronic journals for business students will continue to be used as a guide. With the big picture broken down into manageable pieces, each part can build on the other, and the final product—a written marketing plan—will be much more manageable to draft.

STEP 1   *Describe the User and Library Services*

The purpose of library marketing is to provide users with information about resources and services that they otherwise may not have known about and that also fulfill an active need. The latter piece—that the marketing information fulfills an active need—is just as important, if not more, as providing the information on its own. Therefore, the first step in developing a marketing plan will be to describe the user population and available library services. At this point, descriptions should be kept as general as possible. For instance, an academic library might define their basic user groups as "students" and "faculty," with services that relate to research assistance, whereas a public library might define its basic user groups as "the local community" and "teens" with services that relate to reader's advisory and access to the

Internet. The process of describing the general user group or groups will be discussed in Step 2.

A simple list will do the trick to begin describing users and library services. Again, because this is the first step all examples should be kept very general. See the example lists below:

Academic library users

- students
- faculty
- walk-in users
- staff
- librarians

Academic library services

- bibliographic instruction and information literacy sessions
- reference, in-person and online
- print collections
- databases
- electronic journals and books
- technology and equipment
- study space
- **Interlibrary Loan** and reserves

The sample lists provided here are not exclusive to electronic resources, because electronic resources can influence nearly every aspect of the library. Depending on the needs of a specific library, the degree to which marketing will be specific to a single format or specific resource will vary. Step 2 will focus on how to select marketing opportunities based on specific, target user populations.

STEP 2   *Describe the Target Audience and the Opportunity*

An effective marketing plan cannot target all user groups simultaneously. The next step, therefore, will be to select a specific user group that demonstrates a need that can be fulfilled by electronic resources based on the information gathered while defining the user population. If marketing is designed to reach everyone, the message might end up reaching no one, so be sure to pick a group that can be communicated to easily.

Setting up formal focus group discussions is one way to identify possible user groups. If formal sessions are not feasible, however, online surveys, informal conversations, and reference desk statistics can also supply useful information to identify a resource need within a target user group. Gathering information about user needs directly from the community of users will help prevent distributing unneeded information. Just as marketing to everyone will likely reach no one, neither will marketing to a target user group using a message that is not immediately relevant.

At this point it should be obvious that the target audience and the marketing objective are inherently linked. Therefore, when the target audience has been identified the overall objective of marketing should also become clear. If an objective is not immediately identifiable, then an alternate target audience should be considered. For instance, if the library community has a large population of distance business students and the library has a strong collection of low-use electronic journals in business, a good marketing objective would be to increase use of electronic journals in business. However, if electronic journals in business already show high use, then an alternate target user group and/or goal should be selected for marketing efforts. The sample chart below builds on the chart from Step 1 by describing the target audience within "students" that have strong opportunities for library marketing with a measurable objective.

USER SUBSET FROM PART 1	OPPORTUNITY	OBJECTIVE
Business students	Low use of business journals in electronic format combined with a large population of remote business students	Increase the use of electronic journals in business

Objectives should be results-oriented and include a measurable outcome. For electronic resources, results-oriented outcomes should involve something that can actually be measured, such as **usage statistics**. In the example above, the objective "increase the use of electronic journals in business" will be measured for success using usage statistics. Step 3 will build on how objectives are measured with evaluation methods.

STEP 3 *Set Goals and Evaluation Methods*

After marketing opportunities and objectives have been defined, it will be time to set goals. Goals are the actual efforts that contribute to the objectives which, as stated in Step 2, should already be results-oriented. Although any given objective can include multiple goals, each goal should also have a distinct method of evaluation. Marketing goals should be obtainable but not too artificially easy to achieve. A goal set too low will always succeed, and failure provides opportunities to improve or alter methodology. Because marketing takes both time and money the evaluation of goals should demonstrate progress—but failure is OK, too! The evaluation portion of goal-setting will also ensure that a clear start and end to marketing are visible.

The sample chart below builds on the chart from Steps 1 and 2 by matching the objective to results-oriented goals with clear evaluation.

OBJECTIVE FROM PART 2	GOAL	EVALUATION
Increase awareness of online resources in business	Increase the presence of the library online; actively engage with business students online	Half-annual and annual cost-per-use calculations of using COUNTER reports

Evaluate Goals Using COUNTER

COUNTER statistics are an extremely low-cost solution for the evaluation piece of a marketing plan. If a marketing plan involves demonstrating to a user population the value of any form of electronic resource, then success can be measured with how the usage statistics performed for the periods before and after marketing.

When using COUNTER statistics as an evaluation tool, be sure to collect statistics for the full previous calendar year. Collecting statistics during planning will help set benchmarks for goal-setting and will also ensure that comparison statistics are already on hand for when marketing commences. For more on using statistics to evaluate electronic resources, see chapter 7.

STEP 4   *Define the Medium*

The marketing medium is what will be used to carry the message. For cost-effective marketing, the medium should be a resource already available at the library, or available to acquire at a low-cost. The chart in figure 9.1 outlines example low-cost marketing mediums, along with their requirements for use and considerations to take before implementing.

Any time spent marketing is also money spent. Therefore, if a marketing medium is available at a low cost but will require more time to implement than other methods, consider the benefits and pitfalls of the cost saved versus time spent.

FIGURE 9.1
Marketing Mediums

MEDIUM	REQUIREMENTS	CONSIDERATIONS
Email	Contact list Engaging message	How will contacts be selected? Will messages be read, or considered spam?
Digital signage	Design program Digital display	How long will digital signs display? How often will signs be updated?
Social Media	Social media platform User account Followers Succinct messages	What social media site should be used? What social media sites is the community using? Who will manage the account? How often will messages go out?
Flyers	Design program Low-cost printing Distribution method	Where will the target audience be? How many flyers will be needed? How long will flyers stay up?
Blogs	Blogging platform Content, updated frequently	What blog software will be used? Where will the blog be linked? Who will be in charge of updating it?
Contests	User participation Prizes or giveaways	How will we engage participants to join? How much money is available for prizes and giveaways?
Event booths	User participation Prizes or giveaways	How will we engage participants to join? Is there a pre-existing event happening, and during what time of the year?
Website space	Design program or website coding Scheduled messaging	Is there space on the website to add marketing? How long will marketing remain on the website, and how often will it be updated?

Though many of the marketing mediums listed in figure 9.1 require things such as "design program" and "engaging message," depending on the programs and methods used, coming up with attractive designs and catchy phrases will not necessarily require an advanced degree. The next section of this chapter will go over some tips, tricks, and user-friendly tools that can be used to get up and running without much grief!

STEP 5 *Set a Budget: Financial and Time*

After selecting the marketing medium, the next step will be to determine how much time and money to commit. Use the plan's objective and selected marketing mediums to make this determination by identifying the staff who will be involved in implementing the marketing. Then, identify skills in the group and determine how much time will be needed to complete goals and evaluation.

FIGURE 9.2
Set a Budget: Financial and Time

OBJECTIVE FROM PART 2	MEDIUM	STAFF NAME	ROLE(S)	COST ESTIMATE	ESTIMATED TIME
Increase awareness of electronic journals for business students	Email	Jane Smith	Collect contacts from registrar	Low	Draft schedule: 1 hour
			Create a schedule for when newsletter content will be distributed, 5 times per year		Draft text: 1.5 hours, 5 times per year
	Social Media	John William	Create and manage social media account for the library		Manage social media account: 30 minutes/day
			Draft short, catchy messages about resource availability; respond to users informally on the social media platform		Draft messages: in bulk, once per week during the active school year

Two options—one for an email campaign and one for a social media campaign—are provided for one marketing objective, demonstrating the need to clearly define the roles, cost, and estimated time for distinct aspects of marketing plans.

As stated earlier, for academic libraries marketing plans should include a clear schedule, ideally one that can repeat and build over time to reach current users and future users. In the example in figure 9.2, repetitive scheduling is built into the estimated time.

With Step 5 completed, the direction of the written narrative should be clear. Again, a narrative version of a marketing plan is essential, especially if the plan needs to go through a review before it is implemented, or if a project report needs to be presented to stakeholders to demonstrate success or to make requests for additional funding. Because electronic resources carry yearly costs, having a written document as evidence of project growth and evaluation will go a long way toward advocacy and funding requests.

Tips and Tricks to Maximize Resources

Although a written marketing plan will ensure that any marketing endeavors are done in a deliberate, consistent fashion, a marketing plan on its own is not enough. Marketing requires a bit of, as the French say, *je ne sais quoi,* which theory and worksheets cannot provide. There are, however, methods of acquiring an edge for marketing campaigns. The items listed below are a few tips and tricks to get a little bit of that edge in any kind of library marketing.

Catch Users' Attention with Graphics

By now, the concept of going viral on the Internet should be familiar. Videos, articles, and tweets go viral every day, shared and seen by millions. Internet content goes viral in part because of compelling imagery. Have an image of a cat wearing a watermelon hat, or a video of your grandma demonstrating the latest dance craze? Shared at the right time with the right medium, it could go viral. Lure in library users in a similar way, using striking images that will grab their attention and then keep it for a little longer with the message. When developing a graphic-centric marketing campaign the image and the text combined should convey a clear, compelling message. A good example of this concept are the "Got Milk?" advertisements and Apple's "Think Different" campaign from the 1990s.

To locate compelling graphics, try these resources:

Compfight (www.compfight.com)—an image search engine built on the Flickr API; images can be sorted by Creative Commons licenses for reuse.

Getty Images (www.gettyimages.com)—beginning in 2014, a large portion of Getty images became available at no charge; they can be reused as long as they include a footer with a credit and link to the licensing.

Google Images (www.images.google.com)—search for images on Google, and then narrow results using the Search Tool option for "Usage Rights."

ImageCodr (www.imagecodr.org)—an online tool to quickly reference the Creative Commons licensing rights on any image from Flickr.

Morguefile (www.morguefile.com)—free, high-quality post-production images licensed for reuse.

Noun Project (www.thenounproject.com)—search from thousands of icons by keyword; a free membership account provides access to use icons with attribution, or for purchase royalty-free. See figure 9.3.

FIGURE 9.3

An Example of an Icon Available from the Noun Project, Available for FreeDownload

Free icons from the Noun Project are licensed for reuse with attribution based on Creative Commons Attribution licenses. Image created by Nherwin Ardona from the Noun Project.

Combine images together with text and publish using these resources:

Canva (www.canva.com)—an online tool with templates to drag and
drop content to create presentations, social media graphics, and
flyers; share designs with a free account and direct linking. See
figure 9.4.

Easel.ly (www.easel.ly)—an online tool with templates to drag and
drop content to create professional quality infographics.

Issuu (issuu.com)—quickly upload, publish, and distribute content
online in the form of magazines, newspapers, portfolios,
catalogs, and guides; Issuu offers a free version as well as a
range of price plans.

FIGURE 9.4
Marketing Flyer Made by Using Canva

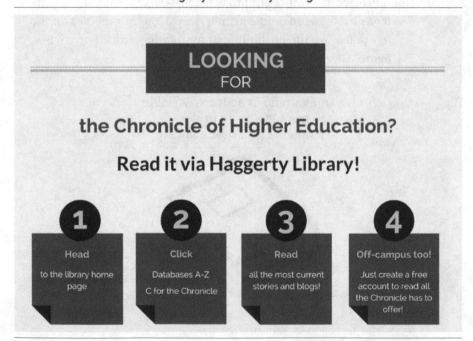

Marketing flyer made by Dan Vinson, the Coordinator of User Services and Library Assessment
at Haggerty Library & Learning Commons at Mount Mary University, for the electronic version
of the Chronicle of Higher Education. The image was created using a free account on Canva
(www.canva.com).

LibGuides from Springshare—if already available, LibGuides are a very cost-efficient method of distributing marketing material to users; embed marketing into subject specific guides to draw in users based on their specific needs.

Microsoft PowerPoint or Microsoft Publisher—these resources are already available at most libraries and have a low learning curve if similar resources, such as Microsoft Word, are already known; use the ready-made templates in Publisher or individual PowerPoint slides to save as PDF and then print as a flyer or upload to social media.

Prezi—though intended as live-presentation software, Prezi provides ready-made templates that make it easy to drag and drop content for professional looking content.

Avoid Jargon

Users will connect with a message that connects with them. This means library jargon does not belong in library marketing! Instead of using library jargon—from specific database names like "EBSCOhost" and "LexisNexis," to service types like discovery layers and Interlibrary Loan—try simplifying the message by focusing on a topic or general resource that connects to the target user group. Then, pick a resource or a couple of resources that can aid in research to that topic. If a specific resource is used for marketing, make sure its name describes what it is and that the message clearly indicates how to get to it, such as with the example in figure 9.4 for *The Chronicle of Higher Education*.

As a rule, the simpler the better. If the library is looking to draw in users with something memorable, considering giving a marketing campaign a slogan. Slogans work best when kept short, so try to keep it at ten words or less. Popular library marketing slogans include:

- Your guide to answers.
- Check it out!
- Enrich your life.
- Far more than you expect.
- Read, learn, discover.

- Plug in @ your library.
- Research made easy.

If ten words are not enough—or if a headline is not appropriate for a marketing campaign—consider using only as much text as can be shared on the social media site Twitter, which limits to 140 characters (including spaces). Reaching exactly 140 characters is a challenge, and it can be a good exercise in editing to convey an information-rich, succinct message.

Cross-Promote

Cross-promotion is the process of embedding marketing into preexisting events and services. When considering cross-promotion, think about what events are already planned, such as semester milestones and holidays, and incorporate your marketing activities.

Cross-promotion can also involve space: strategically place marketing material where target user groups frequent or locations where users already look for information and library resources. Shelf cards, or "read-a-likes," are small signs that can be placed within library stacks that promote databases on a similar topic to the call number. Shelf cards can take the form of DIY book jackets wrapped around a discarded book or a small rectangular box for where an ebook title would be organized on the shelf. Alternately, if a print book is also available as an ebook, bookmarks can be placed inside the print copy on the shelf to direct users to the alternate format. Shelf cards can include QR codes to link users directly to the content using a mobile device (see figure 9.5).

FIGURE 9.5
Shelf Card

SCIENCE
FICTION
Martin, G.

eBook

A GAME OF THRONES
Martin, George R.R.
New York : Bantam Books, 1997, c1996

An example of a bookmark shelf card with a QR code to link directly to the content.

Social media is also a good platform for cross-promotion, especially for topical calendar year content. Figures 9.6 and 9.7 are examples. Cross-promotion on social media platforms will attract a broader audience and might not be appropriate for marketing to target user groups.

Social media is a means of conversation and therefore it is a good way to talk directly to individual users. When using social media for library marketing, try to maintain a one-to-four ratio: for each tweet or post, connect to four other external messages, either with replies, shares, or likes. Additionally, because social media is also always in motion, be sure to post important messages multiple times over a few days.

FIGURE 9.6
Marketing Electronic Resources

 JSTOR @JSTOR · Jul 20
#Apollo11 landed on the moon #OTD in 1969 - how are the artifacts being preserved? bit.ly/29SaSzd

The tweet pictured above is from JSTOR, and is a good example of how marketing electronic resources can be cross-promoted to calendar events and linked to directly. To see more marketing examples from JSTOR, check them out on Twitter: @jstor (twitter.com/jstor).

FIGURE 9.7
Using Social Media

 **MSU Library**
@msulibrary

Did you know Google Scholar can include
your library holdings when not on campus?
Example for scholar.google.com

Montana State University Library uses social media as an opportunity to advertise
library services and specific resources, and to engage directly with users. To see more
marketing examples from Montana State University, check them out on Twitter:
@msulibrary (twitter.com/msulibrary).

Opportunities for Marketing Collaboration

Although some librarians may feel that library marketing is beneficial—
which will be the case if promotion and evaluation is part of their primary
responsibility, such as with outreach or assessment librarians—other librarians may have an adverse reaction to it, feeling that it is too corporate, too
much work, unnecessary, or superfluous. Adverse feelings and behaviors do
not exist in a vacuum and likely have a root cause. When encountering mar-
keting-aversion, treat the situation as an opportunity to listen, similar to the
listening and learning required when developing a marketing plan. With that
said, demonstrated success with any project is marketing in and of itself, and
success in any endeavor may sway even the strongest of nay-sayers.

Some library staff members and colleagues may also have varying levels
of comfort with electronic resources. Therefore, when marketing specifically
to electronic resources, make sure to be clear that electronic resources are not
a threat to more traditional library services, and that training opportunities
are available for any interested party. After all, if library marketing advertises
new products and services, everyone at the library should be aware not only
of their presence but also how to use them. Internal outreach tasks can be
accomplished with internal education, transparent communication, and collaboration.

1. Internal Communication and Education

Just as end users need to be aware of the existence of electronic resources, staff need to also be aware of electronic resources in order to provide appropriate research and troubleshooting assistance. By communicating in a transparent way about new or changed resource availability, staff will be able to better serve the user community. For instance, if a resource has not been renewed it will be important to inform staff about the change so that users are not inadvertently advised to use resources that are not available. Here are a few ways to communicate the availability of electronic resources to staff:

> Establish an internal listserv to announce new electronic resource acquisitions and trials.
>
> Email front-line librarians about known outages with electronic resources, and send follow-ups when access is restored.
>
> Create emails, newsletters, and brochures to announce new electronic resources.
>
> Communicate with departments during serials renewals to discuss possible changes.
>
> Host library orientation sessions for new faculty.
>
> Encourage faculty to sign up for library instruction sessions.
>
> Develop and teach library instruction sessions in collaboration with faculty.

When evaluating whether communication should be a priority in library marketing, take a moment to review with whom the library communicates and how. Communication for communication's sake isn't effective, just as marketing for marketing's sake will not be successful. Figure 9.8 shows a few examples of effective communication to the left, and their not-so-effective counterparts to the right.

Another way to educate and communicate with staff is to involve them when developing workshop ideas or a marketing plan. Electronic resources librarians are not in front of patrons as frequently as reference and circulation staff and asking for advice from frontline staff can be informative to learn about which resources students ask about and which topics have a high demand for assistance.

FIGURE 9.8

Examples of Effective and Ineffective Communication

EFFECTIVE COMMUNICATION	INEFFECTIVE COMMUNICATION
Librarians and library staff are informed of upcoming changes in resources and services.	Resources and services are updated without notification, or without enough advance notice.
Information is dispersed through the same methods each time.	The information chain has inconsistent methods of delivery.
Faculty are informed of changes in products and services available at the library.	Faculty have expectations of collections and services that are not available; the library is not aware of how faculty receive updates.
Library instruction sessions facilitate relationship building with faculty.	Relationships with faculty occur through happenstance.

2. *Collaborate*

Libraries can raise their visibility and leverage their services by teaming up with other departments that have a stake in library services. Consider partnering with faculty who have demonstrated excitement for electronic resources, a high rate of requests for electronic course reserves, or recent requests for acquisitions of electronic resources. Further, faculty are likely the first to hear about the high cost of required course textbooks from their students, and electronic resources provided by the library can directly address such a problem. Faculty can also encourage students to use the library for research, and can incorporate electronic resources into course management systems.

Collaboration with IT departments can also benefit library marketing. For instance, an IT department with expertise in user experience may be able to advise on ways to improve language for marketing (e.g., the kind of language the average user understands), what will draw people in, and jargon to avoid. IT departments can also provide information about design and publishing programs that are already licensed for institutional use, which is useful when identifying a cost-effective marketing medium.

And do not forget about library vendors! Vendors are an extremely beneficial source for collaboration, from ready-made marketing material to on-site workshops. Incorporating vendors into marketing events may also be a good opportunity to demonstrate to staff that vendors are working toward the same goals as the library, and that they are available for additional assistance when problems arise. As a bonus, vendor representatives doing on-site visits might come with swag items, such as pens, flyers, bookmarks, and table cards. Swag items can then be used as event and contest prizes or giveaways, which also solves one of the cost factors when using an event as a marketing medium.

Finally, consider arranging an event or a booth with advocacy groups, such as Friends of the Library, campus clubs, or student senate. Groups such as these are generally good at planning, and may have an event already scheduled that the library can join.

Find Inspiration

Librarians love sharing their work. Check out the following blogs for inspiration, templates, and design tips prepared by librarians, for librarians.

Librarian Design Share
(librariandesignshare.org)

> A great source for inspiration and librarian-made templates. Search for designs by type, software used, or by keyword. All published work on Librarian Design Share is made available in a shared Google Drive folder with a Creative Commons Attribution-NonCommercial-ShareAlike license, so anyone can copy, adapt, and distribute the materials.

The 'M' Word
(themwordblog.blogspot.co.uk)

> A library marketing blog that helps librarians learn about marketing trends and ideas.

The Library Marketing Toolkit
(www.librarymarketingtoolkit.com)

> A companion website to the book of the same name, written by Ned Potter. The site includes links for essential tools and resources, library marketing workshops, and case studies.

3. Librarianship as Service

Good customer service is another way in which libraries can market themselves both with end-users and future collaborators and stakeholders. The perception of the library as a place to go for useful information, with helpful, knowledgeable staff, is a form of general marketing and self-promotion. Although the results from this type of marketing cannot always be quantified, there are opportunities to assess the community's perception of the library from comment boxes, user surveys, and word-of-mouth feedback.

Troubleshooting efforts, such as those described in chapter 6, can also be considered a form of public relations as marketing. For instance, if users reach out to the library for help accessing electronic resources and are provided with friendly, helpful service, they will be likely to turn to the library again, either for more assistance with electronic resources or for other research needs. This concept reinforces how marketing as public relations and service is at the core of library work.

Marketing of library services can also be applied to activities such as roving reference, in which librarians on reference duty move about the library offering assistance instead of sitting at a reference desk. Roving reference can support all aspects of reference and research assistance, and will demonstrate to users that there are people available to help. After all, it is not just electronic resources that can be intimidating—the barrier of an official desk with a sign and staff member can be just as difficult to approach as a new technology!

Conclusion

Marketing, in its strictest, most competitive sense, can be a foreign concept that is difficult for librarians to grapple with on a day-to-day basis. Marketing as outreach, public relations, and customer service, however, is attainable and makes sense for most librarians in their daily work. Added complications arise when electronic resources are thrown into the mix, due to the difficulties associated with their exposure and cost, as well as their perceived competitor, the Open Web. In fact, electronic resources do exist on a more competitive playing field than the rest of the library: users need to learn about the resources and be able to access them, and the institution needs to decide whether their cost is worth the continued subscription. Although libraries and resources do not necessarily need to compete with other libraries, there is increasing need to compete with other outside resources. To this end, Peter Drucker wrote in *The Economist:*

> Given the ease and speed at which information travels, every institution in the knowledge society—not only businesses, but also schools, universities, hospitals and increasingly government agencies too—has to be globally competitive, even though most organizations will continue to be local in their activities and in their markets. This is because the Internet will keep customers everywhere informed on what is available anywhere in the world, and at what price.[4]

The Open Web is perceived as "easy" due to the notion that it contains all things. This perception is detrimental for libraries simply because access to most scholarly resources on the Open Web require payment. If the library has paid that fee to provide access to its users but users are not aware of how to get to them, then both the Open Web and the library have failed to provide access. The easy road to marketing electronic resources is to simply announce that a new purchase has been made and be done with it. However, that type of marketing message is quickly lost if the announcement is not made in the right way; if the right people are not told; and if they, in turn, do not convey the message to relevant users. In short, library marketing requires careful consideration of: user needs, goals, message and communication medium, and scheduling. By using the methods and worksheets described here, and leveraging freely available tools and collaborations, library marketing can transform from a daunting task to a very achievable process.

NOTES

1. American Marketing Association, "Marketing's Evolving Identity: Defining Our Future," *Journal of Public Policy and Marketing,* 26, No. 2, Fall 2007.
2. Association of Research Libraries "Marketing and Public Relations Activities in ARL Libraries," 1999.
3. Cosette Kies, *Marketing and Public Relations for Libraries* (Metuchen, NJ: Scarecrow Press, 1987).
4. Peter Drucker, "The Next Society," *The Economist,* November 1, 2001.

FURTHER READINGS

Al-Daihani, Sultan M., and Suha A. AlAwadhi. "Exploring Academic Libraries' Use of Twitter: A Content Analysis." *The Electronic Library* 33, no. 6 (2015): 1002–15.

Bergstrom, Tracy C., and Alexander Papson. "Promoting Digital Library Services through Workshops." *Marketing and Outreach for the Academic Library: New Approaches and Initiatives* 7 (2016): 71.

Dempsey, Kathy. *The Accidental Library Marketer*. Medford, NJ: Information Today, 2009.

Dubicki, Eleonora I. *Marketing and Promoting Electronic Resources: Creating the E-Buzz!*. Routledge, 2013.

Duke, Lynda M., and Toni Tucker. "How to Develop a Marketing Plan for an Academic Library." *Technical Services Quarterly* 25, no. 1 (2007): 51–68.

Empey, Heather and Nancy E. Black. "Marketing the Academic Library." *College and Undergraduate Libraries* 12, no. 1–2 (2015): 19–33.

Garoufallou, Emmanouel, Rania Siatri, Georgia Zafeiriou, and Ekaterini Balampanidou. "The Use of Marketing Concepts in Library Services: A Literature Review." *Library Review* 62, no. 4/5 (2013): 312–34.

Gupta, D. K., C. Koontz, and A. Massisimo. "Marketing Library and Information Services: Connecting from the Past to the Future." In *Marketing Library and Information Services II. A Global Outlook,* edited by D. K. Gupta, C. Koontz, and A. Massisimo, 13–22. Berlin and Munich: De Gruyter Saur, 2013.

Helinsky, Zuzana. *A Short-Cut to Marketing the Library*. Elsevier, 2014.

Jessy, A., and Mahabaleshwara Rao. "Marketing of Resources and Services with Emerging Technologies in Modern Libraries: An Overview." *International Journal of Information Dissemination and Technology* 6, no. 1 (2016): 15.

Kennedy, Marie R., and Cheryl LaGuardia. Marketing Your Library's Electronic Resources: A How-To-Do-It Manual for Librarians. American Library Association, 2013.

Lisa O'Connor and Kacy Lundstrom. "The Impact of Social Marketing Strategies on the Information Seeking Behaviors of College Students." *Reference and User Services Quarterly,* 50, no. 4 (2011): 351–65.

Polger, Mark Aaron, and Karen Okamoto. "Who's Spinning the Library? Responsibilities of Academic Librarians Who Promote." *Library Management* 34, no. 3 (2013): 236–53.

Potter, Ned. *The Library Marketing Toolkit*. Facet Publishing, 2012.

Pride, Marcy M., and Patricia Fisher. *Blueprint for Your Library Marketing Plan.* (Chicago: American Library Association, 2006)

Profera, Elyse L., Michael A. Arthur, and Barbara Tierney. "Return on Investment: New Strategies for Marketing Digital Resources To Academic Faculty." *Charleston Conference Proceedings*, 2015.

Singh, Rajesh. "Does Your Library Have an Attitude Problem Towards 'Marketing'? Revealing Inter-Relationship between Marketing Attitudes and Behaviour." *The Journal of Academic Librarianship* 35, no. 1 (2009): 25–32.

Vaaler, Alyson, and Steve Brantley. "Using a Blog and Social Media Promotion as a Collaborative Community Building Marketing Tool for Library Resources." *Library Hi Tech News* 33, no. 5 (2016).

Yi, Zhixian. "Effective Techniques for the Promotion of Library Services and Resources." *Information Research: An International Electronic Journal* 21, no. 1 (2016): n1.

Van Scoyoc, A. M. "The Electronic Academic Library: Undergraduate Research Behavior in a Library without Books," *Libraries and the Academy* 6 No. 1 (2006): 47–58.

Emerging Trends and the Impact of Change on Electronic Resources Management

- Access versus Ownership: An Ongoing Dilemma
- What it Means to be Open
- Being Open Is Not So Simple
- Changes in Higher Ed
- Evolving Collections

The management of electronic resources is a stimulating and challenging area of librarianship, driven by changes in technology, publishing, scholarly communication, higher education, user needs and expectations, and the economy. This chapter will highlight the significant changes happening in the field which influence the way libraries build and maintain their electronic collections. Many of these changes are symptomatic of the larger themes and questions in electronic resources librarianship discussed here, such as the impact of transitioning from ownership to access, and the impact of traditional business models getting on board with the **Open Access** movement, which, in light of the mission of libraries is beneficial, but requires a shift in thought regarding how resources are vetted, managed, and kept up to date.

Electronic resources management does not take place in a vacuum. Although libraries' print collections are also influenced by changes in publishing, local workflows, and budgets, electronic resources are much more volatile and vulnerable simply because of their digital presence. Even though electronic resources seem to be ever-transitioning compared to their print counterparts, change on the side of the library can be slow. Despite this, global trends in the marketplace still have a great impact on the ebb and flow of local workflows for electronic resources librarians.

As topics and trends for electronic resources will inevitably continue to evolve, readers are encouraged to consult the list of further readings at the end of the chapter and to remain current with library listservs and conferences.

Access versus Ownership: An Ongoing Dilemma

When print was the dominant format in libraries, material was purchased and access to it was guaranteed as long as there was space on the shelves. For electronic resources, however, the idea of ongoing access is quite different—practically the opposite, in fact! Libraries subscribe to electronic resources that are owned by the content provider, and each electronic resource is licensed and hosted online. Because content is hosted online, libraries have zero control over platform upgrades, system malfunctions, and publisher transfers. Although this situation is certainly a negative aspect of electronic resource management, by switching from print to electronic format libraries have gained access to an incredible wealth of content, with value-added features and enhanced search capabilities. Library users can access content from anywhere, at any time, and content can be integrated into digital citation managers and learning management systems. Despite the uncertainties presented by the fact libraries are essentially borrowing access from providers—that is, licensing content instead of owning it—there is no going back. The fundamental shift in resource access requires that librarians rethink the core mission of the library, its longevity, the impact of resource availability, and the ability of the library to continue to operate autonomously.

Perpetual Access

In a world where nearly all electronic resources are not owned, **Perpetual Access** is paramount. Perpetual access refers to the library's right to access licensed content after the subscription period has expired, such as in the case of a cancelled subscription, ceased publication, or change in title or publisher. Without a perpetual access agreement in the license, libraries are doing little more than renting content which will disappear if the library cancels a subscription or if a publisher ceases to exist.

In recent years, libraries have seen their collections budgets shrink, yet the cost to license content continues to increase at a higher rate than inflation. Such a climate forces libraries to make tough decisions to cancel subscriptions, jeopardizing access to resources and the stability of their collections. Perpetual access answers part of this problem by guaranteeing the library's investment into the future, ensuring ongoing access no matter the cause.

In theory, perpetual access answers the ownership dilemma, but to fulfill perpetual access entitlements, libraries and publishers must make a significant investment. The process to track and maintain perpetual access entitlements is extremely complicated and time consuming, and to date there are few solutions offered by either the library community or content providers to address workflow problems. Issues related to perpetual access include:

- when to enact perpetual access rights
- who to contact to enable perpetual access rights
- how to identify and isolate individual titles for perpetual access
- setting up access for perpetual access content in the library's systems
- creating payment notes in the library's ILS for perpetual access content
- link checking perpetual access content that is hosted locally or by a third-party provider

So, considering all of these time-consuming issues, why bother? Again, perpetual access is critical to building and maintaining robust collections, providing users with ongoing access, and representing a library's right to content. Publishers benefit from perpetual access, too, because it ensures their content remains available to users, which can further drive interest and demand.

Tracking Perpetual Access Entitlement and Ensuring Access

Though most electronic resources librarians become concerned with perpetual access at the end of a subscription, the entitlement process should really begin during the licensing phase. When reviewing a **license agreement**, the specific language and conditions associated with perpetual access should be considered carefully. Advocating for clear language and conditions early in the licensing process will reduce the chance of confusion or unexpected costs should perpetual access need to be fulfilled. Perpetual access clauses should include the following elements:

- Conditions in which perpetual access is allowed
    Example: Termination of subscription, title changes, cease in publication, or new editions.
- Location of perpetual access copies
    Example: Local hosting, or hosting provided by the publisher or third party (such as Portico), and in what format, such as PDF or CD-ROM.
- Associated costs
    Example: Fee to host content on publisher's server or continue to access content on publisher site.

Both the LIBLICENSE and CDL model licenses contain the following four recommended perpetual access terms:

- *Recommended Term 1*
    Perpetual access is provided under automatic termination of subscription.
- *Recommended Term 2*
    Perpetual access will include access to **backfiles**, if backfiles were originally part of the subscription.
- *Recommended Term 3*
    The license should specify the perpetual access location (e.g., publisher server, library server).
- *Recommended Term 4*
    The license should allow for library server hosted perpetual access.

Keep in mind that perpetual access is generally only an available option for **journals** and **ebooks**. **Aggregator databases** and **streaming media** generally do not offer perpetual access rights. For more information on the type of language used to describe perpetual access, see chapter 5.

License review is only the first stage of ensuring perpetual access entitlements. The conditions described in the license must also be locally recorded and tracked to ensure perpetual access is not only legally granted but also obtainable to claim. In the event that perpetual access entitlements need to be fulfilled, clear documentation will enable an electronic resources librarian to verify access and update holdings. Many challenges exist to effectively track perpetual access entitlements, and some libraries may not fully appreciate the problems caused by not tracking and claiming perpetual access entitlements. Information professionals most commonly use the following tools to track perpetual access provisions in the license:

> **Electronic Resources Management System (ERMS)**: License modules within an ERMS generally have an entry to track perpetual access rights as well as dates of access during subscription and post-cancellation.

> **Integrated Library System (ILS)**: Perpetual access rights can be described in local notes in the bibliographic record or order record in an ILS; invoice records can also help track the exact years of subscription.

> **Spreadsheets**: Title lists contained within spreadsheets are simple tools—though siloed and not connected to the library's systems—that can be used to track perpetual access rights at a granular level.

> **Knowledge Base**: Local packages can be created within a knowledge base to enable access to individual titles with perpetual access entitlements.

> **Subscription Agent**: The library's subscription agent can also be a source of information or a good starting point when searching for information related to perpetual access.

Despite the many tools available, tracking and maintaining perpetual access entitlements is a challenge. In his 2014 article, Chris Bulock summarizes the results of a survey that asked librarians about tracking for perpetual access in their libraries:

> The results would indicate a disconnect between the stated importance of perpetual access in surveys such as Carr's (2011) and the effort

> expended on this issue. The present study indicates that many libraries
> are not tracking perpetual access for electronic content, that many librar-
> ians are unsure of their own practices, and that a sizeable number have
> already decided they would take no action if a vendor ceased to provide
> perpetual access.[1]

License terms, dates of access and subscription, and local holdings information are all pieces of the perpetual access puzzle. Unclear license agreements can lead to confusion or even the inability to act upon entitlements.
Libraries and publishers may have different expectations for how and when
perpetual access is made available. Major discrepancies in the format and
placement of perpetual access holdings and the associated costs can severely
impact a library's understanding of its perpetual access entitlements. Some
publishers provide perpetual access in the form of archival access in formats
that are unusable, such as CD-ROMs, external hard drives, or PDFs, whereas
others allow for perpetual access hosting through third-party providers (e.g.,
LOCKSS and **Portico**). When faced with an unexpected fee for hosting content, some libraries are unable or unwilling to pay the cost for access. In
situations of publisher transfers, the new publisher might not have all the
holdings data needed to fulfill the former publisher's agreement. The current "maze," as Bulock calls it, is sure to cause confusion. Many librarians
find the current system of tracking and claiming nearly impossible to navigate because current tools cannot get the job done efficiently and effectively.
Despite its significance to library collections, however, perpetual access is far
from a simple procedure, but it is one of continued interest and of extreme
value for libraries and publishers alike.

Striking a Balance Between Ownership and Access

The argument between ownership and access is ripe with contradiction:
librarians look to perpetual access as a solution to maintaining ownership
to subscription journals and ebooks, but local workflows often fall short of
ensuring that libraries can fulfill perpetual access claims. Because perpetual
access rights can be difficult to track, many libraries do not claim or set up
the access and instead rely on aggregator databases or **Pay-Per-View** access to
fill in for cancellations, which do not include perpetual access rights. Truly,
the process of non-renewal as a method of saving money is a double-edged

sword. Questions associated with ownership, access, and the future of library collections are rooted in the economy, local budgets, and manpower.

Despite these realities there is recent indication that libraries and publishers are finding ways to provide access and preserve content. In their 2014 article, Zhang and Eschenfelder cite an upward trend in the presence of perpetual access provisions in licenses. They found that perpetual access provisions in license agreements increased from 53.3 percent from 2000 through 2004 to 81.0 percent from 2005 through 2009.[2] Additionally, initiatives such

Snapshot of Portico, LOCKSS, and the Transfer Code of Practice

Portico is a digital preservation service from ITHAKA for books, journals, and other scholarly content. When an electronic journal experiences an event that triggers it for archiving in Portico, libraries can gain access to the journal's content via Portico. Trigger events for Portico can include the following:

- A publisher ceases operations and titles are no longer available from any other source.
- A publisher ceases to publish and offer a title, and it is not offered by another publisher or entity.
- Back issues are removed from a publisher's offering and are not available elsewhere.
- Catastrophic failure by a publisher's delivery platform for a sustained period of time.

LOCKSS (Lots of Copies Keep Stuff Safe) provides libraries and publishers with open source digital preservation tools to preserve and provide access to digital content. Using LOCKSS, libraries can preserve and provide access to content into the future and publishers' content can exist in perpetuity.

The **Transfer Code of Practice,** created by the **United Kingdom Serials Group (UKSG),** which moved to **NASIG** in 2014, provides guidelines for publishers to ensure journal content remains accessible to libraries and readers when journals change publishing entities. The Transfer Code of Practice contains best practice guidelines for both the transferring publisher and the receiving publisher. Publishers are asked to endorse the code and to abide by its principles wherever it is commercially reasonable to do so.

as Portico, LOCKSS, and the Transfer Code of Practice address the ongoing need to provide access, preserve content, and for libraries and publishers to work together.

Historically, libraries were judged by the number of items or volumes they owned. These days such a model is unfeasible and irrelevant. Libraries are becoming smarter and more strategic in spending their dollars and building collections. The process of tracking and making perpetual access claims remains untenable. Library advocacy for greater perpetual access rights, streamlined process, and support of access and preservation initiatives is critical, lest the argument of ownership is never won and thousands of resources become unavailable to all institutions.

What It Means to be Open

Chapter 2 addressed the practical and mechanical aspects of managing Open Access content. Due to the increased popularity of and importance of Open Access resources it is also worth examining the philosophical arguments surrounding this kind of publishing. Supporters of the Open Access movement have long argued the need for expanded, low-cost access to scholarly content, because:

> The majority of research is hidden behind a **paywall**, only accessible to those who pay for access or those who are affiliated with subscribing institutions.

> The high cost of scholarly resources causes a global imbalance, because researchers in developing countries cannot afford to access life-saving research.

> Research institutions essentially pay twice for research, first by employing the researchers doing the publishing, and again by subscribing to the research when it has been published.

> Peer reviewers are not paid for their time and the cost of **peer review** is passed onto subscribers.

In short, the traditional journal subscription model is not sustainable. Although library budgets have on average increased since the financial downturn in 2008, budgets have yet to rise to pre-2008 levels and have failed to increase at a rate comparable to inflation. As libraries spend fewer dollars on content, publishers are struggling to find innovative solutions to provide libraries with content while still remaining operational and profitable, and have introduced new business models including the **Big Deal**, Pay-Per-View, **DDA**, and **hybrid journals**.[3]

Librarians are forced to find the most cost-effective means of providing access and rely more on usage and expenditure data than ever. Libraries are collaborating to build collections, reduce costs, and find solutions to all-too-common problems. Collaboration among libraries is hindered, however, by an overall lack of transparency in the publishing industry. Most libraries are required to sign nondisclosure agreements that forbid librarians from sharing price information. Publishers argue that they need these agreements to stay competitive in the marketplace, but libraries then cannot compare costs or negotiate aggressively. This lack of transparency leads to inconsistent or inaccurate reporting on how much publishers spend to publish monographs and journals, and determining potential cost savings by transitioning to Open Access is difficult to measure.

Open Access advocates argue that they have the ultimate solution, but still up for debate is who exactly will see cost savings and how much, because business models for Open Access publishing are not consistent. Although some Open Access publishers charge an **Author Processing Charge (APC),** others do not, and then still others charge a membership fee or have subsidies from society or university presses. Traditional journal publishers would argue that subscription journals are worth the cost, benefit the entire research community, and offer significant advantages over Open Access journals, including a higher editorial quality and peer review process.

As Open Access publishing continues to grow and mature, commercial and society publishers are being asked to demonstrate their value and worth

What Is an Author Processing Charge (APC)?

An APC is a fee charged to authors to publish in an academic journal. In traditional publishing, an individual or a subscribing library pays for access, but in Open Access publishing the author is charged to support the cost of publishing. Ideally, the APC is paid by the researcher's affiliated institution or with a research grant, rather than by the individual author. APCs are sometimes simply referred to as "publishing fees."

in order to stay competitive. Cornell University's arXiv is an excellent example of an Open Access repository that has become critical to scholarly communication in mathematics, physics, and computer science. While arXiv and Open Access repositories like retain prestige in the scholarly community, the subscription journal still reigns due to the academic tenure and promotion process. Scholarly publishing is a major driver in tenure, where a journal's prestige factors heavily in publishing decisions. High-prestige journals with a high percentage of rejections and stringent peer review processes are

Check It Out

Libraries and related information organizations are doing some interesting things to support free access to research.

SPARC (Scholarly Publishing and Academic Resources Coalition)
A global network focused on increasing Open Access publishing, the open sharing of research, and use of OERs in higher education.

CHORUS (Clearinghouse for the Open Research of the United States)
A collection of services and technology built in support of public access to research and enhanced discovery, access, and preservation of research and scholarly content.

Open Access Button
An app used by researchers to report when they are denied access to research because of paywalls. The Open Access Button uses the gathered data to advocate for Open Access and when possible, retrieves full-text articles on behalf of researchers.

Knowledge Unlatched
An initiative to promote the publication of Open Access monographs. Member libraries pledge funds to "unlatch" books. Once the cost of publication has been paid by library pledges, monographs are published under Creative Commons licensing.

Lever Press
Sponsored and managed by a consortium of libraries, Lever Press published Open Access monographs.

considered the most selective, and therefore the most desirable. The incentives to publish in high-prestige journals often outweigh the ethical reasons to publish Open Access.

Open Data

In 2013, the Obama Administration directed Federal agencies with research expenditures exceeding $100 million to make research data freely available to the public after a one-year embargo period. The Office of Science and Technology Policy (OSTP) directive also required federally funded researchers to manage their data by creating data management plans, which outline how the data will be stored and made available in the future. In 2016, the three-year anniversary of the OSTP directive, the program was summarized by Fred Dylla, Executive Director Emeritus of the American Institute of Physics:

> 1) public access policy is in place for 98% of the research funding from US federal agencies starting in the last year, 2) a robust article identification system is in place from Crossref that is already tracking more than 11,000 funding agencies worldwide, 3) CHORUS, a public-private partnership, is actively assisting the agencies with implementing their public access plans, 4) TDM solutions are beginning to appear, and 5) agencies, supported by various stakeholders, are making some headway on data management.[4]

Who Is Making Data Openly Available and Where Is It Accessible?

Some institutions and libraries include open access data within their individual **Institutional Repositories (IRs)**, whereas some host their research data on a separate, multidisciplinary platform. Multidisciplinary, open access data platforms include:

Dryad

Figshare

Open Science Framework

Zenodo

Being Open Is Not So Simple

Although publishers, libraries, researchers, and the federal government are grappling with the fiscal, moral, and logistical issues surrounding Open Access publishing, users have begun to access scholarly, electronic resources in more home-grown—and far less scrupulous—ways. These methods range from individuals sharing articles directly and hosting content on personal websites to using robots to crawl publisher websites to retrieve thousands of articles at once. Some argue that the current system of scholarly communication is so unfair and difficult to manage that researchers have been forced to violate copyright law to gain access to scholarly works.

Researchers have always shared articles as a natural part of the research process. Although traditionally article sharing occurred discreetly between two parties, social media networks such as Twitter have created new and more efficient avenues for scholars to share scholarly materials with each other. On Twitter, the hashtag #icanhazpdf has been used to directly request articles from other Twitter users. Gardner and Gardner describe the #icanhaz pdf phenomenon in their 2015 ACRL conference paper, showing that #ican hazpdf is most often used by academics and students in the United States and United Kingdom.[5] Despite the seeming popularity of #icanhazpdf, this type of exchange is considered piracy and violates both publishers' terms of service, library license agreements, and copyright law.[6]

Sci-Hub, a pirating website that provides illegal access to countless full-text articles, has also caused a stir in the Open Access movement, especially around copyright and scholarly communication. Sci-Hub acquired countless institutional username and password credentials to access content. Alexandra Elbakyan, the site's creator, has been hailed as a Robin Hood by some supporters, whereas critics describe her as a lawbreaker and serious threat to the integrity of the economics behind scholarly publication.[7] Elbakyan herself described Sci-Hub as the result of an unfair system in which researchers in developing countries are denied access to the scholarship they need.[8] As of this book's writing, Sci-Hub is still active despite legal action from the publisher Elsevier as well as an order from New York District Court to take down the site.

Open Access advocates argue that "free" access to research is not the same as Open Access, and are uncomfortable with how Sci-Hub has been associated with Open Access. Other advocates worry that Sci-Hub has the potential to complicate relationships with publishers, many of which have made steps to offer Open Access publishing options in addition to their traditional subscription resources.

Home-grown solutions to accessing scholarly research are symptomatic of much larger issues. They demonstrate that the ways in which we share scholarly communication are flawed, or at the very least can be improved. Electronic resources librarians can be mindful of these issues in their daily work by signing license agreements with perpetual access clauses, purchasing **DRM**-free ebooks, and advocating for more sustainable subscription models and Open Access options. Library users do not understand the license agreements that libraries sign or why some scholarly content is available and some is not. Instead, users become quickly frustrated by access restrictions on and limited functionality of certain resources. Libraries must promote their collections and services, but also educate their users to be lifelong information seekers by teaching students and faculty ways to find and access Open Access content that is legal and sustainable.

Changes in Higher Education

The library plays a prominent role on college campuses and it is no surprise that changes in higher education also impact library services. The increasing costs of higher education, reductions in state and federal funding, fluxes in scholarly communication, trends in online education, applications of social media and new technology in instruction, and, of course, tenure and promotion, all influence college and university libraries. In many ways, the library acts as an incubator to experiment with emerging trends in education. High textbook costs, for example, are being addressed through initiatives begun in university libraries. Issues surrounding scholarly communication and open access to research are reflected in institutional repositories (IR). Finally, researchers' heightened interest in **Text and Data Mining (TDM)** impacts the licenses that libraries sign as well as the nature of conversations between publishers and libraries.

Open Educational Resources

The rising cost of textbooks is a growing problem for students and educators alike. The College Board estimates that the average in-state, full-time undergraduate student at a four-year public college will pay $1,298 each year for books and supplies.[9] For many students, the high cost of books is a barrier to learning and, as *The Chronicle of Higher Education* reported in 2011, seven out of ten students have chosen not to purchase a textbook because of its price.[10] Despite these alarming trends, little research has been published on the impact of high textbook costs on student performance. Complicating matters further, new textbook editions are issued frequently, and while that lowers the cost of the previous editions it also renders them obsolete and outdated. Used textbooks, a more affordable alternative, are then no longer relevant to the class; this also leads to a shorter shelf life for textbooks from the library.

As a response to the high cost of textbooks, educators, librarians, and researchers have begun to create **Open Educational Resources (OERs)** as a textbook alternative. Open Educational Resources are "teaching, learning, and research resources that are free of cost and access barriers, and which also carry legal permissions for open use."[11] OERs are published online and are free for anyone to use. They can be as simple as a self-published PDF, or can live on a website or course management system. As with most things "open," OERs are generally published with Creative Commons licenses that allow users to adapt and share the work in other forms.

Although many educators and administrators are aware of the high cost of textbooks, creating a process and motivating faculty to participate in the creation of OERs is far from simple. As discussed earlier, the tenure process recognizes publications in high-prestige, peer-reviewed publications with traditionally defined impact factors, therefore the time and effort required to develop OERs may seem excessive when compared to the nominal benefits associated with them during the tenure and review process. Library resources, in some cases, can be a worthwhile alternative. Electronic resources are accessible for all authorized users at an institution, and the greatest challenge related to their adoption for coursework may simply be that faculty are not aware of what is available from the library and how the material can be embedded into existing course management systems.

Institutional Repositories

In the past decade and a half, university libraries have curated digital collections from their institutions' research and scholarly output. These local collections make up an Institutional Repository (IR), which plays a significant role in the scholarly communication process by enhancing the visibility and access of an institution's scholarly activity. Institutional repositories, by their very nature, capture and preserve the university's intellectual output and enrich the content with robust metadata that is searchable on the Open Web. They typically hold journal articles, theses and dissertations, datasets, book chapters or sections, presentations, images, and artwork. Institutional repositories make content available as Open Access and, unlike subject-specific or funder repositories, only contain the scholarly work from a single institution. Because institutional repositories adhere to the Open Archives Initiative Protocol for Metadata Harvesting (OAI-PMH), they are interoperable with **discovery systems,** which is critical to discoverability within the larger scholarly body of work.

Institutional repositories offer many benefits. They:

- expose the research and scholarly output of an institution to the world, thereby maximizing visibility and impact
- indicate a university's quality and prestige as well as a record of the university's intellectual output
- provide **usage statistics** on how often documents are viewed and downloaded, which can be helpful measurements when evaluating a particular work's impact on the larger research community
- provide a single location for faculty, students, and researchers to deposit and advertise their work, rather than merely posting scholarly work on personal or departmental websites
- allow faculty and students to provide direct links to their work for portfolios and presentations

Despite these benefits, university libraries have struggled to motivate their faculty to deposit work into their institutional repositories, either for reasons related to scholarly output volume—a senior faculty might have hundreds of articles to deposit—or because faculty might not be aware of the service or understand its benefits. Again, because the tenure and promotion

Find Institutional Repositories

Registry of Open Access Repositories (ROAR) at http://roar.eprints.org/

Directory of Open Access Repositories (OpenDOAR) at wwwopendoar.org/

process recognizes publications in high-prestige publications, many faculty and graduate students fear there will be unintended ramifications from depositing their works. To address this unease, some institutional repositories offer selective **embargo** periods, which researchers can set for themselves or to comply with regulations in author agreements with for-profit publishers (e.g., those related to publishing in **Green OA** journals).

Additionally, some universities have implemented Open Access mandates, which require faculty to deposit publications into an Open Access repository. Harvard University and the Massachusetts Institute of Technology (MIT) have both created Open Access mandates. The Registry of Open Access Repository Mandates and Policies (ROARMAP) is an excellent source to learn about institutional policies and mandates in both the USA and internationally.

Librarians also need to play a role in advocating for institutional repositories by offering guidance on the submission process to users. As stated earlier, one of the greatest strengths of an institutional repository is the interoperability that result from shared metadata standards. Setting up a straightforward and easy-to-use system to record metadata for discovery is critical to a successful repository. A robust submission form will make the process easier for

Strategies to Promote the Use of an Institutional Repository

Demonstrate the value of the IR by using download statistics to track citations and impact.

Develop a simple and straightforward submission process that encourages users to submit research.

Offer workshops and create research guides to educate users on the benefits of the Institutional Repository, and build in opportunities to address common faculty concerns, such as copyright, into these activities.

Create a short and long-term outreach and marketing plan tailored to specific audiences.

Look for potential campus partnerships with academic departments and services.

Advocate for an institution-wide Open Access mandate.

all involved, and concise metadata fields in the forms will facilitate gathering the complete and accurate metadata needed for discovery.

The library should play a prominent role in advocating for the use and support of any institutional repository. Demonstrating the value of the institutional repository is essential for faculty inclusion, as well as continued university support and funding. Advocacy and education are crucial to the success of an institutional repository. A well-designed marketing plan can go a long way toward getting faculty informed and involved. And marketing can extend beyond end-users, too. University administration need to be aware of all the benefits related to an institutional repository and how it can be a useful tool in recruiting new faculty and students.

Text and Data Mining

Text and Data Mining (TDM) has become increasing popular among researchers, especially in the digital humanities. Increasingly, researchers are looking for methods to search and extract information from large amounts of text and data quickly and systematically. In TDM, documents are identified and translated into machine-readable format so that the data can be scraped and used to populate a database for examination. TDM has huge implications for many industries and across languages. As such, publishers are very interested in the evolution and practice of text and data mining.

Publishers, librarians, and information organizations have acted quickly in response to the demand for TDM. Publishers have begun to include TDM clauses in their license agreements. Some publishers have gone further and developed APIs to assist in TDM, such as those from Elsevier's Science-Direct, which facilitate TDM for academic subscriptions for non-commercial purposes.[12] CrossRef has also developed means of supporting TDM through the CrossRef Text and Data Mining Services and the CrossRef Metadata API. CrossRef has leveraged its huge body of metadata to help researchers and publishers navigate TDM using a common system. These APIs—and more are sure to come—aim to address some of the biggest challenges associated with TDM. However, because the practice is relatively new, publishers, vendors, and third-party organizations have yet to develop a truly consistent and systematic process for TDM.

Demand from researchers for TDM will only continue. Electronic resources librarians can support their users in the process during the license negotiation process by advocating for its inclusion when possible.

For more on how TDM can be included in license agreements for electronic resources, see chapter 5.

Evolving Collections

Change is happening everywhere in libraries, especially in collections. Although the authors of this book do not have a crystal ball to see into the future, they foresee continued development in the following areas:

> Scholarly communication and the future of the monograph and journal as we know them today
>
> Discovery and access systems that are more secure, seamless, and intuitive
>
> Open Access and Open Source Technology

Finally, one trend to keep an eye on relates to industry consolidation. Increasingly, library vendors are merging to stay competitive and profitable. During the writing of this book, ProQuest acquired both Ex Libris and Alexander Street Press, and EBSCO acquired YBP and has begun a partnership with Open Library Environment (OLE) to develop an open source Library Services Platform (LSP). It is possible that by the time of publication some of these names will no longer be familiar because of these mergers. Vendors reassure librarians that mergers and acquisitions ensure continued affordable pricing and high-quality products, but still librarians worry about stability, because vendor consolidation relates directly to an ongoing concern for libraries: the ability to provide consistent access to relevant, high-quality research and scholarship now and in the future.

NOTES

1. Chris Bulock, "Tracking Perpetual Access: A Survey of Librarian Practices," *Serials Review* 40, no. 2 (2014): 97–104.
2. Mei Zhang and Kristin R. Eschenfelder, "License Analysis of e-Journal Perpetual Access," *The Journal of Academic Librarianship* 40, no. 1 (2014): 62–69, http://dx.doi.org/10.1016/j.acalib.2013.11.002.
3. Stephen Bosch and Kittie Henderson, "Fracking the Ecosystem: Periodical Price Survey 2016," *Library Journal* 141, no. 7 (2016): 32–38.
4. Fred Dylla, "Three Years After the OSTP Public Access Directive: A Progress Report," *The Scholarly Kitchen,* March 8, 2016, https://scholarlykitchen.sspnet

.org/2016/03/08/guest-post-fred-dylla-three-years-after-the-ostp-public-access
-directive-a-progress-report/.

5. Carolyn Caffrey Gardner and Gabriel J. Gardner, "Bypassing Interlibrary Loan
via Twitter: An Exploration of #icanhazpdf Requests," 2015 ACRL Conference
Proceedings. www.ala.org/acrl/sites/ala.org.acrl/files/content/conferences/
confsandpreconfs/2015/Gardner.pdf.

6. The authors of this text do not support or encourage the use of #icanhazpdf.

7. Simon Oxenham, "Meet the Robin Hood of Science," http://bigthink.com/
neurobonkers/a-pirate-bay-for-science.

8. Julia Belluz, "Meet Alexandra Elbakyan, the Researcher Who's Breaking the Law
to Make Science Free for All," www.vox.com/2016/2/18/11047052/alexandra
-elbakyan-interview.

9. The College Board, "Quick Guide: College Costs," https://bigfuture.collegeboard
.org/pay-for-college/college-costs/quick-guide-college-costs.

10. Molly Redden, "7 in 10 Students Have Skipped Buying a Textbook Because of Its
Cost, Survey Finds," *The Chronicle of Higher Education,* August 23, 2011, http://
chronicle.com/article/7-in-10-Students-Have-Skipped/128785/.

11. SPARC, "Open Education," http://sparcopen.org/open-education/.

12. Elsevier, "Text and Data Mining," www.elsevier.com/about/company-informa
tion/policies/text-and-data-mining.

FURTHER READINGS

Beh, Eugenia, and Jane Smith. "Preserving the Scholarly Collection: An Examination
of the Perpetual Access Clauses in the Texas A&M University Libraries' Major
E-Journal Licenses." *Serials Review* 38, no. 4 (2012): 235–42. doi: 10.1016/
j.serrev.2012.10.005.

Billings, Marilyn S., Sarah C. Hutton, Jay Schafer, Charles M. Schweik, and Matt
Sheridan. "Open Educational Resources as Learning Materials: Prospects and
Strategies for University Libraries." *Research Library Issues* 280 (2012): 2–10.

Blanchat, Kelly Marie. "Optimizing KBART Guidelines to Restore Perpetual Access."
Collection Building 34, no. 1 (2015): 13–16. doi: 10.1108/CB-04-2014-0022.

Breeding, Marshall. "EBSCO Supports New Open Source Project." *American
Libraries,* April 22, 2016. http://americanlibrariesmagazine.org/2016/04/22/
ebsco-kuali-open-source-project/.

Bulock, Chris. "Techniques for Tracking Perpetual Access." *The Serials Librarian* 68,
no. 1–4 (2015): 290–98. doi: 10.1080/0361526X.2015.1017711.

Glasser, Sarah. "Providing Perpetual Access: Results of a Survey." *Library Resources
and Technical Services* 58, no. 3 (2014): 144–52.

Stachokas, George. "Electronic Resources and Mission Creep: Reorganizing the
Library for the 21st Century." *Journal of Electronic Resources Librarianship* 21,
no. 3–4 (2009): 206–12. doi: 10.1080/19411260903446170.

Sullenger, Paula. "A Departmental Assessment Using the Core Competencies for Electronic Resources Librarians." *Serials Review* 40, no. 2 (2014): 88–96. doi: 10.1080/00987913.2014.922377.

Van Noorden, Richard. "Open Access: The True Cost of Science Publishing." *Nature* 495, no. 7442 (2013): 426—429.

Wertheimer, Linda. "Expensive Journals Drive Academics to Break Copyright Law." February 20, 2016. www.npr.org/2016/02/20/467468361/expensive-journals -drive-academics-to-break-copyright-law.

University of North Texas Libraries Open Access Resource Rubric

RESOURCE NAME		DATE	
	EXCELLENT	ADEQUATE	INSUFFICIENT
Quality (Review Process)	Stated peer or librarian review, prefer multiple reviewers (for journals, etc.)	Peer or librarian review is noted but not described in detail, or the process is limited	No review processes are in place
Quality (Contact Information)	Contact information is provided for author/publisher	Contact information for author or publisher is general, outdated, or incomplete	No contact information is provided or is only available through contact form
Quality (Information)	Information is logical and pertains to stated subject of resource (look at titles, abstracts, any other information)	Most (not all) information is pertinent to the subject	Subjects are varied and seemingly incoherent
Authority (Publisher)	Credentials of publisher are clearly and easily identifiable; Preferred domains: .edu, .gov, .org, or .net	Credentials of publisher are difficult to find, or do not match subject very closely; Publisher has positive reputation but not established longevity	Publisher credentials are not included or poor; publisher has limited or no positive reputation

(Cont.)

Guidance based on the Collection Development Policy for Open Access and Born-Digital Resources, for more information please see policy at www.library.unt.edu/policies/collection-development/oa -collection-development-policy.

	EXCELLENT	ADEQUATE	INSUFFICIENT
Authority (Author)	Credentials of author are clearly and easily identifiable; credentials scholarly in nature and relevant to content	Credentials of author are difficult to find, or lacking in some way	Author credentials are not included or irrelevant
Objectivity (Information)	Information provided is open to verification and validation, process for this is stated. Information provides for multiple perspectives and/ or addresses shortcomings of research	Information provided is open to verification and validation in a limited fashion; Information provides for some perspectives and may address shortcomings of research but not completely	Information provided is not open to verification or validation; Shortcomings of research are not addressed or multiple perspectives not allowed
Objectivity (Advertising)	No or minimal advertising	Moderate advertising is present	Heavy advertising is present and interferes with information
Currency	Information is recently published relative to the subject	Information is published fairly recently	Large gaps between publications; infor-mation is out of date
Currency (Frequency)	Publication dates are regular, clearly identified on the resource, and adhered to	Limited larger gaps between publications than those stated on the resource	Publication frequency is not stated or adhered to
Functionality (Software and Registration)	No additional software is needed; no registration is needed to access the resource	Minimal, if any, additional software is needed; no registration is needed to access the resource	Extra software or plugins are necessary to view information; registration is necessary
Functionality (Viewing Options)	Resource has text-only viewing options, or options for optimal viewing	Limited display options available or text-only is not available	Limited or no display options available, limiting usability of information
Functionality (Links)	All citations and links are correct and functional	Most citations links are correct and functional;	Multiple citations and links are incorrect or not functioning

License Review Checklist

License Review Checklist

This appendix has been adapted from a checklist developed by the University of North Texas Libraries, and reused and modified with permission. The checklist below is intended to be a learning tool that can be adapted and remixed depending on the unique requirements of any institution. When using the checklist as a part of active license review, mark the boxes that apply. Some options include "(flag)" references, which indicate the possible need to review a clause further, or modify language before final license approval. Depending on the specific requirements at an institution, the types of items to flag will vary. Before deciding on the types of language to flag, discuss institutional requirements with General Counsel or internal colleagues.

The checklist is broken down into the three most common licensing sections: Part 1: Terms and Conditions, Part 2: Content License and Business Terms, Part 3: Execution, and Part 4: License Attachment, Amendment, or Addendum. The fifth and final part covers the option for a second and third review, or "everything else."

PART 1
Terms and Conditions

License Parties

☐ Both license parties are referenced clearly.

☐ Both license parties are referenced, but need revision. (flag)

- ☐ Only the Licensor is referenced. (flag)
- ☐ The license agreement is silent.

Definitions

- ☐ All required definitions are present and reasonably match the library's model license.
- ☐ All required definitions are present, but some need revision. (flag)
- ☐ All required definitions are not present. (flag)
- ☐ The license agreement is silent.

Jurisdiction/Venue/Governing Law

- ☐ The state of jurisdiction is the library's home state.
- ☐ The state of jurisdiction is not the library's home state. (flag)
- ☐ No state or country is referenced as having jurisdiction. (flag)
- ☐ The license agreement is silent.

Indemnification

- ☐ Both the Licensor and the Licensee are indemnified.
- ☐ The Licensor has indemnified the Licensee.
- ☐ The Licensee indemnifies the Licensor only. (flag)
- ☐ The license agreement is silent.

Force Majeure

- ☐ Force majeure applies equally to both parties.
- ☐ Force majeure applies to the Licensor only. (flag)
- ☐ The license agreement is silent.

Termination of Access/Security Breach

- ☐ The Licensor will give notice prior to terminating access due to an alleged violation.
- ☐ The Licensor will not give notice prior to terminating access due to an alleged violation. (flag)
- ☐ The license agreement is silent.

Notice of Click-Through License

☐ Licensor does give the Licensee an opportunity to review any user click-through licenses before implementation.

☐ Licensor does not give the Licensee an opportunity to review any user click-through licenses before implementation. (flag)

☐ The license agreement is silent.

Authorized Users

☐ References all patron groups identified in the library's model license.

☐ References all or most (circle one) patron groups identified in the library's model license. (flag)

☐ References all or most (circle one) patron groups identified in the library's model license, but includes references to "restricted users." (flag)

☐ The license agreement is silent.

Permitted Uses

☐ Permitted Uses do not diverge from Fair Use, and do not contradict other license clauses; the institution does not claim responsibility for its users.

☐ Permitted Uses do not reference Fair Use; the institution does claim responsibility for its users. (flag)

☐ The license agreement is silent.

Simultaneous Users

☐ Unlimited number of users allowed.

☐ Restricted to _____ users. (flag)

☐ The license agreement is silent.

Authentication (EZ Proxy, VPN)

☐ The library's method of remote user authentication is available.

☐ The library's method of remote user authentication is not available. (flag)

☐ Remote user authentication is not allowed. (flag)

☐ The license agreement is silent.

Interlibrary Loan (ILL)/Scholarly Sharing

☐ Sharing rights are permitted and method of electronic provision is not restricted.

☐ Sharing rights are permitted and method of electronic provision is restricted.

☐ Sharing is prohibited by license. (flag)

☐ The license agreement is silent.

Course Packs

☐ Electronic rights are permitted, does not include record-keeping requirements.

☐ Electronic rights are not permitted; does include record keeping requirements included. (flag)

☐ Not permitted. (flag)

☐ The license agreement is silent.

Usage Statistics

☐ Usage data is available and COUNTER compliant.

☐ Usage data is available and not COUNTER compliant. (flag)

☐ Usage data is not available from the vendor. (flag)

☐ The license agreement is silent.

MARC Records

☐ Available for free from vendor or OCLC. (circle one)

☐ Available at cost ($_____) from vendor or OCLC. (circle one)

☐ Not available. (flag)

☐ The license agreement is silent.

Perpetual Access (for applicable content)

☐ Includes perpetual rights language and cites whether fees are included.

☐ Does not include perpetual rights language. (flag)

☐ Perpetual access does not apply.

☐ The license agreement is silent.

Archival Rights (for applicable content)

☐ Available from the vendor at no charge.

☐ Available from the vendor at an additional charge.

☐ Available from an alternate provider, such as LOCKSS, CLOCKSS, and Portico.

☐ Available via a local copy/hard drive.

☐ The license agreement is silent.

Server Availability

☐ The license agreement does include provisions for a partial refund due to excessive server downtime.

☐ The license agreement does not include provisions for a partial refund due to excessive server downtime. (flag)

☐ The license agreement is silent.

Accessibility/ADA Compliance

☐ The platform is ADA compliant.

☐ The platform is not ADA compliant (flag, depending on the content).

☐ The platform will be ADA compliant by a specific date: __/__/__.

☐ The license agreement is silent.

Text Data Mining (RDM)

☐ TDM is permitted.

☐ TDM is not permitted.

☐ TDM requests will be reviewed on a case-by-case basis.

☐ The license agreement is silent.

User Privacy

☐ The license agreement does include language regarding the protection of user privacy.

☐ The license agreement does not include language regarding the protection of user privacy. (flag)

☐ The license agreement is silent.

Confidentiality of Business Terms

☐ The license agreement does not require non-disclosure of licensing terms or prices.

☐ The license agreement does require non-disclosure of licensing terms or prices. (flag)

☐ The license agreement is silent.

PART 2
Content License and Business Terms

Licensed Content

☐ The content is clearly referenced in the agreement.

☐ The content is not clearly referenced in the agreement. (flag)

☐ The content is not referenced in the agreement. (flag)

☐ Does not apply; the agreement is a Terms and Conditions only.

License Fees

☐ The license fee does match the quote.

☐ The license fee does not match the quote. (flag)

☐ The license fee includes additional fees not negotiated. (flag)

☐ Does not apply; the agreement is a Terms and Conditions only.

License Term

☐ The subscription term is clearly defined; it does not include an auto-renewal.

☐ The subscription term is not clearly defined; it does include an auto-renewal. (flag)

☐ Does not apply; the agreement is a Terms and Conditions only.

Multi-Year Fees (if applicable)

☐ Multi-year price is based on set fees over a finite period of time.

☐ Multi-year price changes are on a fixed percentage increase; auto-renewal does apply unless the vendor is notified of non-renewal ___ days in advance. (flag)

☐ Multi-year price changes are not fixed; auto-renewal does apply but does not include a notice period. (flag)

☐ Does not apply; the agreement is a Terms and Conditions only.

Automatic Renewal

☐ The subscription does not include an automatic renewal.

☐ The subscription does include an automatic renewal, with __days' notice.

☐ The license agreement is silent.

Early Termination

☐ The license is multi-year and does include an early termination/opt-out clause.

☐ The license is multi-year and does not include an early termination/opt-out clause. (flag)

☐ The license is for a single year; early termination and opt-out clauses do not apply.

PART 3
Execution

Signature Line

☐ Signature line is included for both parties.

☐ Signature line is included for the Licensee only. (flag)

☐ Signature line is not included. (flag)

PART 4
License Attachment, Amendment, or Addendum

Content Name

☐ The content referenced in the amendment matches the quote.

☐ The content referenced in the amendment does not match the quote. (flag)

☐ The content is not referenced in the amendment. (flag)

Original License Agreement References

☐ License references do include the original license name, date, and/or license ID number.

☐ License references do include the original license name, date, and/or license ID number, but the reference license is old. (flag)

☐ License references do not include the original license name, date, and license ID number. (flag)

Amendment Exceptions

☐ Language does not include exceptions for license terms, amendment is for content updates only.

☐ Language does include exceptions to original license terms. (flag)

Amendment Fees

☐ The fees referenced in the amendment do match the quote.

☐ The fees referenced in the amendment do not match the quote. (flag)

☐ The fees are not referenced in the amendment. (flag)

PART 5
Everything else

☐ Check for problematic words and phrases. (see chapter section: "Word Search")

☐ Request a colleague to conduct a second, or third, review.

☐ Submit questions and notes to legal counsel.

Glossary

*Acronyms and Everyday Jargon—Things Every
Electronic Resources Librarian Should Know*

Access Only. Access only refers to content acquired from a library vendor or publisher that is only available for the duration of a license agreement, generally ranging from one to several years. Once the subscription period has lapsed, access only content will no longer be available to patrons unless the subscription is renewed. Access may sometimes be referred to as non-subscribed, or complimentary. *See also* Complimentary; License Agreement; Subscribed; Perpetual Access.

Addendum. Also known as an amendment; any update or change to an active license agreement may require an addendum, as specified by a library purchasing office or by a library vendor or publisher. An addendum will generally be shorter than a full license agreement, and will reference the master license agreement and/or Terms and Conditions. *See also* Amendment; License Agreement; Model License Agreement; Shared E-Resource Understanding (SERU); Terms and Conditions (T&C); Terms of Use (TOU).

Abstract and Index (A&I). A category of databases that provide bibliographic citations and abstracts to the literature of a discipline or subject area. An A&I database will not provide full text, but it may have the ability to link to the content through OpenURL. *See also* Index; OpenURL.

Aggregator Database. An aggregator is a reference to a bibliographic database. An aggregator can be a full-text database of subscription content, such as databases provided by EBSCO and ProQuest; a gateway aggregator for an Abstract and Index database; or a third-party hosting service for a publisher's content, such as HighWire Press and Ingenta. Because aggregator databases can be very large, tracking their coverage is not an easy task.

Altmetrics. Non-traditional metrics that measure resource impact from social media, news, blogs, and more. *See also* H-Index.

Amendment. Also known as an Addendum. Any update or change to an active license agreement may require an amendment, either as specified by a library purchasing office or by a library vendor or publisher. An amendment will generally be shorter than a full license agreement, and will reference the master license agreement and/or Terms and Conditions. *See also* Addendum; License Agreement; Model License Agreement; Shared E-Resource Understanding (SERU); Terms and Conditions (T&C); Terms of Use (TOU).

Article Processing Charge (APC). A publication fee that is charged to an author publishing in an OA (Open Access) journal. Often the author's institution or research fund will pay the APC. An APC is different from a fee assigned by predatory publishers, in which money is exchanged by editorial and publication services are not provided. *See also* OA (Open Access).

Archives. Also known as Backfiles. Archives refer to electronic content that is much older, or that has been digitized from older print serials and books. Archives are acquired through a large, one-time purchase, versus as a yearly subscription. *See also* Backfiles.

Athens. A method of remote authentication for electronic resources. Athens authentication provides users with access to licensed electronic resources through a single sign-on, eliminating the need for multiple usernames, and operating independently of authentication by IP Address. *See also* IP Address; IP Authentication; Shibboleth.

Authorized User. A license designation that specifies that qualified individuals affiliated with an institution are able to access licensed electronic resources. For an academic library, authorized users might include students, faculty, and staff. For a public library, authorized users might be much broader to include members of the public using the library.

Backfiles. Also known as Archives. Backfiles refers to electronic content that is quite old, or that has been digitized from older print serials and books. Backfiles are acquired through a large, one-time purchase, versus as a yearly subscription. *See also* Archives.

Big Deal. An arrangement with electronic journal publishers that provides the library with a large collection of journals at a price that is less than the content would cost through individual subscriptions. A few examples of Big Deal packages include the America's package from SpringerNature and the Freedom Collection from Elsevier. Big Deals are licensed for multiple years, with fixed prices increases over each year. *See also* List Price.

Carnegie Classification. A framework for classifying colleges and universities in the United States. A libraries' price for an electronic subscription may be determined by the institution's Carnegie Classification or its Full-Time Equivalent (FTE). *See also* Full-Time Equivalent (FTE).

Ceased Title. A journal that is no longer published. *See also* CLOCKSS; LOCKSS; Perpetual Access; Portico; Transfer Code of Practice; Transfer Title.

Charleston Conference. An annual conference for librarians, publishers, electronic resource managers, consultants, and vendors whose work involves the management of library materials and acquisitions. Also referred to as "Charleston."

Click-Through License. A type of license agreement available on a vendor's website or platform that includes general terms of use, and a button to indicate acceptance. A click-through license cannot be negotiated or altered and must be accepted as-is. *See also* License Agreement; Model License Agreement; shared E-Resource Understanding (SERU); Terms and Conditions (T&C); Terms of Use (TOU).

CLOCKSS. An offshoot of the LOCKSS (Lots of Copies Keep Stuff Safe) program. Content is archived at geographically distributed publisher sites and a group of selected libraries to ensure the long-term preservation of web-based scholarly publications. Content no longer available from a participating publisher becomes available for free through CLOCKSS. *See also* Ceased Title; LOCKSS; Perpetual Access; Portico.

Complementary. Complementary content is content that is not directly purchased by a library, but that is made available free of charge as a result of another purchase or subscription. Complementary content is often only available for use during an active license agreement; if the supporting content is not renewed or has expired, access to complementary content will be lost. *See also* Access Only; Subscribed.

Consortium/Consortia. An association of libraries and/or library systems established by formal agreement, usually for the purpose of resource sharing. Membership may be restricted to a specific geographic region, type of library (public, academic, special), or subject specialization. Examples include CIC (Committee on Institutional Cooperation), NERL (Northeast Research Libraries), and Orbis Cascade Alliance. *See also* Site License.

CONTU. Guidelines that were developed to assist librarians and copyright proprietors to understand the amount of interlibrary loan permitted under copyright law. For example, CONTU suggests if a library requests a book more than five times, it should buy it. *See also* Interlibrary Loan (ILL); Copyright Law.

Copyright Law. Copyright acts as a protection against others copying the work. It is the exclusive right granted by a government to publish a work for a specified number of years. *See also* CONTU.

CORAL. An open source ERMS (Electronic Resources Management System) built by the University of Notre Dame. It includes customizable modules for Acquisitions, Licensing, Administration, Support, and Usage. *See also* Electronic Resources Management System (ERMS).

Cost-per-use (CPU). A common metric to measure the continued value of library materials in electronic format. To obtain cost-per-use data, the total cost of the resource is divided by the number of times the resource was used for a subscription period.

COUNTER. COUNTER stands for Counting Online Usage of Networked Electronic Resources, which is a Code of Practice that covers the recording and reporting of online usage statistics in a consistent, credible, and compatible way. COUNTER enables libraries to: compare usage statistics from different vendors and generate standardized metrics such as cost-per-use. *See also* Usage Statistics.

Course packs. A collection of readings selected by an instructor from a variety of sources to supplement or serve as a textbook. The readings are reproduced, usually by a college or university duplicating service or commercial photocopy shop, for sale under a single set of covers to students enrolled in the course. License agreements for electronic resources will often include a clause outlining whether licensed content can be used in course packs. *See also* Interlibrary Loan (ILL).

CUFTS. An open source Electronic Resources Management System (ERMS) developed by Simon Fraser University. CUFTS facilitates centralizing license terms, renewal dates, contacts, database A–Z lists, and more. *See also* CORAL; Electronic Resources Management System (ERMS).

Database. Searchable online platforms that contain documents, or information about documents. A database could contain citation and abstract information about books and articles, or provide both along with the full text. Database content can include journals, government documents, datasets, conference proceedings, book chapters, book reviews, images, and streaming media. *See also* Abstract and Index and Aggregator Database.

Database A–Z. An access point on a library's website that provides users with the ability to search for top-level databases by name in an alphabetical list.

Demand Driven Acquisitions (DDA). Demand Driven Acquisitions is a method of acquisitions in which libraries make a large collection of ebooks that have not yet been purchased available to patrons. Only when a title is selected for use does the library complete the purchase. Often a purchase is triggered by a multiplier, or a predetermined number of patron uses. *See also* Patron Driven Acquisitions (PDA); Pay-Per-View (PPV).

Denials. Denials refers to electronic content download requests that were denied on the publisher's platform. Denials occur either because of an access error or because a library does not subscribe. COUNTER reports can provide data on the number of times content was denied to users. In COUNTER 4 these reports are: Journal Report 2 (JR2), Database Report 2 (DR2), and Book Reports 3 and 4 (BR3 and BR4). *See also* COUNTER; Turnaways; Usage Statistics; Usus.

Digital Object Identifier (DOI). A code for the identification and exchange of intellectual property in the digital environment. Metadata about the object is associated with the DOI name, which may include the location, or URL, where the object can be found. A DOI remains fixed for the lifetime of the electronic object.

Digital Rights Management (DRM). DRM systems put restrictions on electronic content, limiting its use for downloads, printing, and loan period. DRM may stipulate the number of simultaneous users, the total number of uses allowed by a library, or the amount of time electronic content may be used. DRM is intended to protect intellectual property and is most often used by publishers and other content providers when making ebooks available for download. *See also* ebook.

Discovery System/Discovery Layer. A unified method of accessing library resources, often allowing users to cross-walk archival management systems, institutional repositories, and the library catalog within a single platform search. *See also* Link Resolver; Source; Target.

ebook. An electronic book. An ebook can be born digital, be digitized from the print edition, or be simultaneously published in both print and electronic formats. Digitized ebooks could be considered backfile, or archive, content. *See also* ejournal.

eJournal, or **journal.** An electronic journal or serial. An electronic journal can be born digital, be digitized from the print edition, or be simultaneously published in both print and electronic formats. Digitized ejournals could be considered backfile, or archive, content. *See also* eBook.

eReserve. Materials selected by faculty for required class reading that are digitized or saved from a library database and placed in an electronic reserve system for downloading or printing. Electronic resource license agreements may include a clause that cites the libraries ability to use the licensed content for eReserves.

Embargo. An embargo is a period of time during which third-party database vendors are restricted from offering the most recent electronic journal content. For instance, an aggregator database might offer Journal X up until the most recent three months or year on a rolling basis. Embargo periods are used to prevent libraries from canceling subscriptions with publishers because the content is available in an aggregator.

Electronic Resources & Libraries (ER&L). An annual conference that aims to bring together information professionals who work with electronic resources to discuss the ways in which content is collected, maintained, and made accessible.

Electronic Resources Lifecycle. The ongoing, nonlinear, and repetitive processes associated with the selection, acquisition, management, evaluation, and renewal or cancellation of electronic resources. *See also* Techniques for Electronic Resources Management (TERMS).

Electronic Resources Management (ERM). Electronic Resources Management references the day-to-day processes of an electronic resources librarian and/or electronic resources staff. ERM should not be confused with ERMS, which specifically references a system or software program used to facilitate day-to-day management. *See also* Electronic Resources Management System (ERMS).

Electronic Resources Management System (ERMS). An internal system or software program to assist in the maintenance of licensed electronic resources, such as databases, ebooks, and ejournals. An ERMS may include a means to track license agreements including license and copyright terms, renewals, access management, and collection development. *See also* Electronic Resources Management (ERM).

EZproxy. A web proxy server used by libraries to provide users with off-site access to licensed electronic resources. EZproxy provides off-site users with authenticated access to resources that are otherwise restricted by local IP authentication. EZproxy is currently provided by OCLC. *See also* OCLC; Web Access Management (WAM).

Fair Use. Conditions under which copying a work, or a portion of a work, does not constitute copyright infringement. Fair use may include copying for purposes of criticism, comment, news reporting, teaching, scholarship, and research.

Federated Search. A single search platform that provides simultaneous search across multiple resources. A user enters a search query in one place, which is then distributed to other participating search engines, or databases. Discovery layers provide a similar service to users yet differ in their method of retrieval, which is done using indexes, which is much faster than federated searching. *See also* Discovery Layer.

First Sale Doctrine. One of the few restrictions on copyright holders. The doctrine defines the rights of an individual who knowingly purchases a copy of a work in copyright from the copyright holder. The purchaser is given the right to sell, display, or otherwise dispose of that particular copy, notwithstanding the interests of the copyright owner. For electronic resources and software, however, the copyright holder remains the owner of the work, because the purchased work is essentially a version that has been rented, leased, or loaned.

Fiscal Year. A period of twelve months, not necessarily coincident with the calendar year, used by a library or library system for financial accounting purposes. Most public and academic libraries that depend on public funding use a fiscal year that begins on July 1st and ends on June 30th, although libraries at privately funded colleges and universities may use a fiscal year that coincides with the academic calendar.

Freely available. The term "freely available" may occasionally be used as a synonym for "open access," indicating scholarly content that is available at no cost. For electronic resources, freely available will indicate the ability to download, read, and share scholarly content, such as journal articles. Freely available can also indicate content that is freely available as a result of a Creative Commons license, such as a website, blog, or other born digital work. *See also* Open Access (OA).

Full-Time Equivalent (FTE). A term used to designate a number of full-time staff or students, taking into account part-time students. Publishers and library vendors may use a college or university's FTE to determine pricing for electronic content, because the figure can indicate the volume of content that will be used by an institution. *See also* Carnegie Classification.

Gold Open Access (Gold OA). A method of Open Access publishing in which an article is published in an Open Access journal or a hybrid journal. The publication fee is made possible by an Article Processing Charge (APC) paid directly to the publisher. *See also* Article Processing Charge (APC); Green Open Access (Green OA); Open Access (OA).

Green Open Access (Green OA). A method of Open Access publishing in which authors make their work available through self-archiving in an Open Access repository where it can be accessed for free after an embargo period. *See also* Article Processing Charge (APC); Gold Open Access (Gold OA); Open Access (OA).

H-index. An impact measurement based on the set of a researcher's most cited papers and the number of citations that they have received in other publications. *See also* Altmetrics.

Hybrid Journal. A subscription journal in which some of the articles are available Open Access. A hybrid journal may result from authors paying a publication fee, also known as an APC (Article Processing Charge), to the publisher in order to change the status for their individual articles. *See also* Open Access (OA).

Index. Indexes provide information on the subject, author, and/or title of a particular set of periodicals, as well as a full citation for each article. Article citations will include the title of the periodical, date, volume, pages, as well as the author and title of the article. Some indexes also include abstracts. *See also* A&I (Abstract and Index).

Integrated Library System (ILS). A resource planning system used to track items owned, orders placed, bills paid, and the borrowing records of patrons.

Interlibrary Loan (ILL). A unit of the library that handles the borrowing and lending of materials to other libraries. License agreements for electronic resources will outline whether the licensed content qualifies for external lending.

Institutional Repository (IR). A digital collection of documents produced by faculty, students, and current affiliates of a university. Intended to preserve and disseminate scholarly information, a repository generally has unrestricted access and content. It can be discoverable through a dedicated platform as well as the library's discovery layer. *See also* Open Access.

IP Address. IP, or Internet Protocol, represents the physical address of a computer attached to a network governed by the TCP/IP protocol. IP addresses appear as sets of Arabic numerals separated by dots (e.g., 123.456.78.9). Publishers require libraries' IP addresses in order to set up access to online content via IP authentication. *See also* IP Authentication; Proxy; Remote Access.

IP Authentication. Access that is based on recognizing that a user is retrieving content by an authorized library, because the requesting computer falls within the library's range of IP addresses. A user attempting to access a library's electronic resources from outside the library's IP ranges will need to use a proxy in order to authenticate. *See also* IP Address; Proxy; Remote Access.

Journal. At times, the word journal is used interchangeably with ejournal (electronic journal). *See also* eJournal; Peer Review; Subscription.

Knowledge Bases and Related Tools (KBART). A NISO recommended practice to improve OpenURL linking by addressing the data provided to link resolvers and knowledge bases. A knowledge base depends on the data that publishers and library vendors provide to the knowledge base developer. KBART is a recommended practice for formatting and distributing title lists to enhance data and improve linking. *See also* Knowledge Base; Link Resolver; NISO; OpenURL.

Knowledge Base (KB). A knowledge base is a technology system that stores complex information used by a computer. For electronic resources, a knowledge base combines data about a library's electronic holdings, such as publisher, platform, and individual titles for journals, books, and more. This type of knowledge base may also include information for a link resolver to improve resource discovery. *See also* Link Resolver.

License Agreement. A legal document between a vendor or publisher and a library that defines the use of a product, usually an electronic resource. A license agreement will often include Terms and Conditions (T&C), either contained within the license or as a separate, but referenced, document. *See also* Model License Agreement; Shared E-Resource Understanding (SERU); Terms and Conditions (T&C); Terms of Use (TOU).

Licensee. A term referring the holder of a license agreement. For libraries, the Licensee is generally the library, or the operating institution.

Licensor. A term referring to the person or organization that grants the Licensee with permission as outlined in a license agreement. For libraries, the Licensor is generally the publisher or vendor providing the product or service.

Link Resolver. A software tool that connects an article citation to the full text. A link resolver uses a source or citation, to connect to the appropriate content, which is the target. *See also* KBART; OpenURL; Target; Source.

List Price. The standard price of a product. The list price for electronic resources will not include a discount and will not be adjusted based on the size of an institution. Often libraries do not pay list price for electronic resources, but instead will pay a price depending on Carnegie Classification or FTE (Full-Time Equivalent). *See also* Big Deal; Carnegie Classification; Full-Time Equivalent (FTE).

Lots of Copies Keeps Stuff Safe (LOCKSS). An open source tool that allows libraries to host content on a local server in order to preserve and provide access to digital content that is no longer available by a provider. *See also* Ceased Title; CLOCKSS; Perpetual Access; Portico.

MARC (MAchine-Readable Cataloging). The international standard for the dissemination of bibliographic data. Each field in a MARC record describes information about a single item. MARC is used to encode information about a bibliographic item, such as author, title, publisher, date, language, and format. RDA (Resource Description and Access) and LCSH (Library of Congress Subject Headings) are standards that define the content within MARC fields.

Model License Agreement. A type of template license agreement that can be used to predefine a library's optimal language for license agreements with publishers and vendors. *See also* Click-Through License; License Agreement; NISO; Shared E-Resource Understanding (SERU); Terms and Conditions (T&C); Terms of Use (TOU).

NASIG. An independent organization (formerly known as the North American Serials Interest Group, Inc.) that works to advance the management of information resources. NASIG aims to facilitate the improved distribution, acquisition, and long-term accessibility of information resources in all formats and for all business models.

National Information Standards Organization (NISO). A nonprofit organization that develops and publishes technical standards to manage information in the digital environment. NISO standards are reviewed regularly, protected by copyright, and made available to no cost to the public. *See also* KBART; PIE-J.

Open Access (OA). Research that is made available online with no restrictions. Authors can make content open access either by self-archiving or by publishing in open access journals and books. In hybrid journals, only some of the articles published are available as open access. *See also* Hybrid Journal; Open Educational Resources (OERs); Gold Open Access (Gold OA); Green Open Access (Green OA); Public Domain.

Open Access Workflows for Academic Libraries (OAWAL). A wiki developed by Jill Emery and Graham Stone intended for librarians working on the management of Open Access resources. OAWAL modules cover advocacy, models and mandates, standards, library scholarly publishing, copyright, and discovery. *See also* Open Access (OA); Techniques for Electronic Resources Management (TERMS).

Open Educational Resources (OERs). Online learning materials that are freely and openly available for anyone to use or adapt for teaching, learning, development and research. *See also* Gold Open Access (Gold OA); Green Open Access (Green OA); Open Access (OA).

OpenURL. A URL syntax that facilitates transportation of information about an article from the source website, such as an Abstract and Index (A&I)

database, to the target, which will contain full text. *See also* Abstract and Index (A&I); Link Resolver.

Pay-Per-View (PPV). A "just-in-time" alternative to providing access to journal articles. In this model, libraries pay only for articles requested by their patrons, rather than an entire journal subscription. Some publishers sell tokens to libraries; each token pays for a single user's access to a single journal article. Other publishers have partnered with third parties, such as ReadCube, to host article access and manage payment.

Paywall. A paywall prevents users from accessing database content, either because the content has not been licensed or because of an access error. It will generally prompt the user to pay to access content. *See also* License Agreement; Subscribed; OA (Open Access).

Patron Driven Acquisitions (PDA). A method of acquisitions in which libraries make a large collection of ebooks that have not yet been purchased available to patrons. Only once a title is selected for use does the library complete the purchase. Often a purchase is triggered by a multiplier or a predetermined number of patron uses. Also known as Demand Driven Acquisitions (DDA). *See also* Demand Driven Acquisitions (DDA); Pay-Per-View (PPV).

Peer Review. The established method of validation for scholarly research in which experts in a given field impartially review and evaluate research before publication. There are various types of peer review: Single Blind, Double Blind, and Open Review, with alternate models emerging as open access and research data transparency initiatives become more popular.

Perpetual Access. The ability and right to maintain ongoing access to electronic content. For subscription licensing, access to electronic content is often lost at the expiration of the agreement. Other licensing may include outright purchases in which the Licensee will retain access to the content after the license has expired. *See also* Access Only; CLOCKSS; LOCKSS; Portico.

Presentation and Identification of E-Journals (PIE-J). A NISO Recommended Practice for the way in which journal information is displayed and cited. Recommendations include how to display journal names when a name change has occurred, and citing the correct ISSN to improve OpenURL linking. *See also* KBART; NISO.

Portico. A community-supported digital archive for the preservation of ejournals, ebooks, and other electronic scholarly content. Portico aims to ensure stable access to electronic content that has experienced a "trigger" event, such as if a publisher goes out of business or when content ceases to be available. *See also* Ceased Title; CLOCKSS; LOCKSS; Perpetual Access.

Proxy. A method of remote access authentication to licensed electronic resources. Proxy authentication generally corresponds to a specific proxy IP range and an authentication key, or user name and password, that is provided by the user. *See also* IP Address; IP Authentication; Remote Access; Shibboleth.

Quotation. A publisher or vendor's initial price, which can be followed by a response or negotiation process. *See also* Carnegie Classification; Full-Time Equivalent (FTE); Request for Proposal (RFP).

Request for Proposal (RFP). An official, public document that invites publishers, vendors, and jobbers to submit a bid to provide a service or material. *See also* Quotation.

Shared E-Resource Understanding (SERU). A NISO Recommended Practice that offers an alternative to reviewing and signing individual license agreements for electronic resources. By mutually accepting SERU, libraries and publishers are expressing shared understanding of the institution, authorized users, the nature of the content, the use of materials, privacy and confidentiality, online performance and service, and archiving and perpetual access rights. *See also* Click-Through License, License Agreement; NISO; Terms and Conditions (T&C); Terms of Use (TOU).

Shibboleth. A method of remote authentication for electronic resources. Shibboleth authentication provides users with access to licensed electronic resources through a single sign-on, eliminating the need for multiple usernames. Shibboleth operates independently from IP Addresses. *See also* Athens; IP Address; IP Authentication.

Site License. A license agreement priced and negotiated for a single institution. A site license will grant access to the users affiliated with a single location, whereas a license agreement for a consortium will include pricing and access for multiple sites or multiple libraries. *See also* Consortium/Consortia; License Agreement.

Source. An article or website that is the starting point for a link resolver. A source can be thought of as the citation from which a knowledge base generates an OpenURL to link to full text. The linked content is known as the target. *See also* Link Resolver; OpenURL; Target.

Standing Order (STO). Ongoing purchasing agreement with a publisher for a monograph or serial series. Libraries acquire new volumes annually or semiannually. Not a true subscription because publication frequency can vary, and the acquired set is not a periodical.

Subscribed. Content that is made available to a library as a result of a license agreement. Subscribed content is often access only and the library must renew the content each year. *See also* Access Only; License Agreement; Perpetual Access.

Subscription Agent. An intermediary between purchasers of content and the content publishers. Subscription agents can provide price quotes and invoicing, as well as maintain information on title changes, licensing requirements, and any handling issues that may arise.

Standardized Usage Statistics Harvesting Initiative (SUSHI). A NISO protocol that provides instructions for automating the collection of usage statistics from vendors, which otherwise would need to be manually retrieved. *See also* COUNTER; NISO.

Streaming Media. Film, audio, and other media content that users access via online streaming. Unlike a DVD or CD, streaming media is accessed on the Internet and users can select individual titles or clips to embed into course management software, websites, or presentations. Access is granted to recognized IP ranges and libraries have the option to purchase individual titles, collections, or participate in a usage driven access model.

Target. The destination of a link resolver. The target is the content, such as a journal article, which is requested from the source. *See also* Link Resolver; Source; OpenURL.

Techniques for Electronic Resources Management (TERMS). A project developed by Jill Emery and Graham Stone to create best practices for electronic resources management throughout their lifecycle, from investigating new content to deciding whether to renew. *See also* Open Access Workflows for Academic Libraries (OAWAL).

Terms and Conditions (T&C). Also known as TOU (Terms of Use). The terms that govern the overall use of licensed electronic resources. Often T&C (Terms and Conditions) will govern multiple electronic resources purchases, either through individual invoicing or through the creation of content amendments and addendums. *See also* Addendum; Amendment; License Agreement; Model License Agreement; Shared E-Resource Understanding (SERU); Terms and Conditions (T&C); Terms of Use (TOU).

Terms of Use (TOU). Also known as Terms and Conditions (T&C). The terms that govern the overall use of licensed electronic resources. Often TOU will govern multiple electronic resources purchases, either through individual invoicing or through the creation of content amendments and addendums. *See also* Addendum; Amendment; License Agreement; Model License Agreement; Shared E-Resource Understanding (SERU); Terms and Conditions (T&C); Terms of Use (TOU).

Text and Data Mining (TDM). The process of automatically extracting information from text documents and large numbers.

Transfer Code of Practice. A set of best practice guidelines from UKSG (United Kingdom Serials Group) to help ensure that journal content remains accessible when there has been transfer between publishers. It also tries to ensure that the process takes place with minimum disruption. *See also* United Kingdom Serials Group (UKSG).

Transfer Title. A journal title that has been transferred from one publisher to another. *See also* Ceased Title; Transfer Code of Practice.

Trial. A period of time during which a publisher or vendor makes available electronic resources free of charge. Trials generally run from thirty to ninety days and during which librarians, faculty, and sometimes students evaluate the content and the database platform. In rare instances, trials will require payment. *See also* Complimentary; License Agreement; Subscribed.

Turnaways. Also known as denials, turnaways refer to electronic content download requests that were denied or turned away on the publisher's platform. Turnaways occur either because of an access error or because a library does not subscribe. COUNTER reports can provide data on the number of times content was denied to users. In COUNTER 4 these reports are: Journal Report 2 (JR2), Database Report 2 (DR2), and Book Reports 3 and 4 (BR3 & BR4). *See also* COUNTER; Denials; Usage Statistics; Usus.

United Kingdom Serials Group (UKSG). An international organization interested in promoting the exchange of ideas about scholarly communication among librarians, publishers, and related vendors. UKSG commissioned the original Knowledge Bases and Related Tools (KBART) report that became a joint initiative with NISO. *See also* (Knowledge Bases and Related Tools); NISO.

Usage Statistics. Data about the use of a library's electronic resources. Usage Statistics can include data about the number of searches, sessions, full-text downloads, image views, video playbacks, and more, depending on the type of resource. Project COUNTER is a standard that addresses consistent distribution, credible, and compatible usage statistics. *See also* COUNTER.

Usus. An independent community-run website for anyone interested in usage statistics for electronic resources, including librarians, publishers, aggregators, repository managers, and individual scholars. Usus provides a forum to discuss, troubleshoot, and research issues related to usage statistics and COUNTER. *See also* COUNTER, Usage Statistics.

Voluntary Product Accessibility Template (VPAT). A VPAT is a form that is filled out by a service provider that describes how access is made available for people with disabilities, based on regulations from Section 508 of the amendment to the Rehabilitation Act of 1973. *See also* Web Content Accessibility Guidelines (WCAG).

Web Access Management (WAM). A form of identity management and user authentication that determines access to electronic resources, usually with a single sign-on requirement. *See also* EZproxy.

Web Content Accessibility Guidelines (WCAG). Part of a series of web accessibility guidelines published by the Web Accessibility Initiative (WAI) of the World Wide Web Consortium (W3C) that specify how digital content should be made accessible for people with disabilities. *See also* Voluntary Product Accessibility Template (VPAT).

Index